AFRICA

AFRICA

A Region of Never Ending Conflict

KWANG HO CHUN
Chonbuk National University Korea

CHONBUK NATIONAL UNIVERSITY PRESS

Published by
Chonbuk National University Press
32, Eojin-gil, Wansan-gu, Jeonju-si, Jeollabuk-do, Korea

www.jbnupress.com

The Library of Congress has cataloged the printed edition as follows :
Chun, Kwang Ho.
AFRICA : A Region of Never Ending Conflict / by Kwang Ho Chun

ISBN 978-89-98534-19-6 93340

국립중앙도서관 출판시도서목록(CIP)

Chun, Kwang Ho

Africa : a region of never ending conflict / [written by] Kwang Ho Chun. -- Jeonju : Chonbuk National University Press, 2014
p. ; cm

Includes bibliographical references
ISBN 978-89-98534-19-6 93340 : ₩20000

340.93-KDC5
320.96-DDC21 CIP2014016971

Table of Contents

Acknowledgements

I would like to express my sincere gratitude to Dr. Geo-Suk Suh, the President of Chonbuk National University for his continuous support for my research. He has provided me the valuable opportunity to conduct this project on the topic of developing countries. I also like to thank my lifelong adviser Dr. Chungwon Choue, the President of the World Taekwondo Federation, who continues to inspire me as a researcher in International Relations. Without their support, the completion of such a large project would not be possible.

My thanks also go to Ms. Hyo-jin Jang and Ms. Okju Kim who gladly helped me rectification, Mr. Ricky Bushaway, Mr. Sam Normington, Ms. Vikki Chan, and Ms. Haeri Jeon for their contributions to the editing of this work.

This research required the review of a considerable amount of material and first-hand observations of African region. To do so, many colleagues supported me with their valuable comments and contributed to the sourcing of the large volume of materials required. Prof. Wang Hui Lee, Prof. Hyun Kim, and Prof. Seok Won Song greatly helped me on this.

I also would like to express my special appreciation and thanks to Dr. Duk-Ho Song, Chief Editor of the Chonbuk National University Press for his full support in the publishing of this book.

Life as a researcher and teacher is not a short journey. Whenever I have had difficulties and have become tired, the members of the Office of International Affairs and the Faculty of International Studies at Chonbuk National University have awoken me and made me strong again.

Finally, a special thanks to my family for whom words cannot truly express how grateful I am. The completion of this work in Korea was possible only thanks to my family's full-time support, endurance and sacrifice.

May 2014

General Introduction

A 2006 Wilton Park paper entitled 'Africa–Drivers for Change'[1] highlighted that thirty four of the world's poorest forty nine states sit, tragically, on Conrad's 'Dark Continent'. This statistic in itself offers a stark reminder of the problems facing Africa in the 21stcentury and it is not offered in isolation. Indeed in 2003 the United Nations 'Human Development Report' also listed the worlds twenty-five poorest nations as African.[2] The African continent is comprised of fifty three sovereign states and it is when these aforementioned statistics are set against that figure of 'fifty three' that the enormity of the African challenge is seen in its true perspective. Approximately seventy percent of the world's 'poorest' countries[3] are African. However these rather bland factual statistics could offer the reader a somewhat dehumanized perspective of the reality of Africa's predicament. That they equate to three hundred and thirteen million human beings living on less than one dollar a day, that one third of the continent lives below the minimum dietary energy consumption rates[4] and are therefore by definition in a state of starvation, may go a little way to humanizing these bare statistics. It is of equal note that these figures have been increasing in recent years and that between 1990 and 2001 Africans falling into the 'less than one dollar a day' bracket increased by nearly one hundred million.[5] It isin the face of these crushing statistics of poverty and underdevelopment that the African continent is currently being defined.

However it is within these very statistics that lies the 'paradox' because Africa also holds 89% of the worlds reserves of platinum, 60% of the worlds diamonds, 53% of its cobalt and 28% of the globes Gold[6] to name but four

1 See Roger Williamson, "Africa – Drivers of Change," *WiltonParkPaper*, Dec. 2006, p. 6.

2 United Nations *'HumanDevelopmentReport'*–2011. – bottom 25 ranked nations were all in African nations.

3 Roger Williamson, *Op.Cit.*

4 *Ibid.*, p. 8.

5 *Ibid.*, From 227 million people in 1990 to 313 million in 2001.

6 Manji and Marks, A series of papers - *African Perspectives on China in Africa* – 2007 *'Exploitation of Africa's Natural Resources'*p. 19.

of an absolute treasure trove of resources. When oil is factored into this equation African poverty and underdevelopment offers the world one of the great conundrums of the 21st century. In the year 2000 Sub Saharan Africa produced 3,610 thousand barrels of oil a day, in 2005 it produced 4,866 and in 2010 it is forecast to produce 7,527 thousand barrels a day[7]. Production has grown, the price of oil has more than doubled and yet, as a continent, Africa largely continues to be defined by war, pandemic, starvation and corruption. Further increasing the 'resolution' on this issue, a brief glance at Nigeria offers up a country with an overall average per-capita income of less than one dollar a day and social indicators of development little better than the rest of Sub Saharan Africa. Yet over the last three decades, since independence in the 1960s, Nigeria has enjoyed oil revenues of in excess of $300 billion as well as substantial sums of International humanitarian aid.

The Catholic Relief Services referred to this phenomenon as the 'Paradox of Plenty', in effect an echo of the question raised in this researchs title. They also defined it as being consistent with the fact that fifty percent of Africa's world trade was based on 'extractive' resources, an activity that also accounted for almost seventy percent of all direct foreign investment[8] into the continent. Perhaps a better know and more widely deployed description of this 'paradox' would be that of 'The Curse of Natural Resources'. So far the authors research has failed to identify the exact origin of this phrase although there do seem to be both contenders and claimants. Irrespective of its origin it is how best the continent can deal with this 'paradox' or this 'curse of natural resources' that appears to challenge both Africa and the rest of the industrialized world. However with the advent of globalization and that other great phenomena of the 21st century, the 'emerging market powers' of Brazil, Russia, India and China(BRIC), the ability to influence the African continent has both moved away from old power houses of the richindustrialized West and evolved in both the nature and the balance and its 'drivers'.

Such is the size and diversity of the African continent that it can but defy the simplicity of either a single definition for 'cure' or indeed the 'curse' that necessitates a remedy. It is a continent made up of huge geographical,

---

7 *Ibid.*
8 *Ibid.*

climatic, religious and of course cultural differences. In the North a largely dry Somalia holds a population of seventy seven million of whom 91% are Muslim. A more fertile South Africa hosts a population of forty four million of whom but 1.5% are Muslim and Chad, a country of nearly ten million divides itself almost equally between Islam and Christianity. Botswana has few resources but remains a shining beacon of democracy and good governance, whereas Congo produces three hundred and fifty thousand barrels of oil a day and holds huge mineral resources but has been cursed with conflict for well over a decade. Again Zimbabwe, in spite of recent mismanagement, retains the natural fertility to be the 'bread basket' of the south whereas Ethiopia, in the north, continues to challenge the world with its almost cyclical famine and disaster.

Within this diversity, the dynamic of 'resource abundance', or this 'curse of natural resources', has been and remains empirical fact throughout the region. It is the specifics of definition and attribution of this concept of 'curse' that offers the more elusive challenge. Whilst this research will look at the most recent manifestations of this phenomenon by focusing on the modern era from the end of the Cold War in 1991 to present day, it also will remain cognisant of the historical 'shaping' of the African continent. It is symptomatic of Africa's recent evolution that this was a 'historical shaping' most often seen from a Western perspective and seldom from an African one. However again, whilst this research will strive to demonstrate empathy for this particular perspective, it will also endeavour to avoid allowing 'external interference', be it perception or reality, to abrogate African leadership of any of its 'patrimonial', 'tribal' or 'democratic' responsibilities to constituent populations. In offering a boarder concept of this 'Dark Continent' it is often worth remembering that, in spite of better resourced efforts from both Orthodox and Sino claimants, that Central Eastern Africa is regarded by many within the scientific community as offering us the 'origin of mankind'. It was here that the earliest evidence of 'Hominids' and 'Homo Erectus' were discovered and dated in excess of seven million and two hundred thousand years old respectively.

That Africa's recent historical development has been dominated by various external 'pulses' of exploration, colonisation, exploitation and development is well documented in the history books of Western, Chinese, Arab and of course African cultures. To deny that these external 'pulses' were either motivated or later exploited by what Africa had to offer in terms of resources and ‘favourable’ trade, would again fly in the face of historical fact. Whilst an Egyptian civilization, that rose in 3000 BC and lasted in excess of three thousand years, has offered the world some of the most wonderful examples of early civilization, much of Sub Saharans Africa remained ‘tribal’ in nature throughout these great periods of civilization; a legacy that continues to constrain the development of many areas to this day. But again It could be argued that this offers a purely Western perspective of ‘development’ and who exactly is the West, or indeed the East, to condemn this system of government because it fails to conform with their own perceptions of ‘governance’ and ‘civilization’.

However in the twenty-first century Africa must be viewed in a global context, the world continues to develop and evolve at pace and Africa both wants and overridingly demands, external assistance with its myriad of developmental problems.

PART I

Never Ending Story of Peace and Security in Africa

Chapter I
The African Union and Peace and Security in Africa

Introduction

The African Union constitutes an extremely powerful peace and security resolution tool in Africa. It reflects the Union's Articles of incorporation with an increasing awareness of the importance of enhancing security and stability in the continent, which is something undisputed. Without peace and security, talk about economic development, integration or unity becomes meaningless. In addition, the fundamental law of the Union Constitution puts forward a new vision for challenging conflicts through containment, management or resolution. For the first time it is taking an African approach to African problems. For example, it emphasizes the pivotal role of the continent organization in peace and security resolution through the right of intervention in particular cases, and the right of member states to request intervention. In addition, the constitution provides the opportunity to set forth and coordinate defense policies across the continent. This paves the way for the establishment of an African collective security system on the continent level that was non-existent before.

In this respect, we ask: to what extent can the fundamental law of the African Union be considered as the continuation of the Organization for African Unity (OAU) in peace and security resolution operations within the continent? Does the fundamental law represent a real opportunity for peace and security in the Continent? Is collective continental security possible within the new system?

The African Union's Peace and Security Measures

These are the most important questions that we shall elaborate on by considering the following points. Firstly: the characteristics of contemporary

African conflicts and the problems and challenges before the African Union. Secondly: the relevance of the African Union's experiences. Thirdly: the African Union as the new approach for resolving peace and security.

Firstly, the characteristics of contemporary African conflicts; and the consequent problems and challenges before the African Union. The African continent has faced a fierce wave of conflicts, especially since the end of the Cold War. This wave is characterized by the fact that they are complex and difficult to resolve. That is the difficulty that has faced the Organization for African Unity and will face the African Union in future.

However, the most important characteristics of the African conflicts in the period since the end of the Cold War are as follows. Internal conflicts have surfaced and multiplied, in addition to the remaining cross border conflicts. In the first half of the 1970s half the internal conflicts in the world were spread in Africa. Among the 35 internal or civil wars on the international level, there were about 16 of them in Africa alone, whether due to racial, religious, regional, economic or even tribal factors.[1]

Maybe the main reason for this wave is symbolic to the root transformations of the international order and the inability of Africa to withstand pressures created by such transformations on the one hand and on the other hand the message conveyed by such changes. This is especially true after the collapse of the former USSR which means that the minorities and the ethnic groups especially those overwhelmed, have the right of self-determination, whether by participation in governance or by choosing the appropriate political . The groups that suffered injustice and suppression during the pre-Cold War and Cold War period have seen the opportunity for freedom that has become apparent within the new order.[2]

In this way, peoples, groups and states have confronted each other within this new atmosphere. Some people have classified conflicts in terms of their

---

1 M. Abul-Enien Moh, "Peaceful settlement of African Disputes in the Post-Cold War Era", in Jinadow and L. Adele, eds., *The Political Economy of Peace and Security in Africa: Ethnocultural and Economic Perspective,* (London: AAPS Books, 2000), p. 149.

2 Abdalla Ashaal, *Africa South of the Desertf rom the Colonialist Legacy,* (Cairo: Strategic Studies Center in Ahram, Series of Strategic Brochures, 7thyear,1997).pp. 18-19.

cause. There were 29 reasons for conflicts, and the ethnic conflicts have constituted the most important of these reasons and the most prevalent in continuity. These reasons can be summarized in[3]: military reasons such as foreign aggression, annexation or dominion, intervention, aggression or hatred, supporting rebel or secessionist groups, political and international and ideological reasons, political campaigns, historical regional expansions, regional competitions, terrorism, ruin or segregation in commercial and economic affairs, local political reasons such as: power conflict, hostile groups, population pressures or both, economic and religious disparities, injustice and oppression, democratic claims, ethnic or sectarian violence related to economic, social, religious or judiciary consideration and ethno-political, reasons related to persecution, violation of human rights, refugees' community movements, and poverty and lack of stability due to government mismanagement, apparent government corruption that exceeds accepted traditional tolerance. All these reasons led to huge complications in resolving such conflicts at the continental level. The result was that International solutions were needed for these internal conflicts, especially on settlement phases.[4] Some people have classified conflicts in terms of their causes: First is poor governance; most African leaders recognise only their ethnic groups when it comes to political appointments and provision of social services. Other ethnic groups that are marginalised usually revolt, as there is no avenue for them to attend to political power or have a share of the national resources. If the disaffected groups have their symphafisers in a neighbouring country, the situation becomes worst as they will be support from outside. This is the case with the conflict in Congo, as the Rwandese are support if the rebels in the DRC. There fore, poor governance is one of the major causes of conflict.

Another cause of conflict is the sfruqqle for resources. It has been argued that the rebels of both Liberia and Sierra Leone thought to control the resources in their countries. Diamond fields in Sierra Leone and rubber/ timber in Liberia. Today even water has become so precious that groups or even countries carry arms for.

---

3 Oliver Furley, ed., *Conflict in Africa,*(London:TourisPublishers,1995), pp.3-4.

4 N.M. Blokker and M. Kleiboer, "The Internalization of Domestic Conflict: The Role of the UN Security Council", *LeidenJ ournal of International Law,* Vol. 9, No. 1, 1996, pp. 6-8.

Religious differences have also been identified as a cause of conflict. This happens where one religious followers (mostly the majority) try to dominate the other (the minority), conflict ensue and the society becomes polarised a long religious line. This has been the cause of conflicts in Nigeria and to some extent Sudan. Other causes of conflict are injustice, poverty struggle for powered.

Conflicts differ as to the approaches used to resolve them in terms of intervention or rapprochement, i.e. should we favor the use of intensive preventive diplomacy, conflict management or otherwise establishing peace in the post-conflict or settlement period? Here we should make the distinction between various categories of conflicts. The first category includes internal conflicts, which continue to exist without becoming violent. Usually these are due to long-term dictatorships, the denial of human rights, and poor governance and people's participation. The second category includes conflicts that rapidly flair up and escalate to become human catastrophes which may lead to State's downfall in certain cases, for example Liberia, Rwanda, Somalia and Sierra Leone. The Third category includes the remaining border conflicts such as the case of Cameroon, Nigeria, Eritrea, Ethiopia and Namibia.[5]

Since the end of the cold war, African conflicts have continued to increase and become more complex In reality they constitute a heavy burden that awaits the new African Union, of which the most important difficulties are outlined below.[6]

The African conflicts are associated with and imbued with a wave of intensive violence, particularly against civilians, both those with assets and also against fragile groups such as children, women and refugees. Violence of the latter category includes forms that are atrocious and barbaric as it is characterized by mutilation and inflicting the most hideous and horrible torture and murder methods. In addition, States mostly employ and sponsor

---

5 Funmi Olonisakin, "Conflict Management in Africa: The Role of the OAU and Sub-Regional Organizations", Published in Monograph 46, *Building Stability in Africa: Challenges for th eNew Millennium*, February 2000.

6 Chris Allen, "Warfare, Endemic Violence & State Collapse in African Political Economy", *African Studies*, No. 81, 1999, pp. 367-384.

violence, either by sponsoring special militias or by inciting other groups that are not part of its organs to spark-off such conflicts. The second important difficulty is the spread of the collapsed States phenomenon. The collapsed States have become a phenomenon that is characteristic of Africa under the wave of conflicts that date back to the 1990s.[7] The collapse of the state means the collapse of the legitimate authority, the law and the public order to the extent that it would become imperative to seek ways to reorganize and reestablish the situation all over again or to go back or, more appropriate, to retreat to ethnic nationalism as a remaining or possible identity.

The Collapsed States are probably, taken in this sense, well known and obvious, however, States that are likely to collapse are so many in Africa and to an alarming degree! That is also another issue awaiting the African Union, which has to find solutions to prevent the total collapse of these States.

There are certainly other practical complexities, for example there exist practical problems facing the management and solution process of current conflicts on the African continent. In general, they have a particular significance to the African Union and to its ability to restore peace. Some of the most significant cases and complexities represent the increasing role played by sub-regional organizations in managing and solving conflicts as well as the fears and concerns over political divisions on the settlement of cases and solving conflicts. In addition, there are intervention process difficulties, concerns over regional hegemony, scarcity and decrease of human and financial resources necessary to solve conflicts.

For this, it would be impossible to affirm the existence of institutions or organizations in Africa that are able to act in a peacekeeping framework in a predictable and regular manner, let alone the possibility to take action in precarious conflict situations that require the restoration and imposition of peace and security. For example, with all the intervention in Liberia in 1990, some of the ECOWAS community States lacked officers or high field commanders who could participate in the ECOMOG Force. As their training

---

7 Ali - Mazrui, "The African State as a Political Refugee", in David Smock and Chester A. Chroker, eds., *African Conflict Resolution: The US Role in Peacekeeping* (Washington D.C.: United States Institute of Peace Press, 1995), pp. 9-25

is sub standard and the force was poorly funded. Their equipments were also few and lacked proper maintenance this has there fore affected the ability of the force to restore peace and security in good time.

Secondly: African conflicts solution approaches and the evident experience before the African Union: Conflict resolution in the African environment represents an extremely complex process. On the one hand, it is characterized by multiple aspects ranging from conflict management, settlement and resolution. On the other hand it is characterized by the intricacy between the involved concerned parties that are charged with the task of assuming this huge operation. Also, in terms of whole or partial methods and strategies employed throughout the stages of said operation.

The last 40 years' experience in the field of African conflict prevention, management and solution reflects several facts: the first of which is that the continent has witnessed three major approaches in crises and conflict solution since independence until now. The second of these approaches has been used sequentially, but all of them are employed mostly at the same time. The third is that any of these approaches has its advantages and disadvantages. However, all of them have failed until now to solve African conflicts or to find a successful tool to contain and control such conflicts. It is therefore extremely imperative to reconsider all these approaches within the new system i.e. under the umbrella of the African Union.

Lessons Learnt

It would probably be appropriate to elaborate on these three approaches, by analyzing their positive and negative aspects and the lessons to be learnt, considering that it is a necessary experience for the collective African action under the African Union umbrella.

The traditional approach (The UN and the Security Council): the UN and the Security Council are considered the traditional approach put forward by the international order with a view to deal with conflicts and crises in order to keep peace since the end of the Second World War. International parties have resorted to the UN and the Security Council in order to intervene in several African crises since the Suez Canal crisis and the conflict in Congo

(Kinshasa). This is because the Security Council represents the principal authority charged with international peacekeeping and security in this the world.

However, the wave of African conflicts in the 1990s, mostly internal conflicts as aforesaid, has set the limits to external intervention capabilities in general. This includes UN intervention, whose charter involves– within the framework of several principles – the safeguarding of the state, its territorial integrity and the non-intervention in the internal Affairs of the states.

Nevertheless, UN operated and engineered interventions through the Security Council's discretionary authority have become widespread in the 1990s, due to the huge numbers of refugees, human considerations and the safeguard of democracy.[8] This has led to the emergence of concepts and attitudes threatening peace and security in various regions of the world and the lifting of traditional obstacles that states had been fortified in until then. In view of the developing circumstances conducive to intervention, the African experience revealed defects and deficiencies in this approach during the 1990s. In particular, lessons were learnt in Somalia about the misunderstanding between the intervening American forces and the Somali people that thwarted the UN mission. The Rwandan case also showed the limits of international intervention given the misunderstanding between French forces and the Rwandan people.[(9)]

In addition there has been a lack of interest from the major Western Countries, including the United States, in refusing to join and make efforts in missions aimed at solving African conflicts. Because of this, the major European countries initiated new endeavors. For example France in 1995, England in 1996 or the USA in 1997, built on the concept of the African Crisis Response Force (ACRF). These initiatives were integrated in a common initiative put forward in June 1997 during the OAU summit in Harare. The African States welcomed this as a positive step but made reservations on certain important points such as continuity, guarantees, supports, specifications of intervention operation types, funding, States in African States to assume the task, restrictions and standards of intervention, which

---

8 N.M. Blokker & Kleiboer, *Op. Cit.*, pp. 7-33.

are all issues that had not been conclusively dealt with until now.[9]

The regional approach represents an extension of what some called the Pax Africana that has come to replace the colonialist European role. This trend was reflected in reality in the OAU charter and is one of the organization's chief principles.

On the other hand, the African experience in conflict resolution, internal ones in particular, reflects a development in the organization's role in this respect. During the early stage (1963 – 1993), the OAU was steadfast in its principles and rejected involvement in internal conflicts. In another stage, starting in 1993, upon the creation of a mechanism to prevent, manage and settle African conflicts related to the OAU, the latter started to confront internal conflicts. Some sort of gradual reconsideration in concepts and standards governing the international African relations began to take shape. This is true whether in relation to its internal relations or relations with the outside world. This rethink also applied to its efforts to establish new foundations and standards related to the internal situation and sound governance system.

Despite such transformation, which some regard as a very slow trend, inconsistent with the new era, the OAU has been able to preserve the historic claims of the region and to maintain the respect of borders. Africa has adopted with respect for elections, tolerance, and reconciliation with the opposition, independent judiciaries and sovereignty for minorities.[10]

There is another regional goal which is complimentary to the OAU role that has started to be consolidated in the 1990s, through the sub-regional organizations such as ECOWAS in West Africa and SADC in South Africa and EGAD in East Africa and the horn of Africa. The role of these institutions and regional organizations has included intervention in several conflicts such as those in Liberia, Sierra Leone and Guinea Bissau. In respect of ECOMOG forces, intervention in Lesotho involved response to the

---

9 Astri Sukrke, "UN Peacekeeping in Rwanda," in Gumnar M. Sorbo Etal, ed., *Out of Conflict: From War to Peace* (Upsala: Nordica African Institute, 1997), pp. 96- 99

10 William Zartman, "Guidelines for Preserving in Africa", in David R. Smock and Chester A. Crocker, eds., *Op. Cit.*, p. 97..

military rebellions against the democratic government by SADC. This is in addition to the increasing role in peace settlement fields and conflict solution, such as EGAD's role in Sudan and SADC's role in peacekeeping and elections in Mozambique.

It is worth mentioning here that there exists a point of view that the regional organizations have side stepped the OAU in its role in both inter- and intra-state conflict management. Others argue that the sub-regional organizations have been involved in several conflicts in which they were not originally willing to take this role which suggests conflict of competences. However we can say that the true role of the OAU in accordance with the Articles of Association of the New Mechanism – Mechanism for the Prevention, Management of Disputes, 1993 – would almost be limited to conflict prevention and preventive diplomacy, which is the role that has characterized the organization as different from all other parties whether regional or international.

In general, regional organizations whether continental or sub-regional, face common challenges, of funding difficulties, logistic difficulties, divisions between participants and within governments, as well as weakness in governments that lead them to seek foreign help. This includes security assistance from mercenaries, which indicate the limits of the regional approach, its insufficiency and ineffectiveness in terms of conflict resolution despite the innovations introduced to this type of regional mechanism. Despite the increasing role of the Africans that is exactly what is noted in the increasing growth and build-up of African Armies, whether in peacekeeping operations of the UN in the continent or through regional efforts in this track.[11]

The civil society and special security mechanisms are another approach for conflict resolution that began to take shape a few years ago. Its proponents called for more orientation towards civil society and non-governmental organizations in conflict solution, and in the field of peacekeeping and security.

This trend has become increasingly noticeable in recent years. The role of civil society and non-governmental organizations is no longer limited

11 The Statutes of the African Union (Article 4 Clause 9, 15)

to internal, development, religious and political actions, but demand is growing increasingly for the role of this sector in solving African conflicts. In particular, the role of the Private Security Company (PSC) has grown. There were known to be mercenaries in peacekeeping operations since 1994. Since Rwanda, the focus has been on civil society's role in conflict resolution and not reliance on the state or international organization alone. An example of this was the symposium organized by the AAPSO (The Asian African People's Solidarity Organization) in Cairo, 16 May 2004 on "The Role of Non-Government Organization in the Management of Conflicts in Africa" Therefore, the civil Societies and the NGOS help in the distribution of aid and relief material, to refugees and victims of violent conflicts. Some also help in the post conflict reconstruction and security sector reform.

The new trend was enthusiastic about assigning a role to the civil society groups and private companies in problem solving centers for certain outcomes in particular sectors. An example is the role played by religious institutions such as the World Council of Churches (WCC) and (AACC) All Conference of Churches in Africa, in effective and successful mediation that led to the Addis Ababa Agreement 1972, relative to termination of Civil War in Southern Sudan. In a security environment that has reached its peak in deterioration since independence and with the African experience in peace restoration and conflict solution, there are still some who argue that the present African situation is still characterized by chaos. The powerful States and the most active in Africa such as Nigeria, Algeria and Ethiopia, and even South Africa are still in a state of anxiety and chaos. With regards to medium states that are active such as Ivory Coast, Cameron, Kenya and Angola, they are still suffering from complicated internal problems. In addition to this, the OAU, in its first decade since independence, has been facing increasing pressures due to inefficiency in management and solving African conflicts. This, despite the relative improvement its organs have witnessed- It has not succeeded in the establishment or creation of a mechanism to prevent, manage and settle African conflicts. In such situations, Africa has to deal with the issue of peacekeeping and conflict resolution by assuming as far as possible a dynamism and flexibility that is required to dominate or abandon altogether the principles of national sovereignty and terminate action in part or in whole with the principle of rejecting intervention in internal affairs. Or it can establish a new system that would acquire a more official quality in terms of procedures, characterized by some form of Hierarchy, set on undertaking highly costly operations, allowing outright intervention in internal affairs with a view to resolving internal conflicts and guaranteeing the type of behavior that is consistent with its target high standards.

All this will be dependent on the political willingness of the active African States, on the revival of the concerns for security considerations and on the alleviation of the intensity of internal instability. This is what started to appear by the dawn of the 21st century, with the emergence of the African Union.

Thirdly: the African Union and the new approach to restoration of Peace and Security: The statutes of the African Union were promulgated on 2 March 2001 at the closing session of the fifth extraordinary Africa Summit held in Sirte City, Libya, known as SIRTE 2. By the promulgation of these statutes the OAU was declared in a state of retirement, after 32 years of action under the umbrella of the organization. This ushered in a new era under the umbrella of the African Union, but with a new spirit and new vision characterized by courage, which is ultimately different in many ways from the visions that were once prevalent during the action undertaking by the OAU.

The new vision of the African Union exemplifies a new approach that would generally improve the continent's chances of constraining conflicts and safeguarding peace and security. This would prepare Africa's transition under the Union, from the state of chaos to a state of stability and security and thereby allow Africa to dedicate its efforts to development and raising the standard of living of its people.

What, then, are the landmarks of this modern vision and this new approach? In other words, what are the new objective elements that embody a useful addition to peacekeeping and the conflict resolution process? Are there any negative elements in this new approach? How can such a new approach be activated in a way that would help transform it into an effecting methodological tool for confronting disputes and conflicts in the African environment?

The new approach's components and positive elements; the statutes of the Union which include several major elements that represent a specific vision or method in the field of peacekeeping security preservation, resolution of existing conflicts and the edification of common collective action in the defence field.

This will be expanded, and evaluated by exploring and analyzing the following elements and components. The first element is that the new approach assigns priority to security considerations on the continent through scrutiny of the formulation and stipulations contained in the statute of the Union, which reveals that the African Leaders have given primary priority to Security considerations and to ascribe extreme importance to the reinforcement of Security and stability in the continent. The Statutes reflect the increasing awareness of the danger of instability resulting from the outbreak of wars and conflicts that represent a threat that constitute a danger to development and possible integration. In the introduction of these statutes, there was the following direction: "Aware that the conflict atrocities in Africa constitute the main obstacle before social and economic development of the continent and that there is a need to enhance peace, security and stability as an essential condition to implement or program regarding development and integration.[12] In the third Article related to objectives, there is stipulation on the reinforcement of peace, security and stability. Additionally, this embodies the Union's principles, reflecting a clear emphasis on the importance of security consideration. Clause (9) of the Article stipulates: "Peaceful coexistence of the member States of the Union and the right to live in peace and security" Clause[13] (15) stipulates: "the respect of human life sanctity and rejects evasion of punishment, political murders, terrorists acts, and sabotage activity."[(12)] In this way, we can say that the security challenges have come to occupy, under the Union, in addition to the challenges engineered by globalization, a progressive place which may replace the challenges that colonialism represented under the Charter of the OAU in terms of priorities relative to collective African action. The second element is that the conflict settlement mechanism between States is exemplified by the Conference of the Heads of the States and Governments.

---

12 Gavin Williams, "Reforming Africa: Constituities & Changes", in *Africa South of the Sahara*(London:EuropaPublicationsLimited,2000):and Richard Goseph,"The International Community and Armed Conflictin Africa: Post-Cold War Dilemmas", in Gummer M. Sorbo and Peter Nole, eds., *Op. Cit.*, pp. 9-21.

13 On the OAU concerning the Intervention in Chad, See Dr. Mamoud Abou Ainein, interview with BBC World, 04/09/2011, "Collective African Security".

The statutes refer in the field of peaceful conflict settlement between African countries to two major syndromes in this respect: first principle: conflicts settlements between members of states within the Union by suitable methods determined by the conference; second principle: preventing the threat or use of force between members of States of the Union.

The third element is the new principles in the regional action for peace: this new approach proposed by the statutes of the Union includes undertaking certain standards and principles that are new and important for the continental regional action. This is apparent in two issues, one of them is related to the right of intervention on the part of the Union, and the second is related to the settling of a common defence policy for the African Continent. It has now become the Conference's right, as per the principles contained in the statutes; to adopt resolutions to enable the Union to intervene under restricted or limited circumstances such as for war crimes, genocide and crimes against human rights. The member States now possess the right to request intervention from the Union in order to restore peace and security.

Within this limit, we can say that one of the new values and new standards brought forward by the statutes is the right to intervene in order to restore and impose peace within limited circumstances. That is a qualitative step forward in structural collective action from what existed before.

During the 30 years of the OAU's days (1963-1993), the organization dealt with internal conflicts with condemnation and hesitant handling, generally considering them as internal matters. This was followed by its unwillingness to be involved in Civil Wars. It condemned or ignored claims of groups rebelling against central governments. There was nothing that governed its intervention policy except when there was conclusive evidence of the involvement of foreign powers in the conflict, such as the case of Chad in the early 1980s.[14] However, there has been a recent shift in policy of the body to be more proactive in its handling of security issues in the continent. This in the reason for the organization's proposal for a mandate to allow for peace enforcement.

---

14 However, we understand from the Charter of the UN, the Information and Declarations issued from the International Organization that it is not permitted to use the Principle of non-intervention as a pretext to cover-up violation of the right of self-determinations.

This principle was generally predominant in the organization's stance and remained to draw its force from the Charter's principles, the most important of which was the principle of non-intervention in the internal affairs of the member states and also from the legitimacy of non-intervention as the principle of the UN Charter; where Article 2 stipulates: "Nothing in this Charter allows the UN to intervene in the Internal Affairs that are within the Internal Jurisdiction proper of any of the member States".[15]

Nonetheless, since the 1990s, a new era had started in the relations of the OAU with internal issues, in particular in the case of conflicts. That era was characterized by the establishment of mechanisms for prevention, management and settlement of conflicts in 1993. It was also characterized by the gradual reconsideration by the OAU of concepts and standards that have governed African internal relations, in addition to the awareness of the African Leaders to the threat that the new changes and globalization pose. This is in addition to the New Approach pursued by the OAU, considering the new situations. In effect, peace, security and stability became the issues associated, in the OAU's opinion, with reforming the governance system, in respect of human rights and democracy, which are all new values and standards that have become common worldwide under the new international order.

Nonetheless, the statutes embody a qualitative step in terms of the new continental order with respect to intervention to impose and keep peace. For the first time this issue has been the subject of legislation under the collective African action. This will pave the way in the first place for the adjustment of the continent's new organization in the Post-Cold War period. It also allows for a greater continental role in conflict settlement and peacekeeping, whether by informing or restoring peace.

However, such a new, qualitative step should be rightly placed in its legal context. In fact, the legal significance of the Union's right to intervene is above all determined by several considerations, the most important of which are covered below.

15 Gummer M. Sorbo and Peter Nole, eds., *Op. Cit.*, pp. 9-21.

The Union's right of intervention is embodied in the Article dealing with the principles. Additionally the right of the Union to intervene is not absolute, but limited to particular crimes or specific cases as stipulated in the statutes (war crimes, genocide and crime against humanity). This is also where all of them are cases that require intervention from the international community within the modern international concept of what is now termed the Intervention Section for humanitarian purposes. Then the resolution to intervene is issued by the conference of the Heads of States and governments of the Union. This means that it requires the approval of all member States (unanimously) or by the majority of one third of the member States of the Union, when unanimity proves impossible. This represents a sufficient guarantee for the non-abusive use of rights. In the end the intervention of the regional organizations for the purposes of peacekeeping and imposition is generally subject to the UN Charter and the supervision of the Security Council. This should ensure complete oversight of any intervention operation even if it should be undertaken by regional or sub-regional organizations. This represents another guarantee for the non-exaggeration or immoderation in the use of the right.

The collective intervention of the Union will provide, without doubt, a greater opportunity for the restoration of peace on the continent. Especially when the political will of the member of States is available. On the one hand, this will prevent any harmful interventions; whether on the part of individual African States or sub-regional organizations or by foreign parties. This has been seen several times during recent years. On the other hand, this principle will provide the opportunity for the New Continental African organization to make available a more collective capacity to build more effective institutional structures in the field of peacekeeping and imposition. These will act on the same principles used at the continent level and worldwide. Additionally it will be able to reconsider the organization's mechanism for prevention, management and settlement of conflicts, rendering it more effective compared to its modest track record under the OAU.

Nevertheless, the regional collective principle shall remain fraught with apprehensions and dangers. The first of these apprehensions represents the absence of any regional consensus on certain concepts associated with the intervention process. These include the concepts of war crimes, collective genocide and crimes against humanity. These are all concepts that should be defined with accuracy so as to avoid taking the absence of such specification as an excuse for differences between the intervening States or those calling for intervention. It could also be a justification for the intensification of conflicts themselves to reach a degree where the intervention would become ineffective or unable to achieve positive results.

The second of these apprehensions is one that appears constantly in the African failure to make available an African Force capable of rapid intervention into crises. The causes of these failures remain under the new Union. This matter raises a controversial question embodied in specifying any Authority vested by the African States as a priority in interposing operations, i.e. would it be the UN? Or the AU? or the sub-regional operation? What role will each of these authorities shall play in intervention operations? There is no doubt that these enquiries still need more examination and study under the New African Union. There is still a need for a general and acceptable theory that would govern intervention operation under the African Union.

Secondly: setting up a common defence policy for the African continent: this principle was embodied in the statutes of the Union. Its drafting came in a general manner and without specification. This conveys a sense of opening the door for African collective action in the field of common defence. This might be either at the stage of laying down common defence policies or at the execution and application phase or even as the building the basic structure and mechanism that would serve such a purpose.

The continent's countries under the OAU had endeavored to build a system of common action in coordinating defense policies. In particular against external threats, mainly against any colonialist State or racist régime. However, this matter was not permanently contained in the Charter, where the organization pledges its defence responsibility on Sovereignty, Regional Safeguards and the Independence of its member States. Within this limit, a defense committee was established which was an independent committee consisting of specialized ministers (Defence) and/or Ministers delegated by their Governments, with Headquarters at Addis Ababa where it would act under the supervision of the General Secretariat. This is the case with Ali's intervention in Sudan and its effort to spear head a new initiative for the settlement of the conflict in Congo.

Conclusion

So, in conclusion, a new dawn is appearing for peace and security on the African continent within the African States and through a new mechanism. The values and the standards which prevailed for a long period and were obstructing effective continental organization for peace and security have been changed. A new Standard has replaced them, but it must have support from all the African countries if it is to succeed.

There is no doubt that the formula put forward by the statutes embodying the setting up of a common Defense Policy of the Continent brings hope. This is because of the example of other Regional blocs worldwide who have attained significant progress in building Common Defense Policies. For example, the European Union, which has policies related to Common Defense and the promotion of European Policy in the field of Security and Defense.

However, on the African Level, coordination steps and building a Common Defense Policy has not yet gone beyond the very early stage and would need effective institutional steps. Maybe the European experience related to the intervention process in military arrangements between Regions are considered useful, as the European experience indicates that there is great interaction with some sort of role distribution between the Security, International, Regional and Sub-regional Organizations, such as the UN, the Organization on Security and Cooperation in Europe, NATO and NATO Partners for Peace.

The African Union, through this experience, can coordinate between the African countries, concentrating on non-military components of Common Defense and Security while Sub-Regional Organizations assume military components, provided that effective steps be taken to establish a Continental Organization for Security, Cooperation and Development that would put forward a comprehensive convention on non-aggression and common defense on the Continent level "Conference on Security, Development and Cooperation in Africa".

In general, it is very important that this is done, and it must be done step by step. Maybe the African Countries were well aware of this calculated graduation for establishment of a "Higher Defense and Security Council" because there is the scope to develop, change or create structures and mechanisms to fortify the management of African Conflicts. Finally the law of the Union allowed an African system for collective peace by enabling a combined Continental Defence Policy able to take Africa from conflict towards peace and security. The conflict in Darfur is an opportunity for the African Union to show that it works effectively and can provide peace and security in the region.

Chapter II
African Union and Conflict Resolution : Darfur Crisis

Introduction

The end of the Cold War in 1990 ushered in a plethora of crises around the globe. Conflicts have since then emerged in the Balkans, South East Asia, Chechnya, Iraq, Afghanistan, Liberia, Somalia, Sierra Leone, Democratic Republic of Congo and Sudan among others. Most of these conflicts have taken place in Africa and some are still on-going. Conflict is one of the critical factors affecting the political and socio-economic development of Africa and it has so far defied enduring remedy. The nature of conflict in this region has shifted from inter-state to intra-state conflict. The most disturbing of the latter is the ongoing armed conflict in the Darfur region of Sudan, the largest country in Africa.[1] Sudan had been engulfed in a civil war for more than two decades, when Darfur became a battle ground for a rebellion which has led to the death of about 200,000 people and the displacement of about 2,000,000 others.[2] The American Government has 'concluded that genocide has been committed in Darfur....'[3] Similarly President Olusegun Obasanjo of Nigeria has described what is happening in Sudan as 'genocide'.[4] The United Nations (UN) called it the world's worst humanitarian disaster, even though it has failed to intervene in the conflict.

Conflict itself is inherent in human relations and when not properly managed they escalate into violence, destruction of lives and properties and provoke serious humanitarian crisis as evidenced in Darfur. Therefore, there are institutional frameworks designed for conflict management and resolution. Broadly speaking, the raison d'etre of the UN lies in the

---

1 'Sudan: Tragedy in Darfur',UN Chronicle,No. 3, 2004, p.1.

2 Martin Luther King, "Talking Tough," *Africa Today*, November 2006, p.6.

3 Colin Powell, 'Situation in Sudan', FDCH Congressional Testimony, 9 September 2004.

4 Olusegun Obasanjo, *Op. Cit.*, p. 22.

minimisation of conflict and maximization of cooperation. At the regional level, Inter-Governmental Organizations such as the African Union (AU) have mechanisms for conflict resolution and management.

However, the viciousness of the Darfur conflict has raised vital questions concerning the will, effectiveness and capability of these organizations to deal with armed conflicts. The Commission for Africa has acknowledged that much more must be done to prevent and resolve conflicts in Africa if development in the continent is to accelerate.[5] Thus, the on- going conflict in Darfur presents the AU and the international community with a challenge to back their pronouncements with action.

The AU, which was established in 2002, intervened in the Darfur crisis through the establishment of a Ceasefire Commission (CFC) on 28 May 2004 when it became clear that the UN and other major powers were reluctant to intervene militarily to stop the massacre. The AU's military commitment was later expanded and tagged African Mission in Sudan (AMIS). The AU saw the Darfur conflict as a test case for its self declared mandate to have Africans resolve African conflicts.[6] The AU mechanisms for conflict resolutions may be sufficient in dealing with inter-state conflict, but they are not robust enough to deal with intra-state conflicts such as the Darfur situation. It was not a huge surprise that AMIS was given a narrow mandate hence its inability to prevent the potential genocide despite limited successes in some areas.

Therefore by late 2006, President Obasanjo of Nigeria made a case for the peacekeeping operations in Darfur to be handed over to the UN while the force retains its 'African character'.[7] He noted that the immediate challenges were how the AU could strengthen and sustain the force until transition to UN mission. Although the UN has agreed to deploy a 20,000 peacekeeping force to support/supplement AMIS,[8] the Government of Sudan (GoS) has rejected this offer. Furthermore, the GoS has continued with the escalation

---

5 Nick Grono, "Darfur: The International Community's Failure to Protect", *African Affairs*, Vol. 105, No. 421, October 2006, p.621.

6 G. O'Neill Willam and Violette Cassis, *Protecting Two Million Internally Displaced: The Success and Short Comings of the African Union in Darfur,* (Switzerland: University of Bern, 2005),p.16.

7 Obasanjo, *Op. Cit.*

8 See UNSCR 1706 of 31 August, 2006.

of violence while intimidating AMIS through abduction of its personnel and threats.[9]

It is against the background of these developments that this research seeks to determine the efficacy of AU's mechanisms for Conflict resolution in resolving contemporary and future conflicts in Africa using the conflict in Darfur as a case study. The research will show that the geo-strategic significance of a country is one of the determinants for intervention by major powers in a given conflict zone hence, their reluctance to be decisively engaged in Darfur despite the potential tendency towards genocide.

Similarly, it will argue that African leaders lack the political will required for the functioning of AU mechanisms for conflict resolution. It will also demonstrate that the AU lacks the resources to even sustain a medium scale peacekeeping force without the assistance of the UN and other developed countries hence its efforts need to be directed on conflict prevention rather than resolution.

The research will contend that the approach adopted by the Western nations especially the USA on the Darfur conflict shows a lack of commitment towards an enduring resolution of the crisis. It will also show that China's oil interest in the Sudan is largely responsible for its role in frustrating any UNSC resolution against the government of Sudan. Finally, it will argue that unless a UN force with a Part VII mandate is authorised to intervene in Darfur with or without the approval of the Government of Sudan, Darfur could become another Rwanda sooner or later.

These issues will be discussed in five parts. Part one deals with the introduction while Part Two begins with a conceptual framework on conflict and conflict resolution. It then examines the AU's mechanisms for conflict resolution. Part Three looks at the geo-strategic significance of Sudan, the genesis of the Darfur crisis and the role of the AU in the resolution of the Darfur crisis. The four theories of conflict resolution as propounded by Zartman William were used as a theoretical framework for examining the efficacy of AU's conflict resolution mechanisms. It explores some of the

---

9 This was based on discussions with AMIS sources who want to remain anonymous due to the nature of their current appointments.

extra-regional influence and the obstacles against the supplanting of AMIS with a UN peacekeeping force. The prospects and constraints of AU in conflict resolution and the potential strategies for enhancing its roles are discussed in Part Four. Part Five will conclude by highlighting the major findings of this research.

The Darfur conflict is still on-going and the events are dynamic hence the need to define the scope of this research. The research will cover the period from 2003 when the crisis gained the attention of the international community up to the end of January 2007. However, the analysis of some of the issues will predate 2003 because of the relevance of history in understanding contemporary issues. The research methodology employed was based on a combination of historical and analytical methods derived from primary and secondary sources. There was greater reliance in the latter especially articles and other unpublished materials because the conflict is on-going. The primary data were mainly from unstructured interviews with the past AMIS Force Commander. This is in order to highlight some of the issues not available in the literature. The views of some key AMIS officers were also obtained and are cited as AMIS sources as they do not wish their identity to be disclosed. Again, the civil war between Northern and Southern Sudan which was terminated on the eve of the Darfur conflict will not be covered within the scope of this research because the two are not interrelated.

Conceptual Framework

This part begins with a conceptual framework which includes definition of conflict and conflict resolution. It then examines the nature of African conflicts and their sources in order to set the scene for the examination of AU's mechanisms for conflict resolution in the final part of the part.

Conflict is intrinsic to human nature and it is the result of human interactions when opposing interests converge. Wright Quincy defines conflict as 'a particular relationship between states or rival factions within a state which implies subjective hostilities or tension manifested in subversive, economic and military hostilities.'[10] According to Zartman William, conflict

10 Quincy Wright, *A Study of War*,(Chicago:University of Chicago Press,1983),p. 22.

is 'an inevitable aspect of human interaction, an unavoidable concomitant of choices and decision'.[11] While these definitions remain relevant, they only provide a generic perception of conflict. A more focused definition which is relevant to the main thrust of this research is that provided by Dudley Weeks. He conceives conflict as a relationship between parties that disagree over matters that they value, and thus perceive that their power to attain that which they value is threatened by the other party's values, goals, perceptions, behaviour and/or degree of power.[12] Perhaps directly related to this study is Stagner's definition of conflict as:

> a situation in which two or more human beings desire goals which they perceive as being obtainable by one or the other; but not both,... each party is mobilising energy to obtain a goal or desired object or situation and each party perceives the other as a barrier or threat to that goal.[13]

This research adopts the above definition because it highlights the issues of goal incompatibility and continuous mobilization for struggle which explains the situation between the parties to the Darfur conflict. It is however, important to note that not all conflicts involve the use of arms or are violent in nature. In this regard, Miall's classification of conflict will be relevant to this study. He classified conflicts into five categories namely, peaceful, minor violence, major violence, resolved and unresolved.[14] A summary of their explanations are:

a. **Peaceful** A conflict in which no hostilities took place and there was no use of coercion.
b. b. **Minor Violence.** This is a conflict that involves some coercion or some hostilities but not the use of major force.

---

11 I. William Zartman, *Ripe for Resolution: Conflict andI ntervention in Africa*, (NewYork:Oxford University Press, 1989),p.8.

12 Dudley Weeks, *The Eight Steps to Conflict Resolution*, (New York: Putnanam, 1994), p. 23.

13 R. Stagner, *Psychological Aspects of International Conflicts*, (Balmount: n.p., 1967), p. 16.

14 H. Miall, "Peaceful Settlement of Post 1945 Conflicts: A Comparative Study," in Kumar Rupesinghe and Michiko Kuroda, eds., *Early Warning and Conflict Resolution*, (London: Macmillan Press, 1992),pp. 65 – 66.

c. **Major Violence** This is a conflict which involves major force by at least one of the parties to the conflict.
d. **Resolved.** Resolved conflicts are those conflicts in which major parties have accepted that the conflict was over.
e. e.**Unresolved.** These are conflicts in which major issues were settled while other issues remain outstanding.[15]

While the first three classifications were based on nature of conflict, the last two were based on settlement. In some cases, conflicts are classified on the basis of territorial spread (local, regional, and global) or according to the fundamental issues involved.[16]

This research will argue that the Darfur conflict incorporates two of the above classifications. It is a major violence because a significant amount of force is being used by one of the parties namely, the GoS and the conflict remains unresolved. Although technically, the conflict had been 'resolved' by the signing of the Darfur Peace Agreement in 2005, the failure of the government to implement the provisions of the agreement renders it unresolved.

Having examined the concept of conflict, this research will examine the sources or causes of conflicts in Africa. This will provide the basis for examining the concept of conflict resolution and to evaluate the efficacy of AU's conflict resolution mechanisms in the concluding part of this part. Generally, conflict arises from human interdependence. That is for individuals to meet even their basic needs, they have to rely on the active participation of other individuals. Conflict therefore results from the interaction of individuals who have partly incompatible ends, 'in which the ability of one actor to gain his ends depends to an important degree on the choices or decisions another actor will take'.[17]

However, studies which focussed mainly on African conflicts attributed varying causes of African conflicts. One school of thought has argued

15 *Ibid.*, pp. 69–71.

16 *Ibid.*

17 Robert North and Nazhi Chouri, "Economic and Political Factors in International Conflict and Integration," *International Studies Quarterly*, Vol.27, 1983, p.445.

that the sources of conflicts in Africa could be attributed to the sweeping tempo of democratization in Africa particularly with the demise of the Cold War.[18] They argue that the status quo hardly accepts the process, especially of sovereign national conferences which usually impose a transition time table on the incumbent leadership. In an event where the latter reject such an imposition, which usually does not favour it, the opposition do resort to violence.[19] Another school of thought argued that some sources of African conflict have to do with social resistance against government policy errors and conduct of African leaders in office.[20] Another source of conflict in Africa is the issue of limited opportunities in obtaining legitimate means of livelihood and survival. Africa's poverty coupled with the state oriented economic policies by many countries in post independence Africa, constraints the leadership from providing opportunities to the teeming and aspiring youths.[21] This source of conflict often results in violence as many people struggle for scarce resources. Furthermore, the remoteness of some of the regions coupled with the limited capability of African countries to monitor their borders often strengthens resistance forces and worsens the problems of the regimes they confront. Other causes of conflict include the high level of corruption, weak political institutions and poor socio-economic infrastructure.

From the foregoing, it is clear that scholars have varied opinions on the nature, sources or causes of conflicts in Africa. This research argues that unless the sources or causes of a given conflict in Africa are properly diagnosed, an enduring resolution cannot be achieved. Therefore, the first stage of conflict resolution in Africa must begin by the genuine identification of the sources or causes of such conflict.

The concept of conflict resolution refers to all processes and alternative dispute resolution techniques, negotiation, mediation and arbitration as well as consensus building, diplomacy, analytical problem solving, and

---

18 Dent Ocaya Lakidi, 'Africa's Internal Conflicts: The Search for Response', International Peace Academy Report, March 1992, pp. 7–10.

19 *Ibid.*

20 *Ibid.*

21 Y.M. Dickson, 'Conflict Resolution in Africa: Challenges for the 21st Century', ResearchPaper(NWCAbuja,1997),p.18.

peacekeeping that are intended to address the fundamental causes of conflict.[22] This implies that conflict resolution involves a relatively stable resolution of a deep rooted conflict, which is obtained by identifying the root sources of conflict. It includes instituting socio-economic and political changes that will ensure that the values and needs of all parties to the conflict are met.[23] Kevin Avruch highlights the relevance of cultural understanding of conflicts and stressed the need to place conflict resolution processes in a larger 'socio-cultural context and not isolate them from the encompassing worlds-of-meaning in which, in ongoing ways, they remain embedded'.[24] The nature of intra-state African conflict such as the case in Darfur is a good example of where cultural appreciation of the history of African Arabs (Abbala tribe) is required for an enduring resolution to be achieved. Conflict resolution could be achieved either by agreement of the parties involved, by friendly intervention of a third state or a regional organization in order to help the disputants reach an agreement. The last resort is often the binding or final decision of an international agency such as the UN or an international tribunal or by unlimited armed intervention or war.[25]

Notwithstanding the approaches adopted, conflict resolution refers to the outcome of a conflict situation. Wallensteen Peter also argues that:

The concept of solution, or more specifically conflict resolution, is associated with a purposeful search for ways of accommodating the explicit interests of the parties in conflict. Thus it does not mean the same as termination of conflict through victory, nor does it refer to transformation of conflict.[26]

Conflict resolution in Africa needs to distinguish between two interrelated processes. That is the resolution of specific, manifest conflict and the institutionalisation of long-term stable ways of bounding conflict.[27] This

---

22 *Ibid.*

23 A.K. Kwaskebe, 'Conflict Resolution in West Africa: A Study of ECOMOG Operations in Cote d'Ivoire', Research Paper (Abuja: NWC, 2005), pp. 13–14.

24 Kevin Black Avruch and Joseph Scimecca, eds., *Conflict Resolution: Cross-Cultural Perspectives*, (Wesport:Praeger,1991),p. 15.

25 Heidi Burgess and Guy M. Burgess, eds., *Encyclopaedia of Conflicts Resolution*, (USA,1997),p. 430.

26 Kwaskebe, *Op. Cit.*, p. 14.

27 Francis Deng and William Zartman, *Op. Cit.*, p. 383.

research will therefore consider the factors that account for resolving a specific conflict (Darfur) and what factors within the institutional framework of AU are required to enhance resolution of other conflicts in Africa or at least, prevent them becoming violent. There are four existing theories in literature on peace and conflict resolution. These include the relationship between force and conflict resolution, justice and conflict resolution, community and conflict resolution as well as understanding and conflict resolution.[28] These will be discussed in turn in order to determine their utility for this study.

The relationship between force and conflict resolution was articulated by Zartman's concept of ripeness. He argues that specific conflicts can be resolved when the parties reach 'mutually hurting stalemate.'[29] The sense of stalemate is heightened by the perception that the actors stand on a precipice where the cost of conflict are likely to escalate. Under the circumstances, Stedman Stephen argues, settlement may be reached because the parties are unsure of the implications of continued conflict resulting in a loss by all sides. Crucial to achieving this situation, is the attainment of a kind of symmetry between the parties.[30] There is however a lack of consensus on the efficacy of power alone to settle conflicts. This is because if the resolution does not meet the minimal needs of the parties, there can be no enduring settlement.[31]

This research will demonstrate the usefulness of this theory in understanding the stalemate in the implementation of the Darfur Peace Agreement. Another theory on peace and conflict resolution is justice and conflict resolution. It is equally mistaken to ignore or underestimate the existence of exploitation and the social danger resulting from it. The extremely 'uneven distribution of income and wealth in developing countries, poverty, famine and exploitation as well as horrendous gap between rich and poor . . . are explosive factors'.[32] Obasanjo sees justice, peace and stability as indivisible and places the achievement of justice at the forefront of conflict resolution in Africa.[33] Solutions to conflict must therefore project beyond

28 *Ibid.*
29 Zartman, *Op. Cit.*, p. 384.
30 Stedman, *Op. Cit.*
31 *Ibid.*
32 *Ibid.*
33 Olusegun Obasanjo, *Op. Cit.*, p. 17.

force by ensuring that parties to a conflict perceive solutions based on satisfaction of needs, a sense of fairness, and an acknowledgement of an intrinsic right to participate in decisions about one's fate.

The community also plays a vital role in conflict resolution. By community, Stedman implied values, norms, and institutions.[34] He noted that the development of a bargaining culture has been crucial for moderating conflicts within African States. A sense of shared fate prevents ethnic differences from becoming completely debilitating.[35] The theory is reinforced by Ali Mazrui when he said: 'the future of Africa depends on the extent to which it develops its own capacities to manage conflict with the support of international community and particularly, the UN'.[36] The above comment emphasises the institutional aspect of community in conflict resolution and the AU mechanisms for conflict resolution is a practical application of this theory. The last theory of conflict resolution is that of mutual understanding by parties to the conflict. Zartman posits that parties in conflict must find formulas that satisfy their basic needs. Such understanding according to Stedman centres on the ability of parties in conflict to 'identify and acknowledge the needs of their antagonists and to see how unilateral actions affect the other'.[37] Furthermore, this theory emphasised the need for parties to a conflict to redefine their conflict in such a way as to reduce issues of divergence especially the perception that what one side gains, the other must give up. The theory advocates a critical analysis of the conflict in order to resolve areas of contention. Burton John believes that once each side is accurately informed of the perceptions of the other, of the alternative values and goals, of the alternative means and cost of achieving them, the possible outcomes acceptable to the parties are revealed.[38]

From the foregoing, a conflict resolution is like the two sides of the same coin. On one side is the resolution of a violent on-going conflict and on the other side is the enduring resolution of conflict in general. While the thrust of this research is on former, it will also examine the latter in Part Four. This

34 Stedman, *Op. Cit.*
35 *Ibid.*
36 Dickson, *Op. Cit.*, p. 25.
37 Stedman, *Op. Cit.*, p. 387.
38 John Burton, *Dear Survivors*,(Boulder:WestviewPress,1982),p. 122.

research will argue that African Union's mechanisms for conflict resolution in Darfur and the continent in general should be based on the combination of the four theories enumerated above – force, justice, community and understanding. Derived from the above, this research will argue that resolution of the Darfur conflict must address the termination of the on-going violent conflict and the root causes of the conflict in the short and long terms respectively.

Having established the conceptual framework and looked at the sources/causes of African conflicts and the processes and theories of conflict resolution, this research will now consider AU's mechanisms, for conflict resolution. In order to fully appreciate the modus operandi of these mechanisms this research will give a brief background and structure of the AU. The AU is the umbrella regional organization to which all African countries are members excluding Morocco which withdrew in 1985 following the recognition accorded to Sahrawi Arab Democratic Republic (SADR) by 31 member states of the OAU at its 20th Summit in 1984.[39] The history of AU could be traced to 25 May 1963 when the defunct OAU was established with its headquarters in Addis Ababa Ethiopia. The OAU functioned as a continental organization until 11 July 2002 when it formally metamorphosed into the AU. At the time of the establishment of the OAU, most African states were still under colonial administration, thus its principal objective was the promotion of unity and stability of African states, elimination of colonialism and promotion of international cooperation.[40] However, one of the factors that motivated the winding up of the OAU was that most of these provisions were no longer relevant in a post-colonial Africa.

The AU which was modelled along the framework of the European Union is divided into 8 commissions and 14 directorates. However, the Assembly of the Heads of States and Government is the supreme organ. It consists of a representative from each member nation; usually the head of state and it meets at least once a year. The political organs which will oversee the functioning of the AU and make its policies consist of the Assembly of the Union, the Executive Council, the Permanent Representatives Committee,

---

39 T.A. Imobighe, *The OAU(AU) and OAS in Regional Conflict Management: A Comparative Assessment,* (Ibadan:SpectrumBooksLimited,2003),p.97.

40 *Ibid.*

the Specialized Technical Committee and the Pan African Parliament.[41]

Unlike what obtained in the OAU Treaty which prohibits intervention in the internal affairs of member states – a provision under whose cover many African rulers committed all sorts of atrocities against their own citizens – Article IV (a) of the AU Constitutive Act, provides for the 'right of the Union to intervene in a member state pursuant to a decision of the Assembly in respect of grave circumstances namely: war crimes, genocide, and crimes against humanity'.[42] Article 23 provides for the imposition of sanctions against members who do not pay their dues and budget outlays. While this provision is relevant in order to ensure that the organization is not starved of funds in the resolution of conflict (e.g. Darfur), it is doubtful if the AU can operationalise this Article because most of the members are guilty of not paying their dues.

The Constitutive Act also provided for member states to request intervention from the AU. This could potentially enhance the ability of the Union to prevent the escalation of crises. However, this research argues that the retention of the clause of 'non-interference in the domestic affairs of member states' failed to take cognisance of the intra-state nature of African conflicts. Hence, this constitutional defect reduces AU's capacity for conflict resolution. It is therefore doubtful if the AU can unilaterally intervene in respect of 'grave circumstances' if the host nation denies the right of intervention. Can the AU therefore intervene forcefully? This research argues that the AU lacks the capacity to intervene without the approval of the host nation. Thus the implementation of this provision will depend on the good will of the host nation hence in the Darfur conflict, the AU only intervened when the GoS gave its consent. Furthermore, the intervention of the AU in Darfur conflict was under the provision of 'respect for grave circumstances.' It is therefore a test case for the Union and also an indication of the changes that the African Union has already undergone.

The essay will now discuss the various mechanisms at the disposal of the AU for the resolution of conflicts. These include the Peace and Security

41 'Structure of the AU'. [online]. Available from: http://www.africa-union.org/ [Accessed27December2006].

42 For details, see Article 4(a) of the Constitutive Act of the AU, 2002.

Council (PSC), the Panel of the Wise and the Continental Early Warning System. The major tool for the management of crisis by the AU is the PSC. The Protocol establishing the PSC was adopted by the First Session of the AU Assembly. The PSC Protocol entered into force on 26 December 2003, after it was ratified by 27 member states.[43] Modelled after the UN Security Council, the PSC has 15 members (no permanent members). It is the standing decision-making organ for the prevention, management and resolution of conflicts. Membership of the Council is for a period of 3 years.

According to the AU Constitutive Act, the Council's mandate will include the right of the AU to intervene in member states in respect of grave circumstances, war crimes, genocide and crimes against humanity.[44] The Council can also respond to requests by member states to intervene in restoring peace and security.[45] It can further recommend intervention in member states pursuant to Article 4(h) and (j) of the Constitutive Act, while provision is also made for sanctions against member states in cases of unconstitutional changes of government in terms of the Lome Declaration.[46] It is a collective security and early warning arrangement to facilitate timely and efficient response to conflict and crisis situations in Africa.[47] The objective of the PSC is to anticipate, prevent and manage conflicts in, and between member states. The Council is supported by the Commission, a Panel of the Wise, a Continental Early Warning System, an African Standby Force and a Special Fund.

Another mechanism for conflict resolution is the Panel of the Wise. The Panel of the Wise was to be composed of five highly respected African personalities from various segments of the society who have contributed to the cause of peace, security and development of the continent.[48] The Chairperson of the Commission selects the Panel after due consultation with the member states concerned, taking cognisance of sub-regional representation. The members of the Panel serve for a period of 3 years, and

---

43 AFP Briefing Notes, 'Protocol Establishing the Peace and Security Council of the African Union', 25 May 2004.

44 See Article 4(h) AU Constitutive Act.

45 *Ibid.*

46 AFP Briefing, *Op. Cit.*

47 *Ibid.*

48 *Ibid.*

are generally on an advisory role.[49] The purpose of this Panel is to support the efforts of the PSC and those of the Chairperson of the Commission, particularly in the area of conflict prevention.

The new AU also has an early warning system that would ensure the timely activation of its conflict resolution mechanisms. As the Union's response to potential conflict situation on the continent, early warning system would be established at AU Headquarters in Addis Ababa and the headquarters of Regional Economic Communities (RECs).[50] The system will consist of an observation and monitoring centre, known as 'The Situation Room', located within the Conflict Management Directorate of the AU. It will collect data and analyse on the basis of an early warning indicator module. However, as will be demonstrated in this research, the Panel of the Wise and the early warning systems were not utilised in the Darfur conflict.

In order to provide the above mechanisms with the coercive element to use where necessary, an African Standby Force (ASF) was conceived. A framework for the ASF has been concluded, though not yet operational, to enable the PSC perform its responsibilities with respect to the deployment of peace support missions and interventions. Currently, no AU joint training programme exists for the ASF. As part of the efforts to operationalise the Protocol, the 3rd Meeting of the African Chiefs of Defence Staff (ACDS), which took place in Addis Ababa in May 2003, adopted a 'policy framework for the establishment of the ASF and the MSC.'[51] It called for the establishment of the ASF in 2 phases, up to 2010. Currently, consultations are still on-going with all relevant stakeholders to consolidate the proposals contained in the policy.

Funding is a critical requirement in the resolution of conflicts especially when a military force is deployed like the case in Darfur. It was in anticipation of such situations that the PSC Protocol provided for the setting up of a Peace Fund, which is currently funded by an allocation of 6 per cent

49 *Ibid.*

50 *Ibid.*

51 Alpha O. Konare, 'Report of the Chairperson of the Commission on the Establishment of a Continental Peace and Security Architecture and the Status of the Peace Process in Africa,' May 2005, p. 3.

from the AU's regular budget, as well as voluntary contributions. As at 2005, three quarters of the sum of $96m received for this fund, was from partners of the AU and only one quarter from member states of the Union.[52] This is a pointer to the potential problems that lack of funding would cause for the resolution or management of conflict by the AU.

It is also provided that member states agree to accept and implement the decisions of the PSC. The plans for conflict resolution by the AU appear well grounded on research. The real test of this well-thought out plans would be in their application and workability in conflict areas. It also remains to be seen if the member states of the Union will abide by the decisions of the PSC in the event that it was contrary to their interests.

Directly related to the AU's mechanisms for conflict resolution is an economic programme known as the New Partnership for African Development (NEPAD). It was the New African Initiative (NAI) of 11 July 2001 in Lusaka, Zambia that gave birth to NEPAD as unveiled in Abuja on 23 October 2001 when the Steering Committee changed the name from NAI to NEPAD.[53] The uniqueness of the NEPAD initiative is that it was 'conceived and designed by African leaders supported by their professionals'.[54] NEPAD seeks to address the current challenges facing the African continent such as the continued marginalization of Africa, escalating poverty levels and underdevelopment.[55] This is relevant because as noted earlier one of the major causes of African conflicts is poverty. Therefore this research argues that if this initiative is properly managed, it will help in the prevention of conflict. However, it will be difficult to assess its impact because it is a long term measure.

The NEPAD Initiative is built on the premise that economic growth is only possible in an environment where there is peace and security. It thus has a peace and security initiative which consists of 3 elements; one of which

52 *Ibid.*, p. 7.

53 Mohammed Chambas, 'New Partnership for Africa's Development: Security Implications for the Continent', Graduation Lecture delivered at the National War College, Abuja Nigeria, 23 July, 2002, p.6.

54 *Ibid.*

55 NEPAD in Brief. Available from: http://www.nepad.org/[Accessed20December 2006].

is 'building the capacity of African institutions for early warning, as well as enhancing the capacity of African institutions to prevent, manage and resolve conflicts'.[56] These measures laid the foundation for the present AU's mechanisms for conflict resolution and they both complement each other. It is on the strength of these and other provisions of the AU Constitutive Act that Akinterinwa rightly observed that: 'the AU is the crescendo of all the efforts being made to deliver Africa from the scourge of wars and wanton self destruction. It is a mechanism for self realization, self defence and self preservation . . .'[57] The extent to which these mechanisms are useful in the resolution of the Darfur conflict will be examined in the latter part of this research after considering the nature of the conflict in Darfur.

Cause of Darfur Crisis

In the previous part it was established that an enduring conflict resolution must seek to address the underlying causes of the conflict. This part examines the causes of the Darfur conflict and considers the mechanisms used by the AU in the resolution of the conflict particularly, the African Mission in Sudan (AMIS). It then considers the geo-strategic significance of Sudan and the role of the UN and other major state actors.

The violence in Darfur is a complex ethnic/racial conflict and the history of its genesis is not within the scope of this research. However, in order to appreciate the role of AU, a brief account of the causes of the conflict will suffice. The Darfur region of western Sudan has an area of about 256,000 square kilometres and the on-going crisis is part of a wider and complex conflict that has dragged on for generations.[58] Its origin could be traced to a myriad of tribal/ethnic conflicts, resulting from the lack of recognition of collective grazing rights of people and access to ground water resources, drought, desertification, banditry/rebellion activities, the struggle for political recognition and the meagre government socio-economic activities available. The region was hit by a severe drought in the early 1980s and

56 Chambas, *Op. Cit.*, p.8.

57 Bola Akinterinwa, "African Union: Not New Wine in Old Bottle," *This Day*, 15 July, 2002, p. 14.

58 "Background to the Darfur Conflict," *AMIS News Digest*, February 2006,p. 13.

this forced the Arab herdsmen to migrate in search of water and pasture for their animals. In the process, the herdsmen ventured into areas already occupied by the farming non Arab communities thereby triggering series of complicated conflicts, leading to the current situation. Essentially, the parties to the conflict are the Janjawiid, a militia group recruited from the tribes of the Abbala (Camel-herding Arabs, and the non Baggara people (mostly land-tilling tribes of Africa namely; Masalit, Zaghawa and Fur tribes.[59] The name 'dar Fur' means the homeland of the Fur people and it was 'an African Kingdom that embraced Arabs as valued equals'.[60] It is also worth nothing that all Darfurians (Arabs and Africans alike) are all Muslims and Islam was a state cult in imperial Darfur.[61] By January 1917, Darfur was absorbed into the British Empire under Khartoum and was administered through the native administration system in order to reduce cost. During the colonial era, the Darfur region suffered from lack of development such that by the independence of Sudan in 1956, Darfur had the 'lowest number of hospital beds of any Sudanese province'.[62] The neglect of the Darfur region continued in the post colonial era and the Darfurians complained that they were not being treated as full citizens of the Sudanese State. Darfur region continued to be ignored by the GoS and Darfurains received 'less education, less health care, less development assistance and fewer government posts than any other region'.[63]

This research therefore argues that the neglect of Darfur over the years and the marginalization of non-Arab ethnic groups in Darfur led to a growing dissatisfaction amongst the people. In May 2000, copies of a document titled: 'The Black Book - Imbalance of Power and Wealth in Sudan' was circulated in Khartoum.[64] The document highlighted this marginalization and sensitized the Darfurians because of its revolutionary content which showed that political and economic power in Sudan lay in the hands of only three tribes.[65]

---

59 Julie Flint and Alex de Waal, *Darfur A Short History of a Long War*, (London: Zed Books, 2005),p. 3.

60 *Ibid.*

61 *Ibid.*, p. 10.

62 *Ibid.*, p. 13.

63 Jackson Mwalulu, "The Chad Libya Factor in Darfur Crisis," *African Today*, October 2004, p.22.

64 Flint Julie and de Waal Alex, *Op. Cit.*, p. 17.

65 *Ibid.*

Alex de Waal has argued that the background to the conflict began in 1999 with a split in the Congress Party in which President Omer al Bashir ousted Dr Hassan al Turabi, a Darfurian. Subsequently, the ruling party security officers began replacing local officials within the Darfurian part of the party with hand picked loyalists who will not be loyal to Turabi.[66] New leaders were brought from the Popular Defence Forces (PDF) which, prior to that time, had been the local militia and was relatively unpoliticised. Thereafter, the PDF continued to support certain ethnic groups against others especially for Darfur's indigenous Arabs against group such Masalit, Fur and Zaghawa.[67] This led to a resistance in February 2003 when a large group of farmers turned guerrillas, attacked the police station at Golo in Jebel Marra to seize weapons and 'this was the spark that began the conflagration'.[68] Prior to this time, weapons had been flowing into Darfur through Muammar Ghaddafi's support to various Arab groups across the Sahel in an attempt to create an 'Arab belt'.[69] As guns flowed through Darfur to Chad, so also was an increasing racist ideology of Arab supremacy. This further reinforced the racial/ethnic dimension of one where 'Arab' and 'Africa' assumed a new mutually exclusive and mutually antagonistic meaning.[70]

Also circulated widely, was a document which originated from an Arab organization in Sudan titled: 'Change the Demography of Darfur and Empty it of African Tribes'.[71] Therefore, the Darfur conflict is ethnically/racially based that is, of 'Arabs' against 'Africans'. The resistance to this threat led to formation of the Darfur Liberation Front (DLF) which later changed its name to Sudan Liberation Movement/Army (SLM/A). The SLM/A later formed a coalition with the Justice and Equality Movement (JEM) and in April 2003, they attacked El Fasher Airport in North Darfur which intensified the conflict.[72] Violence escalated further when in response to the attack, the Bashir's government decided to arm the Janjawiid and other government allied tribes against the SLM/A and JEM. The resort to the use of Janjawiid

66 De Waal Alex, "Briefing: Darfur Sudan: Prospects for Peace," *African Affairs*, Vol. 104, No. 414, 2005, p.127.

67 *Ibid.*, pp. 127–128.

68 *Ibid.*

69 William G. O'Neill and Violette Cassis, *Op.Cit.*, p. 14.

70 *Ibid.*

71 Julie Flint and de Waal Alex, *Op. Cit.*, p. 39.

72 William G. O'Neill and Violette Cassis, *Op. Cit.*, p. 15.

is consistent with the government's use of proxies to fight its battle as seen during its 21 years war with the Southern Sudan. Again, since most of the Sudanese military are from Darfur, the GoS could not count on their loyalty hence their resort to the Janjawiid.[73] By the middle of 2003 the rebels were winning 34 out of 38 encounters and the government began to fear that it may lose the whole of Darfur.[74] Subsequently, the Janjawiid and government forces began to operate jointly and attacked African tribes including civilians, raped women and began to destroy 'everything that made life possible'.[75] Therefore, in September 2003 President Idriss Derby of Chad brokered negotiations in N'jamena between the GoS, SLM/A and JEM. It called for a 45-day humanitarian ceasefire which unfortunately, was not respected by all the parties.[76]

Having highlighted the nature and causes of the Darfur conflict and the attempt made by Chad to broker a ceasefire, this research will now examine how the AU applied its conflict resolution mechanisms in the Darfur situation. Julie Flint and Alex de Waal have argued that the AU became involved in the Darfur conflict by default.[77] Peacekeepers were required to monitor the ceasefire brokered by Idriss Derby and the AU was tasked to provide them. However, the AU invoked Article 4 of its Constitutive Act and adopted a combination of dialogue and military approach to the management of the Darfur conflict. The AU formed the Ceasefire Commission (CFC) on 28 May 2004. The CFC was composed of about 60 AU military observers (MILOBS), representatives of the various parties to the conflict and observers from the EU and USA with about 300 soldiers of the AMIS to protect them.[78]

Before proceeding further, it is necessary to first examine the application of the AU Continental Early Warning System (CEWS) at this stage of the conflict. As noted earlier, this mechanism was aimed at early detection of potentially dangerous situation leading to immediate action. Meanwhile, Darfur was first discussed at PSC in May 2004 which means that the CEWS

---

73 *Ibid.*
74 Julie Flint and Alex de Waal, *Op. Cit.*, p. 101.
75 *Ibid.*, p. 111.
76 *Ibid.*, p. 119.
77 *Ibid.*
78 William G. O'Neill and Violette Cassis, *Op. Cit.*, p. 16.

mechanism was not utilised. To this extent, this research argues that the AU CEWS has failed in its first task since the formation of the AU. Had it identified the conflict which effectively became overt in 2003, then an emergency session of the PSC ought to have been held. In either case, the delay in AU's initial response demonstrates a weakness not of the mechanism but the decision making process of the PSC.

Despite the initial delayed response, the AU under auspices of President Olusegun Obansanjo of Nigeria (then Chairman of AU) held a series of meetings with a view to resolving the crisis. This led to the signing of the Darfur Peace Agreement (DPA) in Abuja in May 2006. The process leading to this agreement lasted for two years but Julie Flint argues that the first four rounds of the seven-round talks where dominated by numerous violations on the part of GoS and the failure of the international community to check the wanton carnage in Darfur.[79] She observed that AU mediation was as problematic as the rebel negotiators themselves and that the 30 April deadline set by the PSC was unrealistic. She identified some of the flaws in the process that could possibly hinder its implementation. First, the draft DPA was presented to the parties on 25 April and had only five days to endorse or discard the agreement. Meanwhile, the Arabic version was not ready until 28 April – less than 48 hours before the date line. Second, the people of Darfur were not party to the talks nor were the contents explained to them. Third, there was no provision for individual compensation and no timetable for the disarmament of the Janjawiid militias. Finally, the GoS which is party to the conflict was expected to supervise the implementation.[80] She contends that it was an imposed and partial agreement which favoured the GoS to the exclusion of majority of the people of the Darfur.[81] Although Julie herself was invited to advise the AU during the DPA talks, she noted that the mediators never listened to her advice.[82] As at January 2007, the GoS has failed to disarm the Janjawiid, rather it has continued to support it. In addition, it has continued to threaten AU peace keepers through abduction of its personnel and has refused to accept the supplanting of AMIS with a UN force.

As pointed out in Part 2, for an enduring reconciliation of conflicts in

79 Julie Flint, "Can Darfur Peace Deal Succeed," *Africa Today*, June 2006, p.10.

80 *Ibid.*

81 *Ibid.*

82 Julie Flint in response to a question asked by this author as to the nature of advice she gave the AU.

Africa, conflict resolution mechanisms must be based on the combination of the four theories of conflict resolution namely: justice, community, understanding and force. The DPA however has ignored all these. First, there can be no justice in the resolution of a conflict where a party to the conflict is also charged with the supervision of the implementation process. Second, the community, in this case the people of Darfur were not involved in the peace talks that would affect their future even though they are the victims of the conflict. The pastoralists were not represented at the negotiating table hence their concerns were not addressed in the DPA.[83] Third, there appears to be no sufficient level of understanding and compromise by the signatories to the Agreement beyond their personal desires and the pressure from the AU mediators. To this extent, this essay contends that the AU's violations of these vital theories of conflict resolution have not addressed the root causes of the conflict. Therefore, the DPA needs to be revisited in order to proffer a long term solution to the conflict. However, the AU itself is constrained by the fact that it is not possible to secure any agreement without the active involvement of the GoS which is a state actor and a member of the AU while the SLM/A and JEM are non-state actors. This research will therefore argue that the AU conflict resolution mechanisms failed to fully appreciate the nature of African conflicts which is increasingly intra-state.

Furthermore, despite the provision for the Panel of the Wise, there is no indication that the AU utilised this mechanism. Considering the racial/ethnic nature of the conflict, it would have been useful if the Panel of the Wise, made up of respected personalities of both Arab and African descent, were involved prior to, or during the talks leading to the DPA. Similarly, the DPA did not address the root causes of the Darfur conflict which include poverty and socio-economic neglect among others. A comprehensive peace agreement with potential development programmes for the Darfur region would have been ideal.

The research will now consider the AU's use of force within the theory of conflict resolution highlighted in the previous Part. The African Mission in Sudan (AMIS) represents the AU's use of force as a theory of conflict resolution. In this regard, the mandate of AMIS will be examined before

83 Julie Flint, 'The Arabs are Victims Too', November 19, 2006.

considering its successes and failures. The mandate given to AMIS by AU was to provide secure environment for the delivery of humanitarian relief and return of Internally Displaced Persons (IDPs) and to monitor and observe the compliance of the parties to the Humanitarian Ceasefire Agreement (HCFA). It was also mandated to assist in the process of confidence building; all in order to assist in increasing the level of compliance of all parties to the HCFA and enhance the process of political settlement necessary for peace and security in Darfur.[84] The mandate was drafted based on the assumption that parties will respect the N'djamena Agreement of 8 April 2004. This was the mandate given to the 60 monitors and 300 troops assigned to protect them but the force has since expanded to about 7,000 troops since January 2007 without a review of its mandate.

This use of force in conflict resolution cannot succeed in Darfur because of the limitations of the AU's mandate. The mandate failed to appreciate the violent situation in Darfur hence the AU force cannot protect the innocent civilians in refugee camps. The mandate permits AMIS to protect civilians only if they were being attacked in their presence and only if it feels it has sufficient troops to intervene.[85] The mandate was restrictive and the AMIS Force Commander (FC) said he would have preferred a mandate that 'permits the peacekeepers to bite when the need arises'.[86] He however pointed out that AMIS cannot enforce compliance with limited equipment, finance and logistics. Although, a more robust mandate would require more force on the ground, the AU mediators should have sought for such a mandate so that as AU's force began to increase, the force should have been able to establish at least safe havens around refugee camps. This limited mandate has been the position held by the AU's PSC that the cooperation of the GoS and consent were prerequisites. However, cooperation and consent are relative terms and only makes the task of AMIS cumbersome. The restrictive mandate therefore denied AMIS the ability to stop the ethnic cleansing or genocide. It has been suggested that the PSC should have coerced Sudan to allow greater freedom of action for AMIS.[87] It should be noted however, that some African countries were not comfortable with the restrictive nature of AMIS mandate. For

84 HCFA.

85 Nick Grono, "Briefing–Darfur: The International Community's Failure to Protect," *African Affairs,* Vol.105, No.421, p. 626.

86 Interview with Major General Festus Okonkwo, 3 March, 2007.

87 William G. O'Neill and Violette Cassis, *Op. Cit.*, p. 25.

example, the Rwandan President Paul Kagame has asserted that: 'our forces will not standby and watch innocent civilians being hacked to death like was [done] here [Rwanda] in 1994'.[88] Similarly, the FC has said that: 'We cannot sit down and watch civilians being killed while we are around'.[89] There is however, a significant difference between intentions and capabilities. AMIS lacks the capability to react with force due to its limited strength and the GoS has insisted that increase in troop numbers will be allowed if the mandate does not change.[90]

It was based on this limited mandate and in line with the guidance from the AU Head of Mission (HOM) that AMIS developed its concept of operations (CONOPS). The CONOPS made the following assumptions:[91]

a. All parties will comply with the HCFA.
b. The parties will agree to the strengthening of AMIS as given in the AMIS plan of action.
c. Donors will fund the necessary expenses to allow the execution of the given plan.
d. Protection of civilians is the responsibility of the GoS.
e. The parties will work toward a comprehensive peace agreement.

These assumptions did not hold as the parties continue to violate the HCFA and other protocols. It is against this backdrop that this research advocates the need for AU to reassess the present mandate in order to strengthen the capacity of AMIS to cope with the deteriorating security situation in the region.

Having made those assumptions, the FC's intent was to create a secure environment that will lead to the return of IDPs to their villages thereby creating conditions that will ultimately lead to a political settlement of the crisis. The Main Effort of the FC was 'to degrade the ability of the parties from acting with impunity, as well as enforce compliance with HCFA and this lies with the pro-active monitoring by the MILOBs'.[92] The FC's intention

88 *Ibid.*, p. 28.
89 *Ibid.*
90 *Ibid.*, p. 29.
91 AMIS FC's Handing Over Notes to in-coming FC.
92 *Ibid.*

cannot be achieved because of the inadequacy of his mandate and the limitations of his force size and structure.

The force structure of AMIS includes the Force Headquarters, one Airmobile Special Forces Company (reserve), Force Headquarters Company, one Explosive Ordinance Disposal/De-mining Section, one Light Field Engineer Company, one Military Police Platoon and a pool of military interpreters. It also has eight Sector Headquarters with one infantry battalion in each sector as well as an aviation unit of civil helicopters. Considering the size of Darfur which is 256,000 sq km, the strength of about 7,000 personnel (literarily one soldier per 36.6 sq km) and with the above structure, the implementation of even the restrictive mandate will be a herculean task. It is on this basis that this research will now briefly highlight some of the successes and shortcomings of AMIS in Darfur.

AMIS has recorded some successes despite certain constraints. First, the deployment of AMIS troops in certain areas considered risky and contrary to its mandate, deterred attacks against the civilians. Examples include the AMIS deployment in the town of Labado and other villages in South Darfur in late 2004 and 2005.[93] Second, AMIS personnel have succeeded in the mediation and resolution of local conflicts within their localities where the customary dispute resolution mechanisms have been disrupted by the conflict. AMIS soldiers, most of whom share similar traditions and values with these communities found it easy mediate and resolve conflicts.[94] Some of the Sector Commanders hold regular meetings with the Sheikhs in their sectors to resolve disputes and their efforts are being appreciated by the locals. Third, AMIS patrols in all the sectors are quite flexible in order to cover the varying nature of threats in their areas. For example, while conducting investigative patrols, they frequently divert into other areas under potential threats of attacks as part of confidence building measures.[95] Similarly, they have responded to requests from humanitarian agencies to patrol certain areas where civilians are under threats. In addition, AMIS has expanded its eight sectors through the opening of 'Group Sites' which are small camps

93 William G. O'Neill and Violette Cassis, *Op. Cit.*, p. 35.
94 *Ibid.*, p. 36.
95 *Ibid.*

opened 24 hour/7 days a week presence in order to protect more civilians.[96] The increased patrols by AMIS along the major routes in Darfur have also reduced the level of banditry attacks as compared to the state it was in 2004. On the whole, AMIS soldiers have 'demonstrated adaptability, trying to turn deficiencies into positives'.[97] The force has suffered considerable provocation such as abductions, arson, attacks and killings from the warring parties.

Notwithstanding these successes, AMIS has some weaknesses which are too numerous to be examined within the scope of this research. However, the major ones which relate directly to AU will be discussed. First, there was no strategic guidance and according to the first AMIS FC, 'the strategic directive arrived the mission when I have started arranging for my rotation [almost a year]'.[98] Second, the command and control structure is cumbersome. The present FC reports to the Chairman of AU PSC through the Deputy Head of Mission (DHOM) and the Special Representative of the Chairperson of AU Commission (SRCC). This arrangement is further complicated by the unwieldy bureaucracy at AU Headquarters.[99] Third, although the Head of Mission (HOM) deals with the political groups in the Darfur conflict, there are no political advisors to assist Sector Commanders in developing effective relationship with the parties in conflict within their sectors. The deployment of political advisers is required for the smooth implementation of the peace agreement.[100] However, Major General Okonkwo observes that there is no need to deploy political advisers on a permanent basis but recommends occasional visits to sectors by political advisers.[101] Fourth, there is a serious logistical shortcoming due to the absence of a logistics plan at the inception of the operation.[102] This shortcoming is further complicated by AU's poor coordination of outside assistance from NATO, EU and other bilateral offers of assistance to address the logistics problem of AMIS. For example, at one point, three different countries offered helicopter support but could not get a response from the AU on when, where and how to deliver them.[103] This has

96 *Ibid.*, p. 37.
97 *Ibid.*, p. 38.
98 Okonkwo, *Op. Cit.*
99 William G. O'Neill and Violette Cassis,*Op. Cit.*, pp. 50–57.
100 *Ibid.*
101 Okonkwo, *Op.Cit.*
102 William G. O'Neill and Violette Cassis, *Op. Cit.*
103 *Ibid.*

led the EU to establish a technical support group in Addis Ababa to process and streamline support from NATO and individual states. Closely related to the above is the incapacity of AU to handle the logistics requirement of the AMIS. For example, some troops contributing countries could not supply their countries with basic military equipment at the outset of the mission and key mobility assets were either ineffective or unavailable.[104] The AU also lacks the staff capacity and experience to handle key logistics issues such as contract letting and monitoring, fuel provision, storage and maintenance amongst others. It also has a weak financial oversight thus making donors particularly the EU to demand greater transparency and accountability.[105]

Another major shortcoming is the insufficient impact of the ceasefire monitoring mechanisms which are often not timely and lacked adequate description of the extent of violations. Again, this is a deficiency of the HCFA which did not prescribe punishment for parties that violated its provisions. Similarly, the inclusion of the representatives of the GoS and the rebel groups in AMIS investigations tend to frighten witnesses and victims from testifying. It also allows for manipulation of evidence. For example, even where forensic evidence shows that helicopter gunship attacked a village, the government official would refuse to endorse the report because the joint investigation team had not seen the gun ships' attack.[106]

Although the AU is just about five years old and Darfur is the first test of its conflict resolution mechanisms, the shortcomings identified suggest the lack the institutional framework to support the use of force (AMIS) in conflict resolution. Perhaps the potential solution could be achieved when the ASF concept becomes fully operational.

However, despite the shortcomings of AU in Darfur, its involvement is an indication of Africa's resolve to solve its own problems. As noted by the then AU SRCC Baba Gana Kingibe: 'We stand or fall in Darfur. If we fail here, nobody is going to look to the AU for a solution to other conflicts in the

---

104 Catherine Guicherd, "The AU in Sudan: Lessons for the African Stand-by Force," *International Peace Academy*, March 2007, p. 16.

105 William G. O'Neill and Violette Cassis, *Op. Cit.*

106 *Ibid.*

continent'.[107] Similarly, Obasanjo has observed that: 'it is not in the interest of Sudan nor Africa, nor indeed the whole world, for us to stand by, fold our hands and see genocide in Darfur'.[108] Given the deteriorating security situation which has been described as 'genocide', why is it that the UN and other major state actors have been reluctant to get decisively involved and what has been their roles?

This research will argue that although the UN and other major state actors became aware of the crisis in Darfur by late 2003, they have failed to act decisively because Darfur is of least geo-strategic importance to the major world players. Furthermore, parochial national interests particularly of the US, contributes to this reluctance to act beyond expression of condemnation. The role of China in Sudan has also complicated the situation. Sudan is the largest and most chaotic African country yet it is located in one of the worst geographical area in the continent. Darfur in particular is of little or no strategic importance: it has no water and no oil.[109] Therefore, the US has ruled out the possibility of sending troops now and in the future to Darfur, instead it promised to act only through AU-sponsored peacekeeping force.[110] Even the UK, which was the colonial power in Sudan that ignored the development of the Darfur region, has not responded positively to the crisis. None of the major state actors is prepared to commit their troops in Darfur hence their support for African solutions. The presence of China in Sudan is purely for its oil interests and consistent with its foreign policy in Africa, it does not meddle in the internal affairs of states. It is doubtful if major world players would have reacted in a similar manner in North Africa or the Middle East. This is not to suggest that Sudan is not economically important. It has significant reserve oil and supplies 80 per cent of the world's gum Arabic needs and this product is so vital to international capital that it was exempted from the sanctions placed on Sudanese products in 1997 for allegedly sponsoring terrorism.[111]

---

107 *Ibid.*, p. 38.

108 Olusegun Obasanjo, "Talking Tough," *Africa Today,* November 2006, p.22.

109 Julie Flint, *Op Cit.*, p. 11.

110 Jackson Mwalulu, "Impossible Situation," *Africa Today*, November 2004, p. 16.

111 *Ibid.*

Why then is it that the US which has invested so much resources in the North – South peace process has not reacted positively in the Darfur conflict? This research argues that America is frustrated because as the 21 years civil war in Sudan comes to an end, the Darfur conflict opened another part which affects its oil interest. The GoS had placed a ban on the US and UK firms from exploring oil in Sudan and China had moved in to fill the vacuum. Perhaps more importantly, America is constrained to act decisively because it now has a close intelligence relationship with the GoS in its war on terror. For example in late 2005, it flew Salah Gosh, the Sudanese Chief of Intelligence and one of the architects of the Darfur atrocities on a private plane to the US for consultations with the CIA.[112] However, Williams Paul and Belami Alex have argued to the contrary. They contended that the unwillingness of the West to intervene in Darfur was due to three main reasons.[113] These include the increased scepticism about America's humanitarian interventionism especially over the invasion of Iraq, the minimal western strategic interests in Sudan and the relationship between the Darfur conflicts and Sudan's civil war.

This is not to suggest that America has not shown interest in Sudan rather, it emphasises the lack of decisive action mainly because Darfur is not one of its strategic priority. Although the US has said that President Bush views the situation in Sudan seriously and that Sudan is the centre piece of his African agenda,[114] this has not been substantiated by tangible action. The US has reacted to the Darfur conflict in a number of ways including the determination of genocide in September 2004.[115] In fact, America is the only nation to have made such a determination and the US Government has aggressively sought for a political solution for Darfur as the best way to implement a just and lasting peace. America has provided funds to AU in support of AMIS operations and it played a leading role in the UNSC for action on Darfur and sought for speedy transition from AU to a larger UN peacekeeping force.[116] However, although America is aware that the GoS is

---

112 Nick Grono, *Op Cit.*, p. 628.

113 Williams Paul and Alex Bellamy, "The Responsibility to Protect and the Crisis in Darfur," *Security Dialogue*, Vol. 36, No. 1, March 2005, pp. 27–47.

114 Jendayi Frazer, "Prospects for Peace in Darfur," *FDCH Congressional Testimony*, 18May, 2006, p. 1.

115 Colin Powell, *Op. Cit.*

116 Frazer, *Op. Cit.*, pp. 2–3.

responsible for the deteriorating security situation, it has failed to impose any sanctions because the GoS appears to be cooperating with the US in its war on terror.

On its part, the EU's approach is similar to the US which is to allow the AU to remain as the lead international player in Darfur while it provides the regional organization with the necessary support. The EU's role has been to support an African solution to an African problem by funding AU mission.[117] However, this support has been dwindling as plans are underway to supplant the AU with a UN force. NATO has also provided the AU mission with limited logistics support such as strategic lift and technical assistance but it is not likely to go beyond this gesture. On its part, China has strategic interests in Sudan as it is Sudan's largest trading partner with a bilateral trade of about US$2.521b in 2004 and the China National Petroleum Company (CNPC) owns 40% of stake in the Greater Nile Petroleum Operating Company, a consortium dominating oil production in Sudan.[118] Based on its strategic interests, China has consistently abstained on UN Security Council Resolutions (UNSCR) on Darfur. It abstained on UNSCR 1556 (30 Jul 2004), UNSCR 1564 (18 Sep 2004), UNSCR 1590 (24 Mar 2005), UNSCR 1591 (29 Mar 2005) and UNSCR 1593 (15 Mar 2006).[119] In addition, China has succeeded in diluting the proposals over intervention measures in Darfur including an oil embargo. China's response could be based not only on her strategic interests but also on a long outstanding mistrust of US sponsored interventionism. So far, China's only contribution to the peace process in Darfur was in the form of humanitarian aid valued at about US$610,000.[120]

From the foregoing, this research contends that the conflict in Darfur which is about the size of France requires enormous logistics far beyond what the AU can handle. Perhaps, without the meagre support from the US, EU and NATO, the military component of AU mission in Sudan would have been terminated. According to the then AMIS FC, while these support were appreciated, they were not enough to meet the operational requirements

---

117 Nick Grono, *Op Cit.*, p. 627.

118 Daniel Large, "The Politics of China's Relations with Africa: The Case of Sudan," *Institute of Social and Cultural Anthropology, University of Oxford*, Seminar Paper, 2005,p. 9.

119 *Ibid.*, p. 13.

120 *Ibid.*

of AMIS and that despite AU's requests, 'no country or organization was prepared to provide the highly needed Attack Helicopters'.[121] Thus, the AU's conflict resolution mechanisms must incorporate mission sustainability forecast to determine potential logistics requirements prior to the approval of the PSC for the deployment of peacekeeping force. Alternatively, it should first seek and obtain commitments for logistics support from major world players or seek for alternative source of funding its operations. This research argues that unless the issue of funding and logistics support is addressed, the AU cannot seek for African solution to African conflicts through the employment of force. It may have to rely on the UN framework of intervention.

It is therefore necessary to examine the role played by the UN in the Darfur conflict. Based on the UN's Charter, it was expected that it will be the first organization to react to the violent conflict in Darfur because of the magnitude of the crisis but the UN did not live to this expectation. In addition, the proposal for the UN to provide financial assistance to regional organizations for peace operations is yet to be approved by the UNSC hence the AU could not benefit from any substantial assistance from the UN and this was a major drawback to AMIS. It was also expected that Darfur would test the UN's commitment to Responsibility to Protect (R2P) which was endorsed by the UN General Assembly Resolution 60/1 of 24 October 2005. It states among other issues that:

The international community, through the UN, also has the responsibility to use appropriate diplomatic, humanitarian and other peaceful means, in accordance with Parts VI and VII of the Charter to help protect populations from genocide, war crimes, ethnic cleansing and crimes against humanity.[122]

However, the UN has failed to put pressure on the GoS to disarm the Janjawiid. It was after two years since the conflict became overt that the UNSC in March 2005, belatedly imposed sanctions against those individuals impeding the peace process and committing human rights violations.[123] It also took the UN another one year and in the face of deteriorating security

121 Okonkwo, *Op. Cit.*
122 Nick Grono, *Op. Cit.*, p. 623.
123 *Ibid.*, p. 626.

situation, before it identified four persons for human rights violations.[124] On 24 March 2005, UNSC passed Resolution 1590 calling on the UN Mission in Sudan (UNMIS) to find ways of utilizing its resources to provide 'appropriate assistance to the AU, including logistical support and technical assistance'.[125] The UN has also established an International Commission of Inquiry which has since established that crimes against humanity and war crimes have been committed in Darfur which is no less serious than genocide.

Perhaps the first decisive step taken by UN was when the UNSC passed Resolution 1706 which provides for the deployment of UN peacekeepers to Darfur by the end of the year with a proviso that the deployment would depend on the consent of the GoS.[126] The GoS has taken advantage of the last clause in the resolution and has repeatedly rejected plans to insert 20,600 strong UN peacekeepers in Darfur. Meanwhile, the violence and insecurity in Darfur has escalated and the militias 'are better armed, they are more brutal than ever and their potential to do bad is better than ever'.[127] Again, by the end of 2006, the UN has failed to secure the consent of the GoS by applying diplomatic pressure. Hence Egeland observed that, 'the UN might have made a diplomatic mistake by allowing Western nations to take the lead in applying pressure on Sudan to agree to a UN force'.[128] The AU which had earlier advocated for purely Africa solution to the conflict in Darfur, has realised that it lacks the capacity to cope with the magnitude of the conflict. Hence, it welcomed the transformation of the peacekeeping force into a UN force. However, AU wants to remain relevant in the process as stressed by Obasanjo:

The great challenge before us now is how to strengthen and sustain AMIS until the transition to a UN mission with the support and cooperation of the government of Sudan, while retaining its African ownership and character.[129]

---

124 *Ibid.*

125 UNMIS is monitoring the implementation of the North – South peace agreement which ended the civil war in Sudan.

126 UNSC Resolution 1706, 31 August, 2006.

127 Martin Luther King, *Op. Cit.*, p. 22.

128 *Ibid.*

129 *Ibid.*

However, President Bashir has said that the resolution to replace the AU force with a UN force would only serve the interests of the UNSC to 'effectively put Sudan under the trusteeship of certain parties in the council'.[130] It has been argued that the UN introduced the clause of consent of the GoS because it is nervous of getting involved in a complicated peace support operation in Sudan which is 35 times bigger than Sierra Leone which until recently was UN's biggest mission.[131] Again, the UN could have been conscious that there are Islamic radicals in Sudan who dislike international meddling in their affairs and would not care to give up half of the country to deny such interference.[132]

The adoption of UNSC Resolution 1706 is an indication of the inability of the AU's conflict resolution mechanisms to cope with the violent and complex nature of the Darfur conflict. The fact that AU is desperate for the transformation of AMIS into a UN force suggests that the force has been exhausted and the AU can not cope on its own. The refusal of the GoS to endorse the involvement of a UN force is because the government is a party to the conflict and has been responsible for most of the atrocities. Therefore, having a strong UN presence in Sudan and with the International Commission of Inquiry, top government officials are wary of being indicted and arrested. To this extent, the UN like the EU and US other state actors have so far failed to act decisively in the Darfur conflict.

Constrains and Prospects of African Union

The previous part examined the application of AU's mechanisms for conflict resolution in Darfur and the roles played thus far by major state actors, the EU, and UN. This part will examine the constraints and prospects of AU in conflict resolution in the region. It will then consider some strategies that could potentially enhance AU's capacity to resolve present and future conflicts in Africa.

---

130 Omar Bashir, quoted in Wairagala Wakabi, "Darfur Breakthrough," *Africa Today*, October 2006, p. 26.

131 P. Moocraft, 'Sudan: End of the Longest War?', *RUSI Journal*, Vol. 150, February 2005, pp. 58–59.

132 *Ibid.*

One of the major constraints of AU in conflict resolution is the intra-regional interests of member states in the outcome of a conflict. As noted in the previous part, Libya's desire to create an Arab belt in the 1980s contributed to the influx of arms and bandits in to the Darfur region as well as the creation of a racist ideology based on Arab supremacy. Ghaddafi has demonstrated a keen interest in the outcome of the Darfur conflict and warned in late 2004 that foreign intervention could potentially result in another Iraq - style conflict.[133] In August 2004, he held informal talks with representatives of all parties to the conflict including the AU and Chad.[134] The talks did not yield any result because the SLM/A and the JEM were suspicious of Ghaddafi's intent since he is an Arab and because of his previous antecedents. Again, Chad was not comfortable having Libya taking over the peace process from AU because of its historical rivalry with Libya which began in the 1980s. In the same vein, the GoS at some point in the Abuja Peace talks had advocated the shifting of the meeting to Libya because of what they perceived as Nigeria's sympathy for the SLM/A and JEM.

Furthermore, Chadian President Idriss Derby is a key ally of the GoS and is far from being a neutral arbiter. He is however in a dilemma due to pressure from his advisers not to support a war against his own Zaghawa people.[135] This is partly because the Darfur conflict has been characterised as one of 'Arabs' against 'Africans'. It was no surprise therefore that while Nigeria's Obasanjo has been the first African President to describe the situation in Darfur as 'genocide', the GoS, some countries in North Africa and the Middle East have argued that the genocide determination by the US is a 'cynical use of a new tool to legitimize America's interventionism and demonise Arabs'.[136] Similarly, Julie Flint has argued that the manner in which President Konare of Mali personalised the mediation process in the Darfur conflict during his tenure as the AU Chairman further complicated negotiation between the parties to the conflict.[137]

---

133 Jackson Mwalulu, "No End to Darfur Tragedy," *Africa Today*, October 2004, pp. 22–23.

134 *Ibid.*

135 Ulrich Mans, "Briefing: Sudan: The New War in Darfur," *African Affairs*, 2004, p. 293.

136 Alex de Waal, *Op. Cit.*, p. 133.

137 Julie Flint, in response to a question asked by this author regarding the commitment of African leaders to the peace process.

This research therefore argues that due to ethnic spread of tribes across the national boundaries, ethnic identity tends to override national identity. This has often led to the competing intra-regional interests in the resolution of conflicts in Africa. A similar example to Darfur was the involvement of Guinea in the Liberian and Sierra Leonean conflicts in support of their Mandingo ethnic groups in those countries.

Closely related to the issue of intra-regional interest is the external influence factor in Africa which has sometimes prevented the peaceful resolution of crisis. One of the factors which encourage external influence is the lack of resources on the part of Africa to resolve conflicts without seeking assistance from some Western countries. As noted in the previous part, AU lacks the funds to support her intentions in Darfur and without the support of America and the EU, it is doubtful if the AU force would have lasted this long in Sudan. Quite often it is the interest of former colonial masters that encourage them to take the lead. In the Sierra Leone and Cote d'Ivoire conflicts, Britain and France respectively, displayed this tendency by actively participating. France, which is currently involved in Cote d'Ivoire, aggravated matters when she unilaterally destroyed the Ivorian Air Force. It is however, surprising that in the case of Darfur, Britain has not shown enough interest as it did in Sierra Leone notwithstanding that Tony Blair visited Sudan in 2004. Perhaps, this may not be unconnected with the commitment of British forces in Iraq and Afghanistan. On its part, the US has not acted decisively in pressurising the GoS because the government seems to be cooperating with the US in its on-going war on terror. Since the extra-regional interest particularly of the Western countries are at variance with those of Africa, conflicts are merely suppressed temporarily and its root causes ignored. Hence, such conflicts recur when the aggrieved party deemed fit.

Furthermore, the role of external influences may be complicated in the near future with the increasing incursion of China into Africa particularly, in countries such as Sudan where it has already filled the vacuum created by expulsion of UK and US oil companies. In circumstances where state actors commit their resources towards the resolution of crisis in Africa, they will try to influence the outcome of the crisis in favour of the party that would safeguard their national interest in post conflict. Alternatively, major state actors like China will do everything possible to retain the support of the government in power and thereby safeguard her vital interests in that region notwithstanding ethics and international opinion to the contrary. Already this trend is being played in Zimbabwe where China is now the closest friend to President Robert Mugabe and has remained mute over his human rights violations.

Another constraint of the AU in conflict resolution is the failure of the parties to the conflict to comply with the provisions of the peace agreements they endorsed. For example, despite the signing of the Darfur Peace Agreement (DPA) in March 2006, the GoS has failed to disarm the Janjawiid and protect the civilians as required by the provisions of the Agreement. Rather, it has continued to violate the ceasefire agreement.[138] So far, the refusal of GoS and the Janjawiid rebels to stop all offensive against the non-Arab populations of Darfur is creating credibility problems for the AU. The AU peacekeepers can only check these violations militarily if the force is strengthened and its mandate reviewed to include the disarming of all rebel groups including the Janjawiid. Again, given the nature of African conflicts which is increasingly intra-state, it would be difficult for the AU to ensure compliance with agreements by non-state actors because unlike nation states, it is difficult to apply sanctions against them. Furthermore, this research contends that unless the AU includes punitive measures in its conflict resolution mechanisms, parties will continue to violate agreements.

Perhaps the most critical constraint of the AU in conflict resolution is the lack of necessary logistics and funds to sustain its missions. Majority of the AU member states have weak economic base hence their economies are highly dependent on foreign aids and loans from Western donor countries to carryout their programmes. Most African countries have not been able to meet up with their budgetary contributions to the AU let alone provide additional funding for peacekeeping.[139] Julie Flint and Alex de Waal have observed that 'the AU can only succeed if powerful states offer leverage

138 The ceasefire committee has confirmed that the GoS has violated the agreement more than any other party. This information is based on discussion between the author and some members of the HCFC.

139 Sam Ibok, 'Major Issues and Opportunities in the Interface between the UN and Regional Organizations in Peace Operations: A Perspective from the AU', lecture delivered at the International Seminar on Challenges of Peace Operations, Addis Ababa , 4 June, 2004, p. 18.

and resources to support it'.[140] Hence the lack of funds affects the ability of the AU to set up a force with the requisite military capability to enforce compliance to AU's brokered agreements. The dependence of the AU on external contributions to fund its activities is not in the interest of the organization because it may be constrained to adopt measures which are not in the interest of the AU but of donor countries or organizations. It is in light of the foregoing that this research argues that given the plethora of crises in Africa, the AU must seek an institutional framework for financial support from the UN. Although the UN may be reluctant to grant this form of support due to the tendency to undermine its responsibilities, the AU could advocate for the management of such funds or logistics support by a UN outfit. In addition, the financial/logistics support should be concluded prior to any deployment of AU forces. If the AU cannot obtain such support either from the UN or other international organizations, then it should not embark on a regional peacekeeping operation due to its financial incapacity. However, the AU could review its mechanisms for crisis management and make conflict prevention which is cheaper to accomplish as its main effort. The AU successfully utilized the conflict prevention mechanism in ending the successive crisis in Togo following the death of President Gnassingbe Eyadema on 5 February 2005.[141]

Another serious constraint of AU in conflict resolution is the lack of political will. Although a good measure of political will was displayed in Togo when the AU threatened sanctions following a military coup and demanded a 'return to constitutional legality'[142] and suspension of Togo from AU, it is doubtful if such reaction would be possible in the case of Nigeria, Egypt, Kenya or South Africa. In other words, the AU seems to show political will where the nation involved is small or weak and can easily be coerced into submission. In Zimbabwe for example, despite massive violations of human rights by the Robert Mugabe's administration, no African leader has publicly condemned these acts. The lack of political will has also been identified in the AU's handling of the Ethiopia – Eritrea crisis where it failed to criticize Ethiopia for refusing to accept Ethiopia/Eritrea Boundary Commission (EEBC) decision to award Badme to Eritrea. In the case of Darfur, the lack

140 Julie Flint and Alex de Waal, *Op.Cit.*, p. 127.

141 Ron Bunyan, 'Togolese Political Crisis Spurs Regional Concerns'. Available from: http://www.pww.org/article/articlereview/65361/1/255,[Accessed29March2007].

142 *Ibid.*

of political will has been clearly demonstrated by the fact that out of AU's membership of 52 countries, as at January 2007, only Nigeria and Rwanda are contributing three battalions each while Kenya, Senegal and South Africa have a battalion each and the Gambia has provided a company. Most African countries are only contributing to the military observer mission and not the critical aspect of providing protection which involves more commitment and sacrifice by the troops contributing countries. Other powerful regional players such as Egypt, Ghana, Tunisia, Ethiopia and Uganda could have contributed troops and also, pressurise the GoS to abide by the provisions of the Agreement. Without political will, the AU will be incapable of resolving conflicts in Africa and indeed, without the political will of the leaders of the AU member states, the objectives for which the organization was formed cannot be achieved. It is the political will that could make the difference between the erstwhile OAU and the new AU and without it, Africa's security expectations in the 21st Century will be dashed.

Notwithstanding the constraints enumerated above, there are prospects for the realization of AU's vision in conflict resolution. The organization is barely five years old and the Darfur conflict which provided its acid test happens to be a complex conflict in Africa's largest country and in one of the worst geographical belts of the region. One of the major prospects of the Union is the growing realisation by African states and peoples that their destinies lay in their own hands hence the desire to proffer African solution to Africa's problems. This realization has also led to several developments in the economic sphere particularly the establishment of the NEPAD and some realignments and restructuring in major sub-regional groupings in Africa such as the Southern African Development Community and Economic Community of West African States. Similarly, the democratic reform across the continent is an indication of good prospect for potential development and security in Africa. For instance, as at March 2007, there was no any African country under military regime. This development is likely to encourage aggrieved parties to seek redress through the instrumentality of democratic process rather than the resort to violence. It is also likely that in the era of globalization, the increasing flourishing and near all pervasive impact of NGOs, and civil society organizations would further encourage the culture of transparency, accountability and good governance in African countries. These are vital ingredients not only for democracy and development but for enhancing Africa's security.

The AU is also determined to improve its mechanisms for conflict resolution as contained in the Constitutive Act. For example, Article 4 of the Act includes the prohibition of the use of force or threat to use force among member states. There is also the right of the Union to intervene in any member state under grave circumstances, namely war crimes, genocide and crimes against humanity.[143] The prohibition of the use of force in conflict resolution and the acceptance of preventative diplomacy are both acceptable approaches of managing crisis generally. These are expected to deal with potential conflicts at an early stage. This new approach shows that the AU accepts that national sovereignty is not absolute and that the organization has responsibility to intervene in an intra-state conflict with potentials for escalation. Perhaps, had the AU not intervened in Darfur when it did, the current situation would have been worse than Rwanda.

The willingness of the UN, EU and NATO to work closely with the AU in the resolution of the Darfur conflict is an encouragement to the efforts of the regional organization. Africa is the only region of the world where the UN has encouraged regional intervention of this magnitude.[144] The UN had provided some logistics support to AU to enable the deployment of monitors and peace keepers in Darfur and also organised a donor's conference to raise funds for the AU.[145] This support facilitated the intervention of AU in Darfur which could not have been achieved due to lack of funds. Similarly, the commendation received by the AU from the UN, EU and the international community suggest good prospects for the future of the organization.

On the whole, the prospects of AU in conflict resolution and prevention are bright. It is expected that when other mechanisms such as the Panel of the Wise and the Continental Early Warning Systems become operational, the prevention and resolution of conflicts at an early stage would be enhanced. Similarly, the activation of the African Standby Force in each of the African sub-region would enhance timely employment of force for peacekeeping operations. These mechanisms would in the near future enhance the prospects of the AU in conflict resolution if proper strategies are formulated and implemented.

---

143 AU Constitutive Act, *Op. Cit.*

144 William G. O'Neill and Violette Cassis, *Op. Cit.*

145 Okonkwo, *Op. Cit.*

The rest of this part will consider some strategies that would enhance the roles of AU in conflict resolution. It should be noted that these strategies are based on the constraints and prospects highlighted above. The first strategy required to enhance AU's capacity for conflict resolution is to sensitise African leaders and elite generally to imbibe and develop the political will of ensuring the success of the organization. Kofi Anan has noted that 'with political will, rhetoric can truly be transformed into reality. Without it, not even the noble sentiments will have a chance of success'.[146] Although where financial capability is lacking, the political will may not be there, African leaders need to develop the will to adopt political and diplomatic responses to conflict resolution. They should also encourage the use of democratic channels for pursuing legitimate interests and expressing dissent. In this regard, the NEPAD initiative by African leaders is a good example of demonstrating a renewed political will. However, the major state players in Africa must sensitise and carry others along. Any resolution by the PSC for the deployment of AU peacekeepers should be supported by all member states through the contribution of troops or logistics support. If this has been done in Darfur, the signals to the GoS would have been clearer on the will of African leaders to back AU's resolutions with action.

Another strategy is to seek greater coordination between the UN and AU which will involve the sharing of information and training. The deficiencies of the AU in the technical handling of financial and logistics resources in Sudan could be over come through close cooperation with the UN and other international organizations such as the EU, NATO, the G8 and others. This would facilitate better accountability easy management of allocated resources from these organizations thereby enhancing mutual trust and greater support. In addition, mobilising international support for conflict resolution in Africa would ensure concerted and focused efforts at not only the security dimension but equally the economic and humanitarian aspects. The object of this strategy is to establish efficient and enduring partnership with the UN and other international organizations.

146 Kofi Anan, 'The Causes of Conflict and the Promotion of Durable Peace and Sustainable Development in Africa'. Available from: http://www.un.org/ecosocdev/geninfo/sgreport/report.htm,[Accessed23December2013].

The AU needs to evolve a good strategy of early response to conflicts. The interwoven nature of threats to international peace and security demands that AU demonstrate unity as well as urgency in reacting to situations of potential or actual conflict. Its early warning mechanism should be supported by timely action in order to contain crises at an early stage. For example, the early warning signals of potential conflict in Zimbabwe are clearly visible and now is the time for the AU to act at preventing the conflict by perhaps sending the Panel of the Wise to confer with Mugabe on the situation in that country. This could achieve a greater result than any peacekeeping operations when the opposition parties decide to embark on an insurgency campaign.

Finally, timely response to a potential political humanitarian tragedy by AU would reduce the possibility to deploying a peacekeeping force with its attendant logistics requirements. However, these strategies can only be effective through commitment by African leaders, the international community and the bureaucrats at the AU. The major state players in Africa should also be prepared to shoulder greater responsibilities as demonstrated by Nigeria in Liberia and Sierra Leone and by South Africa in the on-going conflict in DRC.

Conclusion

The central objective of this research has been to determine the efficacy of AU's mechanisms for conflict resolution in resolving the Darfur crisis and other potential conflicts in Africa. This study is unique in several ways. First, the Darfur conflict is still on-going and the situation remains dynamic hence the study did not examine the events that occurred beyond January 2007. Second, there is no existing literature that has examined specifically, this aspect of the study therefore this research has attempted to fill an existing vacuum in the literature. Thirdly, the methodology adopted by using primary sources to corroborate secondary sources gives further substance to the findings and analysis of this study. Based on these reasons, this research will be useful to the AU at various levels as well as organizations and individuals involved in conflict resolution in Africa.

The AU's mechanisms for conflict resolution appears to be tailored to fit inter-state conflicts, hence when confronted with the increasing nature of Africa's intra-state conflict such as Darfur, some difficulties were encountered. For example, how is the AU expected to sanction a non-state actor that has failed to comply with the provisions of an agreement or can the AU deal with non-state actors within a state without the consent of the government? In the Darfur conflict, some of these mechanisms were either misapplied or not used at all.

In the resolution of the Darfur conflict, the AU sponsored Darfur Peace Agreement failed to address the root causes of the conflict and did not apply the theories of conflict resolution hence, parties to the agreement have failed to comply and the Darfur people who were not represented, have rejected the agreement as well. Unless the AU revisits the DPA to ensure that issues of justice, community, humanitarian factors and the root causes of the conflict are adequately addressed, the resolution of the Darfur crisis will remain a mirage. Similarly, while the AU's Constitutive Act and PSC played a vital role in the resolution process, the AU's Panel of the Wise and the Continental Early Warning System mechanisms for conflict resolution were not used prior to the overt stage of the Darfur conflict. These mechanisms are still moribund as they have not been employed in Zimbabwe for example where the potential for conflict is becoming apparent.

The involvement of the AU in the Darfur conflict was more of an accident than the product of any deliberate planning hence, there was no strategic guidance or plan, no strategic planning and mobilisation of the AMIS force were haphazardly carried out. In addition, the GoS, being a party to the conflict, was mandated to disarm the Janjawiid and it has failed to do so. It has also refused to allow the deployment of a UN force that has been authorised by the UNSC and insisted that only the African force will be allowed in Sudan. Meanwhile, the AMIS lacks the teeth to bite and can neither enforce peace nor ensure compliance with the ceasefire agreement. To this extent therefore, the AU's mechanisms for conflict resolution in Africa has not succeeded in resolving the conflict as violence continue to escalate. This research contends that unless the already approved UN force with a Part VII mandate intervenes in Darfur with or without the consent of the GoS, the prospect for peace may remain elusive.

Furthermore, the intra-regional interests of some African countries as a consequence of ethnic loyalty across national boundaries, the absence of a political will by African leaders and poor economic base are some of the constraints militating against the resolution of the Darfur conflict and other conflicts in Africa. Similarly, the lack of political will by African leaders to contribute substantial troops and provide the necessary funds for the sustenance of AMIS force combine to make the force to be seen as a toothless bulldog. This essay also contends that the reluctance of major state actors such as the US and the EU to be decisively committed in the Darfur conflict is largely because the region is of less geo-strategic significance to the interests of these countries. The US for example, has failed to act decisively because the GoS appears to be cooperating with it in the war on terror. Consequently, China has moved in to fill the gap and now constitute a stumbling block at getting UNSC resolution against the Sudanese government.

This essay posits that although Darfur provided the first acid test for the AU and so far it has not been able to resolve the conflicts due to the myriad of issues highlighted, it is still too early to conclude that the five years old organization has failed. However, Africa lacks the capacity to fund even a small scale peacekeeping operation on its own and unless an institutional framework for funding AU peacekeeping force is established, the prospects of AU in conflict resolution in the future will remain a dream. It should be noted that even the strongest regional economic bloc (EU) has been very modest in its Battle Group Concept of about 1800 troops for the Petersberg tasks. The funding and logistics requirement for peacekeeping is beyond what African economies can cope with. Therefore, the AU should lay more emphasis in conflict prevention mechanisms using the Continental Early Warning System and the Panel of the Wise to ensure early engagement with leaders in countries where the potential for conflicts have been identified. This measure is not only cheap but would also prevent possible humanitarian disasters in Africa.

Finally, it has to be emphasized that the AU is still in its infancy and it is more of a regional economic organization than a security bloc hence, its performance in Sudan cannot be compared against the standards of the UN and NATO or indeed the nascent EU Force. Again, the member states of the AU are economically weak and politically young independent countries still suffering from the strings of neo-colonialism. It is on the basis of these issues that the AU's mechanisms for conflict resolution can be better appreciated.

PART II

West Africa: A Region of Success or Failure?

Chapter III
Legacy of Post-Colonialism in West Africa

Introduction

This part of research seeks to give a wider understanding to the development of Liberia, Cote d'Ivoire and Guinea region by looking at a cross-section of countries and determining what factors have affected their post-colonial development. With the exception of Liberia, the region is split between Anglophone and Francophone countries. The basis for the part of research's investigation will be determining whether long-term, post-colonial development was tied primarily to the process of decolonisation and the nationality of the colonial master or less definable and based on a raft of interconnected factors. This part of research will consider Nigeria, Ghana, Sierra Leone, Senegal, Cote d'Ivoire, Guinea and Liberia, providing a short history before considering the method of colonial rule, the de-colonisation process and continued engagement by the former colonial power, and post-independence political and leadership issues and economics.

Africa's ancient, boundary-free pot pourri of city-states, kingdoms and empires, and clan groups[1] were travelled by Greeks and Romans. By the Middle Ages Islam from the Mediterranean had reached western areas. By the 15th century, Christianity was also established and strong trading links existed between Western Africa and both Europe and Arabia.[2] In the 18th/19th centuries the West African coast was dotted with trading posts, run by Europeans who dealt in commodities ranging from slaves to minerals and crops. Later in the 19th century, with Europeans striking inland, more formal control regimes emerged and colonization began: the so-called Scramble for

---

1 Jeremy Herbst, "Responding to State Failure in Africa," *International Security*, Vol. 21, No. 3, 1996/1997, p. 121.

2 Alex Thompson, *An Introduction to African Politics*(New York: Routledge, 2000), p. 9.

Africa. At the 1885 Berlin - West Africa Conference, the European powers agreed to divide the continent (except for Ethiopia and Liberia) amongst themselves.

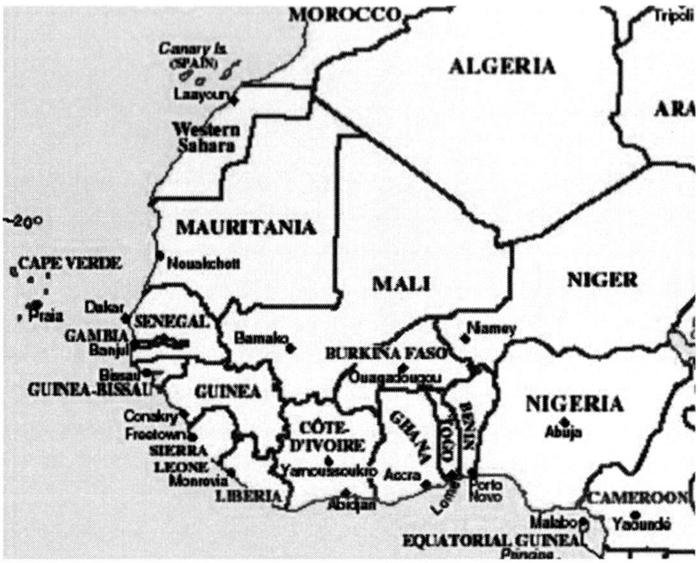

Map of Sub-Saharan West Africa

Independent Countries

Liberia. Niger-Congo speaking peoples representing 13 indigenous groups inhabited the region and with the exception o f the Mandingos, who arrived as Muslim clerics and traders in the 17th century, all had lived in the region since the 12th century. Modern day Liberia was established for freed slaves at Cape Mesurado by agents and colonists of the American Colonisation Society in the 1820s. The nation of Liberia began to develop and in 1847 the colonists announced their independence. The five counties that declared independence were mainly populated by the freed slaves and were governed in a similar way to the USA. The interior, known as the Hinterland and split into three provinces (divided into four and given county status in 1964) was populated by native Africans and treated like a conquered territory; 'the lighter-skinned repatriates lorded over the darker-skinned natives considering them uncivilised, uneducated and unchristian'.[3] The True Whig Party founded at this time ruled until the military coup in 1980 that ushered in the Krahn tribal hegemony.

With no colonial power to provide aid and financial support, resources for public services were scarce and works were neglected. From the late 1800s onwards the country existed on a series of loans; what minimal resources were available ended up mismanaged and corruption became a way of life. A number of times Liberia narrowly missed League of Nations intervention due to its treatment of the indigenous people and inability to integrate them into the political system. In the 1950s foreign investment into newly discovered iron ore started to raise GDP but political infighting between True Whig politicians effectively turned Liberia into a police state and by the late 1970s de-investment had begun. The failure to develop a working political system whilst the economy declined effectively led to the 1980 coup and the installation of Samuel Doe as president.

Throughout the 1980s there were a string of alleged coup plots which led to the execution of a number of Doe rivals. In the 1985 election Doe was declared the winner even though it is doubtful that he secured more than 21% of the vote.[4] The Doe government continued to suppress other political parties and mismanage the economy, which by 1988 was in disarray. By 1990, a coup attempt a year earlier by Charles Taylor (an ex-minister wanted on embezzlement charges) had become a full-scale insurgency. The rebel National Patriotic Front of Liberia (NPFL) subsequently split into two camps (under Taylor and Prince Johnson) with Doe finally being overthrown and killed by Johnson's men. Taylor and Johnson then both proclaimed themselves president. Neither was recognised by the Nigerian led ECOWAS ceasefire monitoring group which in February 1991 installed an interim government. The disarmament process was slow with numerous infractions; it was not until 1997 that elections were held, after which Taylor was declared president.

---

3 Adedeji Adebayo, *Comprehending and Mastering African Conflicts: the Search for Sustainable Peace and Good Governance* (London: Zed Books Ltd., 1999), p. 111.

4 *Ibid.*

In the late 1990s the Taylor government was accused of supporting the Revolutionary United Front (RUF) rebels in Sierra Leone in exchange for diamonds and in 2001 were the subject of a UN embargo for that continued support. This period saw increased opposition to the Taylor government and by 2000 dissident attacks against it by the Liberians United for Reconciliation and Democracy (LURD) rebels, led by Kromah and Johnson (the leaders of two of the former warring factions), had escalated. A vicious civil war ensued with thousands of civilians being displaced or killed while ECOWAS leaders tried to broker a peace deal between Taylor and the rebels. By mid-July 2003 Taylor had accepted a Nigerian brokered plan that saw him go into exile. The deployment of peacekeepers and installation of an interim government stopped the rebel movements gaining power by force. The majority of the infrastructure in the country was destroyed during the civil wars and a large UN force remains to oversee disarmament of the former warring factions. The November 2005 presidential elections were won by Mrs Johnson-Sirleaf who became Africa's first female head of state.

Francophone Countries

Senegal was the first of the French landfalls in Africa; its St Louis settlement dates from 1638. Throughout this time the country was dominated by a Muslim dynasty until it was overthrown in 1893 by the French. Of all the Francophone countries Senegal was the most integrated with France. By 1914 there was a Senegalese deputy in the French parliament and its people were offered French citizenship. In 1946 Senegal joined the French Union and in 1958 became an autonomous republic within the French Community. Following independence a number of military assistance and defence pacts were signed with France; who still maintains a garrison in Dakar. Politically, Senegal was the only country in the region where the people were given the choice of political party to vote for; in fact President Abdou Diouf was finally beaten in elections by his long-time rival Abdoulaye Wade in 2000. During this period the country had taken an active involvement in regional politics and organisations. From 1983 onwards there has been small-scale, internal conflict between the government and the Movement of Democratic Forces of Casamance (MFDC) who are seeking autonomy for the predominantly Christian region of Casamance. This conflict is now subject to a ceasefire, with the MFDC now set to enter the political arena.

Modern day Guinea lies on the edge of the area once influenced by the Empires of Ghana and Mali. Major changes occurred in the 18th century when Muslim Fulani began migrating into the Fouta Djallon highlands and created a Muslim state. This pushed the Susu and Jallonka farmers towards the coast. The French became involved in the 19th century, starting a major push into Guinea. By this time the Fouta Djallon was mainly Fulani, the coastal area Susu and the Niger plain Mandinka, with other tribes inhabiting the forest region. The protectorate was established in 1849, but strong resistance in the interior meant that real occupation was not complete until 1898. On independence in 1958 Guinea opted to leave the French Community and was left without any aid or technical assistance. President Sekou Toure initially turned to the USSR then the USA as major providers of aid. Politics under the Toure regime were characterised by a cult of personality and swift suppression of dissent. Following Toure's death in 1984 Colonel Lansana Conte became president and began to foster closer links with France. Overall the Conte years have seen the country face serious internal problems, threats from across its borders from two neighbours and rebel groups operating within its territory. Recently, the depreciation of the Guinean Franc has led to rising food prices, high utility bills and unpaid salaries, whilst the EU, as the principle donor country, has withheld aid as the government failed to implement political and economic reform.

Cote d'Ivoire first established an outpost in 1687 the French did not send armed forces to control the country until after the Berlin Conference of 1885 when the territory became part of the Federation of French West Africa. Like Senegal, Cote d'Ivoire became an autonomous republic within the French Community in 1958 and achieved independence in 1960. From the Second World War until 1993, Ivorian politics were dominated by one man: Felix Houphouet-Boigny, a Baoule (the largest ethnic group) who maintained extremely close relations with France. Although some anti-French feeling amongst the youth has accelerated "Africanisation" this has been much slower than elsewhere in the region. Under Houphouet-Boigny, Cote d'Ivoire was one of the wealthiest and most politically stable countries in West Africa but with economic decline in the 1990s came internal unrest.

On Houphouet-Boigny's death the speaker of the parliament, Henri Konan-Bedie, declared himself President which brought him into a battle for succession with Prime Minister Alassane Ouattara (a northern Muslim). The main opposition party, under Laurent Gbagbo insisted that a transitional government be implemented so a true successor could be found. In the 1995 elections Konan-Bedie allowed only himself and one other to run; he promptly won. In the late 1990s the country came under increased scrutiny for administrative fraud within the government, resulting in a military coup in which General Guie seized power. He set dates for presidential elections in 2000 but constitutional amendments prior to this meant that only individuals with two Ivorian parents could stand; this discounted Ouattara from standing. In a country where more than one-third of the people are of foreign descent and foreign plantation workers cannot vote this caused outrage. Guie ran as an independent and at his behest the majority of other candidates were disqualified. After a blanket boycott by those candidates' parties, Laurent Gbagbo won the most votes. Guie initially declared himself president but fled when the police and army withdrew their support. Gbagbo was declared president but results from the postponed elections in the Muslim northern region left his governing party without a clear majority, undermining his ability to run the country and deepening the north (Muslim)-south (Christian/animist) divide.[5] Following a civil war in which the northern half of the country fell to rebel forces, the country is currently subject to a shaky UN-brokered and monitored peace process.

Anglophone Countries

Sierra Leone acted as an important source of slaves for Europe during the 18th century. Freetown was established as a place for slaves freed from Britain and British West Indies in 1787 and became a crown colony in 1808. In 1886 the interior became a crown protectorate. Between 1951 and 1961 power was gradually devolved from British officials. Locally elected officials took some responsibility for ministries in 1953 and by 1958 responsibility for all but external affairs and defence had been devolved. As a result, Milton Margai became Chief Minister in 1954, Premier in 1958 and, upon independence, in 1961 Sierra Leone's first Prime Minister.[6]

5 *Ibid.*

6 David Pratt, *SierraLeone: Danger and Opportunity in a Regional Conflict, Special Envoy to Sierra Leone,* (Canada, 2001), p. 52.

In 1971, after a coup attempt against the government of Dr Stevens, Sierra Leone was declared a republic. In 1978 the government moved to establish a single party (All People's Congress or APC) state with Dr Stevens as the executive president. The APC were mainly Temne (approximately one-third of the population) from the less well-developed northern areas whilst Sierra Leone People's Party (SLPP), which could no longer contest elections, were mainly Mende (approximately one-third of the population) from the south and east. Economic difficulties due to spiralling energy prices and a fall in domestic agricultural output were further exacerbated by the cost of hosting the annual Organisation for African Unity (OAU) summit in 1980. In 1981 a state of emergency was declared to deal with a general strike against continued price rises and food shortages. This period also saw several major financial scandals and widespread corruption. In 1985 Dr Steven's personal choice of successor, the armed forces commander Major General Joseph Momoh was appointed leader of the APC and inaugurated in January 1986. Throughout the late 1980s there were rumours of coups, plots and counter plots, and civil unrest. Although political reform was discussed in 1990 the president declared that the country would remain a one-party state.

From 1990 there was fighting along the border with Liberia between government forces and the RUF supported by the Liberian NPFL. In 1992 military units who failed to receive government support for the war quickly and quietly took control of the state apparatus' forming the National Provisional Ruling Council (NRPC) chaired by Captain Valentine Strasser and banning all political parties. His government then strived to improve the country and at the same time fight RUF and other rebel military forces. Civilians were added to the Strasser regime and in 1995 the ban on political parties was lifted. Strasser was ousted in 1996 by Brigadier Maada Bio and civilian elections followed in which Alhaji Ahmed Tejan Kabbah's SLPP won.

Just prior to the elections the RUF agreed to a ceasefire and a peace agreement was signed at the end of the year, but within months this looked fragile as sporadic three-way fighting between the RUF, government forces and Kamajor traditional hunters erupted. In May 1997 Kabbah's government was overthrown in a coup by Major Johnny Paul Koroma and elements of the Army, RUF and the Kamajors. The Armed Forces Revolutionary Council (AFRC) government which included Foday Sankoh, the exiled leader of the RUF, and Lieutenant Soloman Musa, the exiled second in command of Strasser's NPRC government, stated it would work towards national reconciliation and eventual democracy. Kabbah requested Nigerian intervention and by June there were 3000 Nigerian troops in Freetown. Throughout 1997 and early 1998 violence between the Nigerian-led ECOMOG forces and the military Junta continued whilst talks progressed in the background. Eventually, in February 1998, ECOMOG forces took control of Freetown and by the end of March Kabbah's government had returned. Junta loyalists and RUF then continued to fight the government culminating with their assault on Freetown in January 1999 which was repulsed by ECOMOG forces. Fighting continued until a final ceasefire and disarmament programme was implemented towards the end of 2001 under the guidance of ECOMOG, and then UN peacekeepers. President Kabbah was re-elected in 2002 in what were described as free and fair elections; he chaired the first sitting of parliament in that July signifying a return to normal political process[7] but the rebuilding of the country remains a significant challenge.

Ghana, in the 15th and 16th centuries some 30 trading posts had been set up along the so-called "Gold Coast" by European traders. By the 19th century the powerful Asante kingdom had spread out across the region. At the same time the European powers started to shift towards a more direct role. The British initially annexed the Gold Coast to form a Crown Colony; this was followed in 1900 by the northern territories and was completed by the defeat of the Asante in 1902. Little by way of development was undertaken until after the First World War when the idea of indirect rule, already used in Nigeria, was implemented. In the interwar years a strong anti-British intelligentsia grew and in 1947 the United Gold Coast Convention (UGCC) was formed; the secretary of which was Dr Kwame Nkrumah, the eventual post-independence leader. Nkrumah split from the UGCC in 1949, forming the Convention People's Party (CPP) and campaigning on a radical nationalist agenda. The CCP won the 1956 elections and an independent Ghana based on Gold Coast and the British part of former German Togoland was formed in 1957. Nkrumah's vision was to reawaken African nationalism and he started to evolve an ideology of "Nkrumanhism" and "African Socialism".[8]

---

7 *Ibid.*
8 *Ibid.*

Ghana became a one-party state in 1960 and Nkrumah began to distance himself from what he saw as European neo-colonialist interference. He was overthrown in 1966 in a military coup and, after 3 years of military rule, a mixed civilian-military government was elected. This government was overthrown in 1972 in a military coup led by General Acheampong, who in turn was peacefully replaced in 1978 by General Akuffo. The significant event of the Acheampong years was a rapid decline in the economy. In 1979 as Akuffo was about to handover to civilian rule he was overthrown by Flight Lieutenant Jerry Rawlings. This was followed by a period of violence before Rawlings allowed a return to civilian rule at the end of 1979. Although the new President dealt well with internal affairs this did not stop a second successful coup by Rawlings at the end of 1981. The remainder of the 1980s saw an improvement in economic policies but the political situation remained unstable with a number of alleged coup attempts, alleged involvement in neighbouring countries and student unrest. In the early 1990s the economy continued its modest improvement and a new constitution was voted in, which allowed the return to a civilian government and a multi-party political system.[9] Rawlings was elected president in November 1992 and, although the elections were bitterly contested, the opposition New Patriotic Party (NPP) remained fully engaged with the government to ensure that the needs of the country remained paramount. The run up to the 1996 elections which re-elected Rawlings saw inter-communal conflict between ethnic groups over land and resources. This has continued in the period up to the present day but all parties have remained engaged in the political process. Economic growth has remained steady and the country fully engaged with worldwide development organisations. In 2000 the 19-year dominance over the political arena by Rawlings ended when his vice-president was defeated by the NPP who then went on to win subsequent elections in 2003. Ghana remains relatively stable and the economy continues in steady growth.

Nigeria was dominated by a number of Kingdoms: in the southwest the Yoruba Kingdoms of Ife and Oya; in the southeast the Igbo Kingdoms of Onitsha, Nri and Arochukwu; in the north the Hausa Kingdoms and Kanem-Bornu Empire were eventually replaced by an Islamic Fulani Empire. From the 17th to 19th centuries Europeans traded first for slaves and then for commodities from well-established coastal ports. In 1879 the

9 *Ibid.*

British purchased all of the foreign trading stations in the Niger delta and in 1885 obtained a royal charter for the Royal Company of the Niger which made rapid territorial gains. These came under the control of the British government in 1900 and saw Nigeria become a British protectorate in 1901. During British rule the country was run on an increasingly federal basis but education and economic development was more rapid in the south than the north.

At independence the country was effectively a federation of three regions. The northern region was dominated by the conservative Muslim, largely Hausa NPC, the eastern region by the Igbo and Christian NCNC, and the Yoruba western region by the AG. In 1963 Nigeria became a Federal Republic and a fourth region was established. At this time the AG was manoeuvred out of power and replaced by a pro-government Yoruba party; the NNDP. The national election in 1965 saw the northern-dominated NPC ally itself with the NNDP, leaving the Igbo NCNC to join with the remnants of the AG. The results were disputed and in early 1966 a group of mainly Igbo army officers overthrew the NPC-NNDP government, assassinating the key leaders. Six months later a counter-coup by mainly northern officers led to the massacre of thousands of Igbos in the north and helped fuel the Igbo secessionist movement. In 1967 the military governor of the eastern region declared the independent "Republic of Biafra". The ensuing 30-month civil war was bitter and bloody, ending in the defeat for the secessionists.

Although reconciliation was rapid and economic growth was sustained by the oil industry, 1975 saw another coup. The country returned to civilian rule in 1979 but the elections 4 years later were marred by violence and allegations of vote rigging, and the government was soon overthrown again. This was to usher in 16 years of military rule during which there were a number of attempted coups and changes in head of state, strikes by unions, widespread human rights abuses and repression of the people. The country returned to civilian rule in 1999 under Obasanjo, a former general who had returned the country to civilian rule in 1979 and subsequently stood up to the military regimes. Obasanjo was re-elected in 2003 and both human rights and democratic processes have improved during his rule. The country's economy needs to be rebuilt following years of mismanagement and corruption and further development remains marred by communal violence and long-standing ethnic and religious tensions.

Colonial Rule

Although not a European colony, the way in which the Liberian repatriates governed the indigenous population was similar to the harshest aspects of colonial rule elsewhere on the continent. The repression of all opponents of the True Whig government and continued marginalisation of the indigenous people from political and economic involvement fuelled their resentment and ultimately led to the violent overthrow of the government. Having no experience of real democracy the Krahn under Samuel Doe tried to keep power at all costs.

French colonial rule in West Africa was characterised by a policy of assimilation. This presumed the inherent superiority of French culture; it was a duty to civilize the inferior Africans.[10] French language, institutions, laws and customs, and even religion, were imposed throughout their colonies and they were open in explaining that this was for France's benefit and that development of Africans was merely a spin off.[11] The positive side of the policy applied to the educated African elite only. The administration, which was largely directed from centralized offices in Paris, governed by dividing and ruling the local population.[12]

British colonial rule contrasted clearly in principle and practice. The majority of colonies were run by indirect rule, whereby London empowered traditional, indigenous authorities as allies to operate the internal governmental systems.[13] This system of indirect rule maintained tribal differences and was to be the root of inter-communal violence in a number of Anglophone colonies post independence, for example the Muslim north and Christian south in Nigeria. The amalgamation between these two regions finally occurred in 1914 but they were kept as two distinct entities rather than breaking down into smaller provinces, thus emphasising their differences.

---

10 Aguibou Yansané, *Decolonization in African States with French Colonial Legacy,* (Cambridge: Schenkman Publishing, 1984), p. 3.

11 Donald Rothchild & Naomi Chazan, T*he Precarious Balance-State & Society in Africa*, (London: Westview Press, 1988), p. 5.

12 Laurent Gbagbo, *Côte d'Ivoire - Économie et société à la veille de l'indépendance* (1940-1960), (Paris: L'Harmattan: Paris, 1982), pp. 42-43.

13 Richard Brown, *European Colonial Rule in Africa: Africa South of the Sahara 2001,* (London: Europa Press, 2000), p. 21.

The educational system, largely provided through Christian missions, ensured a cadre of local people were able to fill clerical and - for graduates - decision-making posts in business and government at a level not widely paralleled in the region.[14] Some sat on the judicial bench and the legislative council. Britain's strategy envisaged eventual political independence for the colonies[15] and political movements were allowed early in the century.

Decolonisation

Although countries were created by straight lines drawn on maps, splitting tribes, all have honoured the organisation of African Unity declaration that colonial frontiers were to be regarded as sacrosanct.[16] The immediate development of countries post-independence was directly influenced by the way in which it occurred. The colonial legacies bequeathed to most countries in the region were either French or British and they deepened the differences by their contrary approaches to ongoing post-colonial engagement. The French followed the idea of "protected child" whereas the British tended to "cut loose" their former possessions.

In 1945, each French colonial territory elected African deputies to sit in the French Constitutional Assembly. Although it was a requirement that these deputies should join one or other of the metropolitan parties that flitted in and out of the coalition governments, in practice only the French Communist Party (PCF) showed any readiness to welcome this first generation of African politicians into its ranks.[17] There were two distinct camps of politicians; those like Toure of Guinea who supported the PCF policy of immediate independence and rejection of economic and political links with France, and those realists like Houphouet-Boigny of Cote d'Ivoire who favoured cooperation with France. For independence over the period 1958-60, the initial proposal was of "Communaute Francaise" where key decisions were taken jointly with France. Guinea was the only country that

---

14 David Birmingham, *Independence and Neo-colonialism in Western Africa: the Decolonization of Africa,* (London: UCL Press, 1995), p. 27.

15 Richard Brown, *Op.Cit*.,p. 21.

16 J. B. Wright, *Francophone Black Africa Since Independence,* (London: ISC, 1982), p. 2.

17 *Ibid*., p. 6.

voted against and, although her drive for total independence meant that all the other countries would follow suit within 18 months, most came to some compromise with France. Guinea then lurched from crisis to crisis until it embraced steady economic reform under Western guidance whilst Senegal and Cote d'Ivoire maintained extremely close links to France. Cote d'Ivoire was seen by some as a classic case of neo-colonialism due to not completely Africanising key posts and its reliance on international money markets. However, quadrupling of GDP and a prosperity shared by most Ivorians as a result of good management and one of the freest economies in Africa[18] led some to argue it as a model case. Others would argue that, although the country prospered, a failure to address the underlying issues caused by colonial rule postponed the disorder faced by other nations until the French withdrew from internal politics in the late 1990s.

On the contrary, the British believed that to constrain the enthusiastic and emerging native leadership to work within a system appropriate for colonial rule, and which did not have in place the necessary checks and balances, was naïve and arrogant; they left countries to develop themselves within the Commonwealth framework. This British policy coupled with the inertia of the move towards independence ensured that many well-recognised issues such as regionalism and minority groups were suppressed, only to surface with disastrous consequences in the years after independence.

Political Leadership

State or political authority can be defined as a psychological relationship, between the governed and their governors, which engenders a belief that state personnel and institutions should be obeyed.[19] The "governors" can achieve political authority by utilising one or a combination of coercion or legitimacy. Commanding authority by coercion involves the threat or actual use of violence whereas legitimacy gains authority because the electorate associates the governors with the provision of security, social and economic welfare, and is generally termed in modern parlance as "good governance".

18 *Ibid.*, p. 22.
19 Alex Thompson, *Op. Cit.*, p. 89.

The modern African state arrived almost overnight, and its character owed little to the existing society. On independence countries were given advice by ex-colonial powers, UN Special Agencies and other international organisations, the USSR and the Chinese communists. But, apart from a wrinkle here and a slogan there, all this has made little difference to the political systems that they have developed in the long term.[20] Most Africans were left out of any representative relationship between government and people. Consequently, trust and shared political values never developed between the rulers and the ruled.[21] State institutions never sought or gained the respect of the people and there was a "crisis of legitimacy" right from the start. This created the situation whereby regimes gained political authority through coercion rather than legitimacy. This situation can be sustained in the short term but when the "governors" no longer control adequate sources of coercion then the state's political authority is threatened. As a result, countries often developed highly centralised and often weak political systems which could not meet the challenge of nation building and were also, in the main, alien to the traditional cultures.[22] These weak political systems often led to unitary systems where one ethnic group dominated to the detriment of others as in Liberia and to some extend Sierra Leone. It is no coincidence that Senegal, who for the whole post-colonial period has offered its people political choice, seems more stable. It has had a continually developing political system whose main feature is competition between the two main parties.

Francophone countries based their constitutions on De Gaulle's 1958 constitution for France but the forces calculated to offset the power of the executive in France were either not available or easily brushed aside. The tendency in Africa was to concentrate more and more power in the hands of the President.[23] Strong individual leadership became the norm amongst African leaders. Typical of this approach was Houphouet-Boigny of Cote d'Ivoire who manipulated the political arena to maintain power. Very early on he became sensitive to diminishing support for the PDCI and its radically left-wing policies and switched approach entirely, abandoning association

20 J. B. Wright, *Op. Cit.*, p. 2.

21 Alex Thompson, *Op. Cit.*, p. 4.

22 Adebayo Adedeji, *Comprehending and Mastering African Conflicts: the Search for Sustainable Peace and Good Governance* (London: Zed Books, 1999), p. 43.

23 J. B. Wright, *Op. Cit.*, p. 3.

with the French Communist Party, moderating the Rassemblement Democratique Africain, rejecting PDCI militancy, and cooperating anew with the French. It was a turning point and marked the start of 40 years of warm relations between Côte d'Ivoire and France with Cote d'Ivoire becoming France's strongest supporter in the region.[24] The turning point in Cote d'Ivoire came as France announced that it would no longer intervene in internal political debates, thus apparently ending 40 years of reliable and paternalistic support for its favourite African colony whilst at the same time the fight to succeed Houphouet-Boigny raged.

Like Cote d'Ivoire, Anglophone Ghana was well-placed and pioneering following independence but swiftly descended into an economic and political abyss.[25] Nkrumah rejected involvement of the former colonial power as neo-colonial meddling and tried to build a strong Ghana based on "African Nationalism". Whilst he laid good foundations there was a gap between official rhetoric and actual actions/performance.[26] He was undermined by advisors and followers who had different agendas to promote personal wealth. Following mismanagement by a series of military rulers it took the strong leadership of Gerry Rawlings to improve the situation. His first coup attempt failed but at his trial Rawlings was given a chance to outline his proposals for reform which led to his release by junior officers and a successful second attempt. The Rawlings regime was authoritarian but it used tight control to improve the situation in the country, eventually leading it back to civilian rule.

The involvement of outside forces driven by the wider political environment cannot be ignored. Libya; and the "external patronage" offered by Qaddafi for the radicalisation programme of West Africa was supported by its principal ally, Burkina Faso, who provided training, arming and fiscal support to both NPFL and RUF. During the Cold War both the West and the USSR were actively involved in supporting regimes within Africa. The USA supported the Doe regime in Liberia with millions of dollars in return for running a listening station within the country. There is a view that the

24 *Ibid.*, p. 23.

25 *Ibid.*, p. 2.

26 Akwasi P. Osei, *Ghana: Recurrence and Change in a Post-independence African State*, (New York: Peter Lang, 1999), p. 35.

phenomenon of state collapse in Africa began shortly after the conclusion of the Cold War. Dr Karen von Hippel from the Centre for Defence Studies, Kings College London, shares this view: she writes, "...the recent increase in state collapse has been a by-product of the end of the Cold War".[27] Once the Cold War was concluded, the strategic importance of many African countries diminished along with the sponsorship offered by Cold War donors, in effect leaving them high and dry.

The final element within the political arena is that of corruption and the patronage system. Chabel and Daloz talk of African corruption not being the exception but rather the rule – "it is a habitual part of everyday life, an expected element of every social transaction".[28] The result is the lack of investment in development as personal gain takes precedence and also a break down in efficiency within the state apparatus as posts are filled with leadership cronies and the normal political process is circumvented. Coupled to this is the traditional patronage system which rewards loyalty with money and power. Houphouet-Boigny used this to his advantage: he distributed patronage evenly as a way of maintaining the status quo and pacified tribal tensions by including tribal leaders in the government. The opposite effect was seen in Liberia where Doe distributed power exclusively within his Krahn tribe and allowed economic dominance to be held by the Mandingo. The issues surrounding patronage are further compounded when the money runs out; former allies can quickly turn into enemies.

Economics

Crucial to providing political stability in the region post independence was sound management of the economy, the ability to sustain economic growth and development without the "Colonial Crutch". At Independence much of the region was in reasonable economic health. In Anglophone countries many agricultural and industrial operations were owned by locals. For example, in Sierra Leone palm kernels were the chief export[29] until diamonds,

---

27 House of Commons, International Development, Report 28 July, 1999, para 11.

28 Patrick Chabal & Jean-Pascal Daloz, *Africa Works: Disorder as Political Instrument*, (Oxford: Oxford University Press, 1999).

29 David Pratt MP, *Op. Cit.*, p. 52.

discovered in Kono in 1938, replaced them. Subsequently extensive iron ore deposits were discovered in Port Loko and soon earned almost 30% of the colony's revenue. The exploitation of these mineral resources became influential in migration from Freetown into the interior and the evolution of Sierra Leone's modern cash economy. The development of the economies within Anglophone countries was very much dependent on the polices of the respective governments and tied into the wider economic climate.

On independence, the Francophone countries maintained aid and financial arrangements with France and a common currency; the franc CFA which was tied to the French franc. This supported Senegal's ready-made industrial base and Cote d'Ivoire as an important coffee and cocoa producer. In contrast Guinea rejected French economic and political ties on independence and withdrew from the franc zone. Refusal to join regional economic ventures cost the country dear. It was not until 1978 that conciliatory overtures with France and other countries in the region were made. The fortunes of the various countries showed that membership of the CFA franc zone was both supportive and stabilizing. It tied the economies of all participating Francophone countries to each other and to France. An anomaly in the region was Liberia. From an early stage the country had no formal economic development policies. The few who were enterprising enough to proclaim independence monopolised political and economic life to the detriment of the remainder.[30]

A number of factors led to the economic problems within particular countries which, in turn, contributed to instability. Initially governments followed socialist policies and kept tight control, stifling economic growth. It was observed by Adebayo that markets cannot play a dominant role in the way in which an economy functions unless allowed to do so by those in power and authority.[31] In the majority of colonies agriculture had been directed away from feeding the population towards cash crops for export, with some becoming reliant on a predominantly mono-crop agricultural base. Spiralling energy prices and unfavourable exchange rates (certainly amongst the Anglophone countries) reduced agricultural output and drove migration

30 Adebayo Adedeji, *Op. Cit.*, p. 119.
31 *Ibid.*, p. 299.

towards the cities. This led to a lack of reinvestment in the economy and therefore no agricultural reform. With economic stagnation came rising unemployment "[which] may be perceived as a sign of more general social disintegration"[32] and increased the potential for violence.

The region is blessed with an abundance of mineral resources, from oil in Nigeria's Niger Delta, diamonds in Sierra Leone to bauxite reserves in Guinea. Where governments have been able to invest aid money into exploiting these resources, bring in foreign partners and most importantly re-invest the capital countrywide, economies have seen growth and stability. In contrast, lack of funds to develop these resources has led to exploitation by foreign companies and/or mismanagement to support personal gain which has meant no re-investment in the wider community and a continuing downward spiral. In Liberia, from 1926 The Firestone Plantations Company effectively ran the economy, supplied with indigenous "slave labour" by the government. The transfer of land to these foreign companies eroded the local subsistence economy making it unsustainable in the long term whilst capital earned either left the country or only benefited the ruling elite.

Finally, for both Liberia and Sierra Leone, the cost effect on their weakened economies of hosting an annual Organisation for African Unity summit compounded the problems and alienated the poorer sections of the population further. Without a coherent agricultural sector (both subsistence and for export) properly developed and regulated mineral exploitation, the eradication of corruption, and the re-investment of capital into all areas of society, economic stability is unsustainable. The result is a rise in unemployment and increased social disenfranchisement of significant sections of the population. In politically underdeveloped or repressive countries this often ends in violence.

32 *Ibid.*, p. 118.

The Role of Military

Finally, the significant part played by the military in post-colonial West Africa cannot be overlooked. The reasons for military involvement in politics have been varied, received differing levels of acceptance and manifested themselves in numerous coups across the region. In a lot of cases it has been to guard corporate interests, for instance when Nkrumah sacked the majority of the military hierarchy; a hierarchy with a strong British military ethos that was already at odds with the government's socialist policies and alignment with the Soviet Union.[33] When the Nigerian military overthrew the government in 1983 there was no widespread civil disgust at the undemocratic methods due to the corruption, mismanagement and nest feathering that was rife within the government. General Ocran, one of the leaders of the 1966 coup in Ghana, stated that "in Africa, a contented army, however small, is the pillar of economic security and economic growth". [34] However, in Sierra Leone where the army was heavily politicised and described as a brutal and corrupt organisation full of criminals this was not the case. In Liberia the military had its own agenda and was naïve enough to believe that the coup gave it the right to impose its rule on the people.

There have been notable successes. The Nigerian led ECOMOG forces were instrumental in policing the ceasefire at the end of the Liberian civil war in the early 1990s and saving Freetown and Kabbah's government during the rebel onslaught of January 1999. However, even these successes were marred by widespread looting. Until political institutions are strengthened to the point where the military realises that it has no place in politics governments remain vulnerable. An example from Sierra Leone highlights the misunderstanding between supporting "a democratically elected government" and supporting "the government". The Chief of Defence staff briefing the officer corps prior to the local elections told them that the Army existed to support the government and should therefore vote for Kabbah's SLPP.

---

33 Akwasi P. Osei, *Op. Cit.*, p. 75.
34 *Ibid.*, p. 87.

Conclusion

At first glance Francophone countries faired better than their Anglophone neighbours. Rapid British disengagement compared unfavourably with ongoing French support for their former colonies. France's close relationship with Cote d'Ivoire and Senegal supported the argument that most neo-colonialism was constructive and that the model for post-colonial development should have been that of close cooperation. Whilst this simplistic comparison initially holds true, there are a host of inter-related factors, specific to each country that then guided their development. Before colonial rule West Africa was a patchwork of ethnic groups and religions between which there was a perpetual cycle of alliances and conflict both between ethnic groups and internally. On to this were then drawn artificial borders. Although France and Britain had different approaches to colonial rule the result was to maintain the differences between ethnicity and religion; low-level inter-communal violence remained the norm. In his part of research Odunga surmises that conflict within post-colonial African states (which also often had a direct effect on its neighbours) was inevitable.

"Conflicts are violent expressions of dissatisfactions against prevailing situations among communities within a country or region. Conflicts in most African countries are an outgrowth of the legacy bequeathed them by colonial rule because the colonial powers that created them had little regard for cultural affinity and the political practices that existed. Large nationalities and/or ethnic groups were split between states while others which had little in common, besides some aspects of a history or warfare and enmity, were drawn into new state boundaries..."[35]

On independence the majority of states had colonial-style political systems that were designed to support the colonial power and were not generally suitable for governing an independent country. Strong personal leadership was essential but needed to be coupled with robust democratic systems supported by traditional structures to have a significant effect on development. Countries such as Senegal with its continually developing inclusive multi-party political system faired better than one-party states like Liberia and Sierra Leone where both political power and economic control

35 Adebayo Adedeji, *Op. Cit.*, p. 221.

were held by the ruling elite. Assuming that African leaders at every level knew what the development issues were; their policies on the whole had little effect. With corruption rife and operating within the patronage system the majority were more concerned with their own self-importance, keeping themselves in power and maintaining the status quo.[36] Into this political arena was thrown the military; they ranged from highly professional to no more than a brutal uneducated mob. With weak political systems and highly politicised militaries that did not understand their role in upholding democracy, they often acted to guard their corporate interests. As a result most of the region experienced coups and elements of military rule. Even when this had been to counter corruption and mismanagement the military often came to resemble the civilian regimes that they had replaced.

As Osei sums up, "[Africa is] potentially the richest landmass on the face of the earth, the continent is also widely acknowledged as the poorest in terms of generally accepted indicators".[37] There were a host of economic factors that contributed to post-colonial development. With the exception of Senegal, the majority of countries relied on an agricultural base where emphasis had been shifted from sustaining the population towards cash crops for export. These were susceptible to price and exchange rate fluctuations that in turn directly affected revenue. Although rich in minerals, those such as diamonds were extremely difficult to bring under government control. Without the capital to exploit the mineral resources weak governments relied on foreign companies; what revenue remained in the country then invariably enriched the ruling elite rather than developing the wider society. Lack of capital to re-invest, misuse of aid money, corruption and ill-advised economic policies led to economic decline. Overall, states embracing the international political economy fared best.

Experiences in the immediate aftermath of independence were very much dependent on the nationality of the former colonial power. Francophone countries that remained closely tied to France faired better than those countries that were left to "go it alone". Whatever the methods of decolonisation, the underlying issues caused by the drawing of colonial

36 Akwasi P. Osei, p. 117.
37 *Ibid.*, p. 116.

borders were generally not addressed. As countries across the region interacted with their external environment how they faired became dependent on a wide range of interrelated factors such as the strength of their leadership, the maturity and development of their political system, levels of corruption and patronage, management of the economy and engagement in internal affairs by the armed forces.

Chapter IV
Lasting Peace in Africa?: Back to West Africa

Introduction

The end of the Cold War between the Union of Soviet Socialist Republics (USSR) and the United States of America (USA) was expected to usher in relative peace, security and stability globally, and the corresponding calm was to enable meaningful economic and technological growth in most nations of the world. But unfortunately these expectations have not been realised, as the world began to experience new form of conflicts, more complex and devastating.

The two gulf wars (1991 and 2003), the Yugoslavian civil war, the war in Kosovo, Afghanistan and the multiple ethnic wars in Africa are among the conflicts which ended with massive destruction of lives and properties along with gross violations of human right. Kornblum stresses that the post Cold War proliferation of local conflicts have strained the resources and credibility of governments and international community almost to a breaking point.[1]

These conflicts have dampened the initial euphoria and raised doubts about the present strategies for conflict management and resolution. While there is increasing rapprochement among actors in some regions, those in Africa have taken perennial crises proportions, the situation has became more critical with the breakout of inter and intra-state conflicts that resulted in the death of millions and an upsurge of refugees and displaced people. These conflicts which lacked appropriate management at global and regional levels have resulted in the collapse of the Somalian state, genocide in Rwanda and an unending circle of violence in the Democratic Republic of Congo (DRC), Burundi, Sudan and Angola to mention but a few.

---

1 J. Kornblum, *Human right and Conflict Resolution: An agenda for the 21st century*, (Copenhagen, 1999), p. 1

In the last decade, Africa has witness more armed conflicts than any other region in the world; increasingly, the conflicts have taken a regional character especially along the great lakes region.[2] Between 1970 and 1997, over 30 wars have been fought in Africa. The wars involved a quarter of the continent and accounted for more than half of the entire war related deaths world wide, while leaving almost 8 million refugees around the continent.[3]

The African conflicts, most of which are still on going, are threatening the stability of the region. The West African sub-region is not left out in this dilemma; most countries within the sub-region are still being afflicted by wars since independence. Apart from massive destruction to lives and properties, the conflicts have also created an upsurge of refugees within the sub-region. Besides, they provided excuses for extra African powers to interfere in the region's domestic affairs, while giving way for arms trafficking and other African states to interfere in neighbouring states. These have contributed in no measure to the underdevelopment of the sub-region.

The causes of conflicts in Africa in general and West Africa in particular are many and they frequently reoccur. As the world transits into the twenty-first century, the precarious position of African states is brought into sharper focus vis-à-vis the globalisation of the rest of the world. In the West African sub-region, Nigeria, Chad, Liberia, Sierra-Leone and Guinea have all had their shares of these conflicts. Consequently, in the face of erupting horrors, Africa's collective and global attentions have been diverted from the developmental needs of the continent to the management of tension, human misery and militarism.

It is such concerns for peace and stability in the continent that led to the creation of the African Union (formerly known as OAU). At the sub-regional level, the Economic Community of West African States (ECOWAS) was created in 1975 to promote economic co-operation and integration in the region.[4] Due to necessity, ECOWAS objective was later amended to include cooperative security. With crisis erupting one after the other in West Africa, what are the prospects of procuring lasting peace in the region?

---

2 UN report (July 1999), p.1
3 UN reports (1997), para4
4 ECOWAS Brochure (1998), p. 2

Despite the complexity of these conflicts, the prospect for peace is high. However, it will involve a coordinated comprehensive approach involving all the stake holders. This part of research will show how it can be achieved by first looking at the concept of conflict and national security in West Africa, thereafter, the origin of conflicts in the region will be traced. A general description of the nature, causes and effects of conflicts in West Africa will also be examined. Peace keeping and the roles of the international community particularly the 3 major western powers, UN and ECOWAS will be highlighted. Lastly, the part of research will consider the way forward.

Concepts of Conflict and National Security

In the past few years, efforts at interpreting African conflicts have generated heated debates. Recent study of the dynamics underlying some of the violence has resulted to a number of theories. Amongst them is Paul Collier's, where he argues that economic agenda appears central in the understanding why conflicts breakout, he further posits that conflicts are far more likely to be caused by economic opportunities than by grievance.

Another enduring paradigm is the patrimonial concept of Bratton and De Walle. The position of the theory is that process of rule and leadership are personalised and through personal patronage rather than through ideology or law, the resultant effect of such process is that violence become part of everyday life.[5] However, this framework does not explain why states in similar position do not reflect similar violence.

Chris Allen, editor of the magazine 'Review of African Economy' also argues that African violence can be explained by the internal dynamics of 'spoil politics' in which self enrichment is a key issue. Another theory has attempted to use rational choice to explain the senseless violence and brutalities that occur in some of the African conflicts. The argument is that social action and reaction are closely related to either group or individual calculus base on self interest and the exploitation of gain.[6] This theory again

5 M. Bratton, & Van de Walle, *Neo-patrimonial regimes and political transitions in Africa, World Politics*, Vol. 46, No. 4, July 1994.

6 D. Keen, "A rational Kind of Madness, Oxford Developmental Studies," Vol. 25, No. 1, 1997.

does not explain the rebels' rationale for beginning wars.

Stagner describes conflict as a situation in which two or more parties desire a goal that they perceive as being obtainable by only one, the parties consider each other as a barrier and mobilize their energy and resources to embark on the objective of attaining to that goal.[7] Stedman however, offers an insight into the nature of conflict in Africa. He argues that African conflicts arise from problems basic to all populations, the tugs and pulls of different identities, the different distribution of resources, access to power and conflicting definitions of what is just, fair and right.[8]

Burton defines conflict in utilitarian context. He sees it as a means to a change by which our social values of welfare, security, justice and opportunities for personal development can be achieved, it is an essential creative element in human relationship that is neither to be deprecated nor feared.[9] The contradiction is that this utilitarian principle has not benefited African states; rather, conflicts have compounded their problems as it is a major obstacle to the economic and socio-political transformation of these states. This study therefore identifies with Stedman's definition that African conflicts are largely caused by quest of interest groups for access to power and distribution of resources.

In general terms, security could be defined as actions taken in order to keep someone or something safe. It is also defined as measures taken to guarantee the safety of a country, person or thing of value.[10] From both definitions, it will be safe to infer that security provides the enabling environment for peace. Without a sense of security, there can be no quiet, freedom, harmony or friendship.

National security as viewed by the traditional realist approach is the defence of state's territorial integrity. This approach considers security as the most important national interest. However, other areas that have direct

7 R. Stugner, *Psychological Aspect of International Conflict*, (Belmont: Belmont books, 1967), p. 16.

8 Stedman (1997), p. 23.

9 J. Burton, "The Theory of Conflict Resolution," Peace and Violence, Vol. 9, No. 8, 1986, pp. 125-130.

10 *Ibid.*

bearing on national security as observed by Barry Buzan are economic, social, environmental and political sectors. Therefore, developing West Africa socially, economically and politically will not only improve the living condition of the people but also enhance their security.

It is only such a beneficial development that will motivate the people and give them confidence to defend the system that they see as worth having.[11] Robert Macnamara, a onetime World Bank president, also claims that in a modernizing world, security means development and not military hardware, and without development there can be no security.[12] Thus, security is a variable for the attainment of peace and consequently a prerequisite for development and growth. Underdevelopment is therefore a threat to West African security. The citizens of a state and foreign investors require security to engage in productive activities, likewise, without security, a nation or state would be unable to harness its human and other resources for meaningful development and the wellbeing of its people.

Security was initially viewed by some experts to be the ability of a nation to build military defences to protect its territorial integrity from both internal and external aggression. This concept suggests that a state is secured to the extent that it can contain or deter aggression.[13] After the Cold War, the turndown in world economies coupled with environmental pollution and resource degradation warranted a redefinition of security, which was to account for the evolving realities. Therefore, security was no longer limited to protection from military threats, but also from economic vulnerability, ecological threats and natural disasters.[14]

Subsequently, a third and broader concept evolved which was to cater for the whole range of human needs. Security in this view connotes freedom from threat, not only to the physical existence of the state, but also to its ability for self-protection, development and enhancement of the wellbeing of

---

11 Abdoulaye Bailey & Eboe Hutchfild, *Military and Militarism in Africa,* (Dakar: Codesia,1998), p. 123.

12 Robert Mcnamra, *The Essence of security: Reflections in Office,* (NY: Harper and Row, 1968), p. 149.

13 Imobighe, *An overview of theoretical issues in African security*, (1999), p. 2.

14 Ann Tickner J., *Revisioning Security as cited in TA*, (1999), p. 2-3.

its people.[15] It is this broader concept which recognises human security that aptly reflects the African situation.

From the foregoing, security in the region could be defined as the ability of the states to tackle all forms of threat to their survival while contending with the challenges of nation building and good governance. These threats would usually range from external aggression to environmental, economic, social and political insecurities. Thus, the prospect for lasting peace in West Africa is largely dependent on the state of security in the region. It is therefore expedient that the causes of insecurity in West Africa be clearly understood, as it will affect the way in which international responses are shaped.

Causes of Conflict in West Africa

West Africa is comprised of 5 Anglophone, 9 Francophone and 2 lusophone countries, which form the ECOWAS States. The countries that make up the West African sub-region are shown at Annex A.

Historically, most African states had democratic traditional institutions with their political systems that were represented by kings and chiefs. These systems satisfied most of the aspirations of the people. Unfortunately, at the Berlin congress of 1885 European countries including Spain, Italy, Portugal, Germany, Belgium, Britain and France partitioned the African kingdoms and communities into protectorates and colonies. This partitioning was carried out arbitrarily without any consideration to the existing boundaries or socio-political structures. The result was that people with different cultures and traditions, from different nations, kingdoms and communities were arbitrarily joined together.

It was here that the stage was set for most of the conflicts that were to erupt in future (the Nigerian civil war is a good example). Most African countries gained their independence in the 1960s. The post colonial regimes inherited the boundaries, economies and laws from the colonial authorities. They were left with the challenge of building nations out of people that share little or nothing in common. They faced this challenge by centralising political

15 *Ibid.*

power and suppressing any form of political pluralism. However, the political monopoly eventually resulted in corruption, nepotism and abuse of power.[16] Meanwhile, agitations started brewing from the communities that were being marginalised.

The political, commercial, educational and social order and infrastructure established by the colonial powers in West Africa were designed to satisfy their need. This need was the production and transportation of raw material to Europe. Little was done in terms of education and physical infrastructure to support the ever increasing indigenous population and its economy.

The post independence period coincided with the Cold War era. The ideological contest between the two blocs availed political and financial support to their friendly and allied oppressive regimes in Africa. Hence these regimes were able to sustain physical, financial and social securities of their states. With the end of the Cold War, the West African states no longer enjoy the relevance they had, the super power support was withdrawn and they were left to cater for themselves. Most of the states that could not meet up their security requirements became prone to internal unrest. Even when the signal for such unrest was clear, the international community showed little interest. The identity problem that resulted from the partition is the major source of disunity amongst the people of West Africa. It has been argued that if Africans had been left with their indigenous pre-colonial boundaries and political system, with time they would have improved on it just like others did. This would have suited their future requirements and perhaps averted the present conflicts.

The desire by an individual, ethnic group or a section of a society to capture and retain political power in a multiethnic and/or multicultural society is another very significant source of conflict in West Africa. Most often the 'winners' share neither political power nor the privileges attached to it with the rest. Any form of protest against the rulers is always crushed with brute force. In the absence of justice, transparency, accountability and the adherence to the rule of law, the disadvantaged party feels marginalised, unsecured and its very survival threatened. With no peaceful means of accessing resources or political power, they resort to violence.

---

16 UN Report (1998), para 8.

This lack of relatively equitable distribution of scarce but allotable resources, and the monopoly of political, social and economic power by a dominant group to the exclusion of all other groups, aggravated by greed and poor leadership, has created a significant source of insecurity in the form of social cleavages in West Africa.[17] This is also the major reason for the coups and counter coups, and over politicization of religion and ethnicity in Africa.

Another causative factor is the external interference. It was expected that the end of the Cold War would also end external interference in the domestic affairs of sovereign states. This is not completely the case in West Africa. Countries with natural resources like oil, diamond, gold, etc still witness interferences in their domestic affairs both from distant powers and neighbouring states. Other interferences are neither for political or economic reasons but the settlement of personal grudge. The Ivorian leader Felix Houphouet-Boigny was said to have supported Liberian rebels because the Liberian leader (Samuel Doe) executed his (Felix's) son in-law during the bloody coup of 1980 that brought Doe to power.[18] In the same vein, Libyan leader Muammar Qaddafi trained and armed the Liberian rebels in order to punish Doe for closing down the Libyan embassy in 1981, in support of US anti Libyan policy.[19] Interference could be in the form of instigating, fuelling or sustaining conflicts.

There are other catalytic factors to West African conflicts. Not minding the devastation caused by conflicts to human and material resources and the environment, there are those who benefit from it. The armed factions, international armed dealers and other foreign companies were identified to have benefited immensely from the conflicts in Liberia and Sierra Leone. Adeleke argues that Charles Taylor (a rebel) derived $75m per annum from the export of resources in the area under his jurisdiction and $10m from a consortium of North American, Japanese and European miners.[20] He further claims that diamond and gold worth between $300m and $500m, $53m timber and $27m rubber were exported to Europe and South East Asia by the

---

17 Elaigwu(1997), p.18.

18 Adeleke Adebajo, *Op.Cit.*, p. 48.

19 African affairs, 94, No.375.

20 Adeleke Adebajo, *Building Peace in West Africa: Liberia, Sierra Leone, and Guinea-Bissau*, p. 47

Liberian warlord during the Liberian civil war.[21]

In Sierra Leone, the quest to plunder resources and loot central bank was also identified as the key motivation of the rebel groups that toppled the elected government of Ahmed Tijjan Kabbah of Sierra Leone in May 1997. [22]

The issue of ownership of land and other resources has also resulted in several conflicts in West Africa. Claims over farmland or water sources by a family or a community have resulted into severe internal conflicts in the region. In communities where precious resources like oil, gold, diamond, etc are extracted, several complains of inadequate compensation or governments insensitivity to environmental degradation and pollution arise. This is currently the cause of conflict in the Niger Delta region of Nigeria.

Similar to the above mentioned is boundary disputes (both land and maritime) among states, though the OAU decided in 1963 to accept the boundaries African states have inherited from the colonial authorities, there are still some cases that have been causing serious tension. Amongst them are the disputes over the Bakassi peninsula between Nigeria and Cameroon, and that of Gabon and Equatorial Guinea over the Islands of Mbanu, Cocotiers, Corisco, Elobey Grande and Elobey Chico.[23] Some of the disputed areas are rich in mineral resources such as oil, and hence of strategic importance to the countries in question, particularly with the present decline in the economies of the region.

Once hostilities breakout, there is every likelihood of outside interference both from far and near with arms traffickers also exploiting the situation. Another catalytic factor to African conflict is poverty aided by illiteracy. Collier once more argues that a country with large natural resources, many unemployed young men and little education is much at risk of conflict.[24] Even though this theory hasn't explained why countries with similar or worst proxies manage to avoid conflict, no doubt poverty, illiteracy and unemployment facilitates the ease with which rebel groups and warlords recruit fighters in West Africa.

---

21 Adeleke Adebajoi, *Op. Cit.*, p. 48.
22 UN Report(1998), para 14.
23 Elaigwu, *Op.Cit.*, p. 32.
24 P. Collier, *Op.Cit.*, p. 97.

Effects of Conflict in West Africa

The costs of war for West Africans, their cultures, societies, and economies have been immense. As was experienced in Nigeria, Chad, Liberia, Sierra Leone and guinea, civil war does not only devastate the lives of civilians, it damages the environment, wreaking havoc on social, educational and health services. It also traumatises whole generations and forces people to abandon homes and farming land, engulfing once stable family units into a flood of refugees. The direct consequences of war can best be appreciated by looking at its effects on people and the economy.

The end of colonialism marked the beginning of conflicts in West Africa. Since then, wars in the sub-region began to take tolls in human lives on an unprecedented scale. Millions of people have died as the direct or indirect result of war. Estimates of the number killed in the Nigerian Civil War alone run as high as 1 million. In 1998, the UN secretary general claims that armed conflicts in Africa has accounted for more than half of all the war related deaths in the world.[25] Africa as a whole has experienced many internal conflicts including coups, riots and demonstrations that had little potential for escalating into war, yet they are marked by high death tolls. Such is the case with the religious strives between the Christians and the Moslems in Nigeria.

Injury is one of the tragic hazards of war, creating destitute who will not be able to support themselves in the future. It is a heavy burden which relatives bear in caring for the wounded for years to come. Also, injuries caused to civilians either directly or indirectly by rebels are of very grave concern. With the Revolutionary United Front (the rebel group) in Sierra Leone, civilian populations rather than being afforded protection have become both targets and tools of war. Here, several thousand civilians amongst them women and children have been dastardly amputated. Refugee camps and hospitals are full of victims who have had one or more limbs amputated.

Africa accounts for one third of the World's refugees with a substantial percentage emanating from West Africa. While refugees have been returning

25 UN Report (1998).

to neighbouring Liberia, those from Sierra Leone have continued to flee. At present, nearly 500,000 refugees are stranded in the corridor between Guinea and Liberia. The increasing burden resulting from refugee situations constitute a severe drain on the already lean resources of most West African states. Africa's wars are also typified by human rights violations. War has brought widespread violations of personal security and integrity. Summary executions, mass kidnappings, forced labour, rapes, robbery, mass murders, mutilations and torture characterise most wars in West Africa.

War undoubtedly devastates the economy of a country. The empirical evidence of this is overwhelming. It also destroys capitals, leaving shattered infrastructure in its wake. It diverts portfolios away from domestic investment, and triggers massive capital flight.[26] Armed conflict also distorts foreign aid budgets, which are now being increasingly devoted to emergencies, and most fundamentally, it diverts massive government expenditures away from provision of economic and social services towards military expenditure. Disruptions to agriculture, transportations, mining, and industry have further drained national economies.[27] Regrettably, there can be no serious thought of development in the countries that are undergoing war of any dimension. The effect of these conflicts on the people and the environment has posed a serious obstacle to peace and development of West Africa, and the integration of the region into the global society. It has also impacted on the security of some developed countries that are already suffering from immigration related problems.

The Role of International Community

In order to understand the dynamics of what drives the West African security complex, it is important to explain the roles of the international community and the historical context of the geo strategic rivalry between Nigeria and France during the Cold War. France colonised the West African countries with the exception of Nigeria, Ghana, Liberia, Sierra Leone and Gambia.

---

26 K. Y. Amoako, *Address of the UN Under-Secretary-General and Executive Secretary of Economic Commission for Africa*, to the 70th Session of the Council of Ministers of the Organisation of Africa Unity, Algeria, 9 Dec, 1999.

27 *Ibid.*

During the Nigerian civil war France and some of its colonies in West Africa not only recognised Biafra (state created by the rebels in Nigeria) but also supported the secessionist. After the civil war, Nigeria championed the creation of economic community of West African states (ECOWAS) in 1972. This is designed to reduce the influence of France in the region. Paris in a counter move engineered the creation of an exclusive Francophone Communaute Economique de'l Afrique del'Ouest (CEAO) in 1973.

France maintained military bases in four West African countries including Senegal and Cote d'Ivoire. It had always regarded Nigeria as a geostrategic rival and opposed what it perceived as Nigeria's hegemonic ambition in West Africa. The end of the Cold War saw a dramatic shift in France's African policy. It began with its diversification of economic relation beyond the Francophone countries and became the largest foreign investor in Nigeria after Britain. Nigeria also became France's largest market in sub-Saharan Africa.

The French president told French diplomats in August 1997 that France should abstain from "all interference of whatever nature" in Africa and that "France would not accept it herself".[28] Despite its military presence in Cote d'Ivoire, France refused to intervene when the president of Cote d'Ivoire was over thrown in December 1999. Meanwhile, the rivalry between Nigeria and France ended with President Jacque Chirac visiting Nigeria in July 1999 during which he praised Nigeria's continental leadership role. Nigerian president Obasanjo also visited Paris in February 2000. Paris closed down 2 of its military bases in Central African Republic in April 1998. France's disengagement in Africa began to draw Francophone countries in the region into closer security cooperation with Nigeria.

Non Francophone countries are for the first time invited by France to attend a regular military exercise Renfocement des capacities Afrique de la paix (RECAMP) designed to strengthen African peace keeping capacity. While France has reduced its high profile military role in West Africa, its historic rival Nigeria which is the richest country in the region, with a standing army more than that of the remaining 14 countries in the sub region put together, stakes its claim to be a new sub regional military power.

28 West Africa Magazine, No. 4170, 13-19 October, 1997, p. 16.

The security roles of US, UK and France in West Africa were influenced by the Cold War and the decolonisation of Africa. While the US was locked in the ideological contest with a strategic rival the Soviet Union, the major colonial powers Britain and France emerged from the WWII fatigued and economically exhausted. This might have accounted for their inability to evolve a coherent security strategy in Africa. It is in the light of this development in the international system that the roles of the 3 western powers in West Africa need to be considered.

In 1958, President De Gaulle returned to power in France in the heat of Algerian war of independence. Having failed to retain control in Algeria, he tried to maintain some influence in the sub-Saharan Africa. France was indeed responsible for security in all its African territory up to 1960. Until the end of the Cold War, France maintained a high security profile in Africa than did the British and the US. Its security policy permitted active intervention and that is why French military camps are still found in a number of places in the region, though in a much smaller scale.

Amongst the colonial powers of Africa, only France maintained military presence with its colonies. Between 1960 and 1995, there were hundreds of French military interventions in Africa. While some were conducted against communist incursions, others were in support of or crushing rebellions. Some of these interventions are; Gabon (1964, 1990), Senegal (1968), CAR (1979), Chad (1965, 1973 and 1983), Togo (1986, 1990), Comoros (1989), Zaire (1978) to mention but a few.[29]

In terms of economic assistance, Paris recently influenced a Franco-British cooperation on Africa which is aimed at increasing EU and G8 developmental assistance to the region through its programme 'New Strategy for Africa (NSA).[30] The aid will mostly be directed towards education and healthcare.

The British came out of WWII victorious but appeared somewhat fatigued and ready to foreclose the empire. The labour government that came to

---

29 J. Chipman, *The French Power in Africa*, (Oxford: Basil Blackwell, 1989), p. 126.

30 http://www.diplomatie.gouv.fr/en/afrique2286/index.html

power after the war was faced with huge demand for independence from its colonies. Unlike the French who fought to retain their colonies, Britain ceded the empire, leaving behind the commonwealth in its exit strategy. There were other contributory factors like the Suez in 1956 and Ghana in 1957.

In the beginning of 1960 there was a growing difference of attitude in interventionism in Africa between the British and the French. While the French were in their best neo colonial form, the British were reluctant to respond to the call of the governments of the newly independent states of East Africa (i.e. Uganda, Tanzania and Kenya) who were faced with mutinies. During the Nigerian civil war of 1967-1970 Britain rendered only a passive support to its former colony. At the end of the war, Nigerian federalist felt Britain was 'no ally'.

The British passivity was a reflection of the British government's foreign policy. As far as security in West Africa was concerned, the British maintained a very low profile since independence. Unexpectedly, Britain made a swift reversal in its African policy by staging a military intervention in Sierra Leone in 2000. Ironically, it came at the time the French started disengaging in the region. The British PM made several assertions on prioritising assistance to Africa after the Foreign and Commonwealth Office (FCO) recognised the violent conflicts in Africa as a threat to global security and an impediment to the development of the continent.[31] The UK government has indicated interest in preventing conflicts in Africa through its establishment of joint conflict prevention initiative, and plan to work with US, UN and EU in developing a programme that will enhance Africa's peacekeeping capacity.[32] It is in line with its plan that the UK sent troops to Sierra Leone and supporting a number of other projects in Nigeria and Ghana to improve the peacekeeping capacity of their troops.

Having led the allied to victory in WWII, US emerged as an undisputed economic and military power in the world. Its foot print was very visible almost everywhere in the world less Africa. It seems to have left that flank to

31 http://www.fco.gov.uk/africa (UK policy on Africa).
32 *Ibid.*

its NATO allies (Britain and France). After granting independence to African states, the withdrawal of western political control left an unstable situation in the emerging states. Meanwhile the resentment of African leaders towards the West offered opportunities to Moscow and Beijing.[33] This drew US attention into the region. Finally, the Congo crises of 1960-1965 defined US policy in Africa during the Cold War.

In 1960 US administration considered Patrice Lumumber of Congo a Soviet puppet and an enemy of the highest order, referring to him as 'the Castro of Africa'. The CIA recruited Mobutu to replace Lumumber who was later assassinated.[34] The Katanga rebellion that followed the assassination of Lumumber was crushed by a US led UN peacekeeping force in Congo in 1963. It was in Congo that the US first employed mercenaries in Africa before Angola in 1975.[35] After falling out with Mobutu, US lacked a Base and resorted to proxy wars against the Soviet rivals using either war lords or rebels like Jonas Savimbi. Like the British, US also maintained a low profile when it comes to African security.

In 1993 President Clinton launched US troops into Somalia in operation 'Restore Hope'. This was the sole US intervention in Africa since the end of the Cold War. The operation ended in a disaster after 18 US soldiers were killed and 84 were injured. US pulled out of Somalia living top military brass like Colin Powell wandering what US forces went there to do. This may be responsible for the US reluctance to intervene and stop the genocide that took place in Rwanda in 1994.

After the events in Somalia, US presidential policy review was ordered in 1993, which came up with stringent measures that are bound to limit the scope for direct military involvement in Africa. The US made a proposal in 1996 for an African crisis response force consisting of 5,000-10,000 troops drawn from and manned by various African countries. Since then, the US policy as far as African security is concerned is that of regionalisation of African peacekeeping force, "African solution to African problems". Hutchful remarks that "the division of labour between US support and African

---

33 CIA World Fact Book, 2011.

34 Docummentary programme on "Mobutu Roi du Zaire" by Thierry Michel.

35 J. Stockwell, *In Search of Enemies: CIA Story*, in New York, Norton, 1978, pp. 182-185, 216-226.

peacekeeping raises new issues and questions that are different from those that have traditionally driven peacekeeping research." [36]

The US presidential peacekeeping policy review asked that every intervention must be defined in US own national interest. But how much does Africa mean to US national interest? In 2000, the total export of African countries into the US was put at $28bn, with crude oil and petrochemical products dominating, which accounted for 2.6% of total US import.[37] And the US export (goods and services) to Africa in the same year stood at $10.9bn with aircraft and automobile parts, oil and gas equipment dominating. Whether this figures are enough to secure US attention in African security remains to be seen. Meanwhile, Ibrahim argues that with the end of the Cold War, African conflicts no longer constitute a threat to US national interest (containing communism, access to strategic resources and promotion of American values). [38]

On 27 May 2001, while on his plane to Budapest after his first tour of Africa as secretary of state, Colin Powell was asked by the press what conflict prevention measures US would consider next time in Africa, considering the calamity in Rwanda and Congo where millions have died. Powell replied "I think it is still the best policy for us to provide assistance to nations that are willing to put forward forces from the region....the approach we have taken is increasing the capability of indigenous forces to respond to these kinds of things and picking up quite a bit of the bill. In Sierra Leone, the force is now moving up to 17,500 troops with just a few US troops there serving a liaison function. But we are picking up $300m of the bill and that seems to me to be pretty good allocation of the effort, as opposed to the American Army going into every crisis area in the world.[39] US gives aids and conducts a number of military exercises with African countries annually, this is in order to strengthen their security and improve their peacekeeping capacities.

---

36 Eboe Hutchful, *Peacekeeping Under Conditions of Resource stringency*, A paper Read at Conference Titled, From Peacekeeping to Complex Emergencies, Jointly hoisted by the Southern African Institute for International Affairs and iss, 1999, pp. 97–98.

37 USIS, Africa news Report, 11 June, 2001, p. 7.

38 Ibrahim Elbadawi, *Op.Cit.*, p. 18.

39 *Ibid.*

Following the event of the 11th of September 2001 and subsequent US declaration of global war on terror, America has recently deployed about 14,000 troops in Djibouti to keep watch on Somalia. In the economic front, US have maintained an annual budget in financial aid for most African countries. For 2006, African Development Foundation is estimated to receive \$18.85m and \$135.7m for African Development Fund. These amounts do not include the aids given to other areas like healthcare, education, etc.

West Africa is a region that is endowed with natural resources that are vital to the world. Efforts to establish West African Economic Union (WEU) was only realised in 1975 when a treaty formerly establishing the Economic Community of West African States (ECOWAS) was signed in Nigeria by the heads of governments within the sub region. The sole objective was the promotion of economic integration in West Africa.[40]

However, the security challenges that followed the end of Cold War compelled the organisation to adapt its machinery into conflict management, having realised that without peace and security, economic integration would not succeed. The outbreak of war in Liberia resulted in a formation of a military force known as ECOWAS Cease fire Monitoring Group (ECOMOG). In all three cases the conflicts were intra state and ECOMOG had to fight with the war lords. Despite the deficiencies and shortcomings of the force, the peacekeepers made enormous sacrifices and recorded positive achievements.

ECOMOG put off the interconnected bush fires that raged on from Liberia to Sierra Leone to Guinea to Guinea-Bissau and to Senegal. The reliance of the sub regional force on its own resources to end the civil war in Liberia and restore a democratically elected government that was overthrown in Sierra Leone was the first time any sub regional organisation would undertake such an action. It was also the first time UN would send military observers to support an established sub regional force anywhere in the world. The UN established peace building offices in the region and is currently maintaining its largest peacekeeping force in Sierra Leone. The success recorded by ECOMOG is driving the leaders of the sub region to institutionalise a security mechanism to manage future sub regional conflicts.

40 Adebajo(2002), *Op. Cit.*, p.35.

The coming together of West African leaders to take the lead in the effort to manage the conflicts in the region represent a significant trend in conflict management, and raised the prospects for peace in the region. Since then there has been an increase in sharing of responsibility between regional actors and the over burden UN. In his 1992 report to the Security Council on Africa, the UN secretary general Boutros Ghali argued that regional security arrangement is used to ease the UN's heavy peacekeeping burden.[41]

This ECOWAS initiative is also a credible alternative, in the light of increasing reluctance of the 'casualty shy' western countries to send their own troops to Africa after the debacle of Somalia in 1993.[42] Nigeria is the most influential member of ECOWAS. It led the operations in both Liberia and Sierra Leone, providing over 90% of the troops, logistics and finance, and Nigeria's absence in the operation in Guinea-Bissau was blamed for the premature termination of that mission.[43] A conservative estimate of $2bn was said to have been spent on ECOMOG mission by Nigeria, and no fewer than 1,000 of its troops were killed in the operation.[44]

However, Nigeria is heavily criticized for its unilateralism and pursuance of hegemonic ambitions. Burkina-Faso's interior minister Yero Boly accused Nigeria of doing what it wants and going to ECOWAS for approval.[45] The Nigerian foreign minister Tom Ikimi contends that Francophone members of the organisation were only trying to undermine ECOMOG's effort in order to satisfy Paris.[46] General Diarra of Mali also described Nigeria as the problem and the solution to the problem.[47]

In any case, the new administration in Nigeria has already signalled its intention to discontinue playing the role it has been playing in the region. In his address to the UN general assembly on September 1999, barely 4 months

---

41 UN report, 1994.

42 Adeleke Adebajo & Chris Landsberg, "Back to the Future: UN peacekeeping in Africa," *International Peacekeeping*, Vol. 7, No. 4, 2000, pp. 161-188.

43 Adeleke Adebajo, *Op.Cit.*, p. 35.

44 Adeleke Adebajo, *Op.Cit.*, p. 37.

45 Africa Research Bulletin, Published in 1999.

46 Interview With Ikimi

47 Personal Interview with General Diarra on Nigerian television Documentary Programme, 'ECOMOG' Monitored on 1 May, 2004.

after being sworn in to office, Nigerian president Obasanjo says " for too long the burden of preserving international peace in West Africa has been left almost entirely to a few states in our sub region,..... Nigeria's continual burden in Sierra Leone is unacceptably draining Nigeria financially. For our economy to take off, this bleeding has to stop."[48]

Nigeria demonstrated its seriousness by reducing its troops in Sierra Leone from 12,000 to only 4,000. Efforts within the region to persuade Nigeria reverse it's decision failed and the international community became concerned about the future security of the region without Nigeria's financial and military muscle.

The US president Bill Clinton paid a visit to Nigeria in August 2000, and in his address to the countries national assembly says "I know that many of you have often felt that the burden of your peacekeeping is heavier than the benefit.......But there is no one else in West Africa with the size, the standing, the strength of military force to do it. If you don't who will do it? But you should not do it alone and should not pay the enormous price. That is what's been wrong with what happened in the last several years. I am determined, if you are willing to lead, to get you the international support you need and deserve to meet these responsibilities."[49] With the present interest and determination of the major stakeholders to work together in supporting West African countries politically and financially, it is highly likely that violent conflicts in the region will begin to wind down while the socio-economic life of the people improves. The prospect for peace and security returning to the region will also increase tremendously.

The Way Forward

The military in Africa was created by the colonial powers not to deter external aggression but to protect the colonial state through the suppression of internal opposition. With the exception of few, most African armies retain this posture to date, as the threat in most countries remains internal. This is partly responsible for West Africa witnessing more military coups than any

48 http://www.Sierra Leone.org/slnews
49 The Airman(2003), p.12.

other sub region in the world. The military officers belong to the political class that is most threatened by democracy. An assessment of the military in West Africa has revealed that the military is not only a threat to security of the region but to the socioeconomic development of the sub region as well. Ironically, the military always portrays itself as a stabilizing force against corruption, social unrest etc. The military's involvement in politics erodes professionalism in the institution. Rather than providing aid to civil power, the African militaries are the major source of instability and disorder in the region.

The military coups in West Africa were masterminded by either top ranking military officers or junior officers. In some cases even non-commission officers, as was the case with Samuel Doe of Liberia, and Gnassingbe Eyadema of Togo. There have been 75 successful coups in the sub Saharan Africa since 1956 (See Annex B). While democratization is believed to be part of the solution to the West African political problems, the military has on a number of occasions toppled democratically elected governments and replaced them with dictatorship. Some few case were Nigeria (1966, 1983), Sierra Leone (1967, 1997), Ghana (1972, 1979), Togo (1963), Gambia (1994) and Niger (1998).

When pressure builds against dictatorship, rather than handing over to an elected civilian government, the military only transforms itself into a civilian government, trading its uniform for mufti. This again was the case with Samuel Doe in Liberia, Rawlings in Ghana, Jammeh in Gambia and Kampore of Burkina-Fatso. This action neither de-militarizes the politics nor de-politicizes the military. Military coups in West Africa reinforced the primacy of domination over legitimating, exacerbating tension between states and society, and in some cases transform violence from tool of domination to a means of criminal extraction.[50]

Considering the enormity of the damage caused by conflicts in West Africa, it is most important to prevent crisis early enough from escalating into violence. The international community needs to have in place a source of intelligence that will provide early warning of impending conflict. This is to be followed immediately by a strong UN diplomatic intervention to diffuse

50 Abuja conference (1998).

the tension and address the grievances of the contending parties.

The UN needs to involve AU and ECOWAS through its recently established liaison office in AU HQ.[51] It is very critical to ensure that internationally respected personalities do the mediation timely, and a commission to immediately verify the causes of the dispute and a transparent settlement arrived at. Where necessary, a preventive deployment could be considered in order to build confidence in the populace and show them the level of commitment of the international community in resolving the crisis. Preventing a conflict is much cheaper for the international community, saves lives and property from destruction, prevent refugee crisis, and above all avert the spread of violence into neighbouring states.

Another preventive strategy is a peacemaking mechanism that will continue to encourage disputing parties to negotiate. In this, a correct assessment of the causassive factors to the dispute is vital. Where poverty and lack of social services is identified as a catalyst to the crisis, the UN could provide incentives like roads, water, farming implements and fertilizers (to farmers), health care, etc to the people. This may help to calm down the tension.

The chapter VIII of the UN charter has provided for cooperation with regional organisation in the maintenance of international peace and security. Articles 52-54 encourage and empower the regional organisations to settle regional conflicts including enforcement actions. The UN will drive huge amount of benefit in working with the regional organisations in Africa. Bellamy claims that the peacekeeping potentials of regional organisations range from their knowledge of the local environment to geographical proximity to the conflict area.[52] Besides being stakeholders in the conflict, regional organisations also provide a wider diplomatic window of opportunities, and some warring parties will prefer them to external bodies.

Many West African conflicts in the past have escalated out of proportion due to lack of common approach in settling them by the international community. This often happens as a result of variety of interest from the various external actors. As soon as conflict breaks out, protagonist usually

51 UN Report(1994), para 20.
52 Bellamy(2004), *Op. Cit.*, p.214.

seek for allies and neighbouring states begin to take sides. If the situation is allowed to continue for long, intervention becomes more difficult, as parties to the conflict are now more in number. Enforcing sanctions and arms embargo also become more difficult as neighbouring states may undermine that effort.

The collective approach should include all interested parties to the conflict including ECOWAS and AU, with a special envoy from UN as mediator. This will help maintaining common front and harmonising both political and financial efforts. Once a framework is established for the resolution of the conflict, it is important that all parties adhere to it. This will minimize the chances of division amongst the parties and protagonist playing them against each other. Charles Taylor did just that during the Liberian conflict.

Political and economic isolation together with arms embargo can be a very effective tool in resolving a conflict if implemented properly. It has the capacity to starve the protagonist of funds and arms to sustain the war, and leave negotiation as the best available option. A very careful assessment is necessary to ensure that only the decision makers are targeted and the impact does not have an adverse effect on the population. A needed development in this area is to criminalise the violation of the Security Council arms embargo by member states.

The UN in collaboration with AU and ECOWAS need to identify the sources (including merchants and routes) of arms flow into the region, particularly to conflict areas. The UN needs to address these issues seriously.

Prior to the setback caused by Somalia to the UN, the world body showed enthusiasm to keep peace in Africa. The UN has its largest deployment anywhere in the world in Africa. The setback in Somalia resulted in a reluctance to deploy in the continent; Rwanda became a victim of that action, where the UN displayed grave reluctance in the face of one of the most horrific genocides in recent times.

The UN needs to maintain its credibility by restoring its willingness and commitments to keep peace in Africa. There is therefore the need to identify key lessons from Somalia to guide against future operations. The UN played a vital role in ending starvation in the failed states of Somalia, but it was first time ever that UN had its peacekeepers withdrawn ahead of completion of their mission. The UN progress was hampered by total lack of commitment to peace by the warring factions.

The UN secretary general argues that the memories of Somalia continue to hobbie the organisation's capacity to respond swiftly and decisively towards any crisis particularly in Africa.[53] Perhaps if the UN's diplomatic machinery had secured the consent of all the parties in Somalia before deployment, the outcome would probably have been different.

In Mozambique the UN played a role that could serve as a model for subsequent engagements in Africa. It maintained continues dialog with all the parties to the conflict, presenting a harmonised front through which all the peace efforts were directed and pursued. The success in Mozambique is an indication that the world governing body retains the capacity to bring together under one umbrella, all parties involved and resolve a conflict that will otherwise be manipulated by external forces and degenerate into a catastrophe. Other successful UN involvement in Africa includes the Cold War battle fields of Angola and Namibia.

Most countries that are undergoing or have undergone through a conflict in West Africa lack an effective institutional capacity to mobilize and distribute aid to those that need it. Since it is very important that aid reach those it is intended for in good time in order to avert human sufferings, it is imperative to evolve a more efficient process of distributing the aid. In a number of cases, failure to do this rendered the aid programme ineffective and the aid eventually became an incentive to the warring factions.

Roles of UN and Major Actors

The UN has the responsibility of maintaining peace in West Africa irrespective of any setback suffered in the past by the organisation in that region. The UN has done that very well in Angola, Mozambique and Namibia, and is still doing well in many other parts of the continent including

53 UN Report(1997), para 31

Congo, Eritrea, Liberia, Sierra Leone and Sudan. There is no other country, regional or sub regional organisation that has the capacity and experience and also recorded the success the UN did. Despite the success recorded by ECOMOG in Liberia and Sierra Leone, it had to fall back on the UN to achieve a comprehensive settlement of the conflicts.

The US, Britain and France are all permanent members in the security council, therefore their support is imperative if there is to be a lasting peace in West Africa. However, their efforts need to be harmonised and channelled through the UN. This will present a common front in resolving any conflict or crisis and eliminate the complications that arise from divergent interests and approaches.

The collective effort will also be more credible and likely to have wider support and acceptance by the protagonists. Also, UN resolutions passed in respect to any conflicts will be sincerely implemented with less supervision. In addition to the UN's traditional peacekeeping strategy of deployment while diplomatic efforts are being pursued to resolve the conflict, a 'comprehensive approach' to peacekeeping is likely to represent a better idea. This will involve civil organisations that will rebuild and strengthen public institutions in war torn areas.

NGOs and UN humanitarian agencies and commissions that will distribute aid and protect human right and a force to reform the security sector of the affected area could all be part of it. This will accelerate the recovery of the state in question and its reintegration back into the stable community of nations. It will also reduce the chances of the state slipping back to anarchy as was witnessed recently in Liberia.

The UN charter again provides for cooperation with both regional and sub regional bodies in matters relating to international peace and security. Considering the cultural complexities in Africa, it is desirable that the UN work closely with these regional organisations. With UN political, financial and logistic support, the AU and ECOWAS have the human resources and expertise to compliment the UN effort in containing the security problems in West Africa. This will prove valuable especially with the recent increasing reluctance by the West to commit its troops in that region.

Absolute care has to be taken by the UN to ensure neutrality is maintained, as the possibility of some regional forces taking side cannot be completely ruled out. Deployment of multinational supervisors could help in that direction. Such collaboration will give the AU and ECOWAS more legitimacy, better recognition, international support and remove the major impediments of logistics and suspicion suffered by the regional efforts in the past.

The nature of African conflicts involving rebels and militias make it difficult at times to secure the consent of all the warring factions before deploying peacekeepers. Considering the level of destruction that takes place and human suffering especially to civilian in most of these conflicts, it may be necessary to forcefully intervene where necessary in order to avert what may sometimes result into genocide. It will also minimize the destructions to properties and damage to the environment. Such were the cases for the UN intervention in Somalia, NATO in Kosovo and ECOWAS in Liberia and Sierra Leone.

The gradual withdrawal of western countries from the security needs of Africa was followed with a call from both sides for African countries to handle their own destiny. Some countries like US, France, Britain, Germany and Belgium have developed a number of initiatives directed at reinforcing the peacekeeping capabilities of African countries. One of the most laudable is the French programme "Reinforcement de capacities de maintien de la paix" (RECAMP), a military exercise that was conducted for French speaking African countries. However, Nigeria has recently been invited to participate. Such programme assists in the area of training for peacekeeping. However, the divergence in opinion has lead to the countries conducting their exercises separately as opposed to a collective training. Harmonising these exercises under the aegis of the UN could further help in some of the doctrinal conflicts that arise when troops are deployed together in combine operations.

The international law of conflict provides for the protection of civilians, unfortunately, warlords in intra state conflicts do not abide by these laws. Civilians in most cases are targets in such conflicts, with women and children as the worst affected. The atrocities against women and children in Bosnia, Sudan and Sierra Leone were some of the most horrific images seen in the last decade.

The UN must get all combatants irrespective of whether the conflict is inter or intra state, to abide by international rules and regulations guiding a conflict. Any violations must be severely punished to serve as deterrence. The increasing number of dimensions and actors involved in the conflicts also require a 'Collective Approach' in handling, if the conflicts are to be resolved permanently and the victims resettled. Safe havens need to be established early enough and be secured by the UN, it most be free from arms and arms bearing persons other than those securing it. Humanitarian organisations need to be part of the force elements in UN contingent; they should also monitor and report to the head of the UN mission all violations observed. The UN can take measures that include sanctions and military action where necessary against violators.

In addition to the provisions of food, clothes and shelter to refugee camps, the office of the UN high commissioner for refugees need to ensure that vaccination against common outbreaks in war torn areas is administered to all that are in camps. The recruitment of children to bear arms by any faction should be viewed as a serious war crime by the UN and treated as such.

Countries accommodating a large number of refugees need to be protected and assisted by the UN in order not to strain their resources. Guinea has about 10% of its population as refugees from Liberia and Sierra Leone. Their presence over strained the resources of the local communities and raked havoc to the environment in Guinea.[54]

Conclusion

The dramatic change of events in West Africa started shortly after the end of colonial period and the beginning of Cold War. However, the potential for conflict in the region originates from the Berlin congress of 1885, when the 'scramble for Africa' led to the arbitrary partition of the continent amongst European colonial powers. After the partition, most African countries turned out to be multicultural and multiethnic societies. The countries were also not prepared politically, socially and economically for the independence they achieved around the 1960s. This made the challenges of the post colonial

54 UN report(1997), para56

regimes enormous. Unfortunately, most post-colonial West African leaders resorted to some undemocratic and unconstitutional means in tackling these challenges. Reliance on ethnic loyalty, centralisation of state power and use of brute force to suppress opposition was prevalent.

The ideological contest between the two super powers during the Cold War availed the required support for corrupt African regimes to function. However, the withdrawal of this support following the end of the Cold War left most of the regimes weak and unable to meet up their obligations.

Loans were secured from western countries and international financial institutions in order to secure regimes and sustain state machinery. This was also short lived as the countries soon became credit unworthy. It was not long before the security situation in the region deteriorated and violent conflicts started to erupt. From the time West African countries started becoming independent to date over 50 wars have been fought in the continent, with most of them being intra state. Millions of people died in these wars and many more were made refugees. These conflicts are responsible for the instability and lack of economic prosperity in Africa.

This study identifies the cause of these conflicts as multidimensional. While the composition of the states is in itself a potential source of conflict, embedded in it are greed and grievance. Greed is in the sense that African Leaders hold on to power and all its privileges, leaving no constitutional or democratic means for a change. Grievance mostly emanate from the groups that feel politically and economically marginalised by nepotism and corruption practiced by the regimes leadership. In the absence of a legitimate political order and a constitutional means of replacing the regimes, the opposition is left with violence as the only viable option. This makes most regimes in Africa as the most serious threat to their national security.

In addition, lack of political consensus in these countries deprives their societies of national cohesion and core value identification. This again is responsible for the passive reaction by the people whenever their regimes or territories are challenged from within.

Poverty and lack of earning opportunities, aided by illiteracy amongst the young men, in countries that are blessed with resources increased the risk of conflict in most of the states. External intervention also fuelled the conflicts when and wherever they erupted in the region. Today, proliferation of rebel movements, small arms and refugees adversely affect the ability to govern some West African countries. During the Cold War period, U.S. and the former colonial powers in region (Britain and France) played a role in the security of the region. While their role fuelled some conflicts, it nonetheless prevented a lot more from erupting.

However, the post Cold War era witnessed a decline in the security roles of these powers, but 9/11 coupled with the increasing urge for energy by the competing powers has changed this situation. The ECOWAS which was established to promote economic integration in West Africa has since been re-coursed to manage conflicts in the region, when the major stakeholders became reluctant to do so.

Just as the causes of conflict in West Africa are multidimensional, so also are the responses that will guarantee lasting peace in the region. This study opines that building post Cold War security architecture in West Africa requires a collective comprehensive approach that involves a sustained diplomatic, economic and military line of activity. The approach entails the West African countries to take 'ownership' of local solution to violent conflicts. They should also address indigenous causes which include political, economic and social exclusion, poor governance and corruption, manipulation of ethnicity, abuse of human right and the rule of law.[55]

The international community (lead by the UN) on the other hand is required to bring together all the stakeholders including the UNSC, international financial institutions, the G8, etc to speak with a common voice and act with a common front in preventing or resolving a conflict.[56] The stakeholders should also consider the promotion of economic, political and social developments, abusive exploitation of West Africa's resources and the proliferation of small arms.[57]

---

55 http://www.fco.gov.uk, UK policy on Africa : Accessed on 18 Feb, 06.

56 *Ibid.*

57 *Ibid.*

Lastly, the international community should cooperate with, and help to improve West Africa's regional security structure and conflict prevention mechanism. These are keys to eradicating poverty and improving security in the region. Ensuring peace and security in the entire African continent is a worthwhile investment for the international community. It will not only sustain the bi-lateral trade with the West which runs into billions of dollars but also deny sanctuary to organised crimes and terrorist.

Instability in West Africa pose a threat not only to the region but the world, as the ripple effect will end up impacting on global security. Above all, it is only when there is peace and security that Africa will guarantee a stable supply of energy and other raw materials to the industrialised countries of the world.

Chapter V

Prospects African Integration : On the Experience of West Africa

Introduction

A major feature of the international system since the end of WWII has been the tremendous leap towards regional economic cooperation and integration in the various parts of the world. This had much to do with the post-war reconstruction efforts as well as the nature of international economic relations, which has become a feature of the contemporary international system. This process towards economic integration, as distinct from political integration, has become so widespread that the post- World War period has been, to some extent described as an 'era of regional integration'.[1] Indeed, the vigorous interest in regionalism may also have been created by the difficulties in concluding the Uruguay Round of trade negotiations; an awareness that gave the impression that the world trade system may in future gravitate towards trade blocs, aligned around the European Union, the United States, and Japan.[2]

It has been seen, over the years that trade blocs have emerged as viable economic entities that assure their members guaranteed access to larger markets, efficient intra-bloc trade, lower business transaction costs and easier movement of goods and services. Trade blocs also act as shields for their members, as they create customs unions and treat non-members as third parties. The creation of a large number of economic groupings in virtually every region of the world has resulted from the massive liberalisation of world trade, as well as easy access to international finance. Interestingly, some sixty percent of this trade took place within regional integration blocs, to which

1 S. K. B. Asante, *The Strategy of Regional Integration in Africa,* (Accra: Friedrich Ebert Foundation Books, 1996), p. 1.

2 S. K. B. Asante, *Regionalism and Africa's Development; Expectations, Reality and Challenges,* (Ipswich: Ipswich Book Co. Ltd., 1977), p. 1.

almost every country in the world now belongs.[3] One other phenomenon that has lent more vim to the tendency towards integration or trade blocs is the inevitable strive towards common currency. This latter development has been successful within the European Union (since the Maastricht Treaty of 1992), to the extent that regionalism everywhere has as its optimal aim the achievement of a 'monetary union'.[4] Meanwhile, there is the growing concern that the success of regional trade blocs in the developed world, especially among the rich countries of the north, would invariably deny poor non-member countries, particularly those in Africa, access to world markets. It is this growing concern that makes the case for regional integration in Africa a more plausible choice, and efforts towards this end have of late seen more vigour than ever before.

The case for Africa's integration was made as far back as the days prior to decolonisation. The Manchester Conference (Pan-Africanism) of 1945 spelt out in detail, the need for African Unity. The period of decolonisation also saw Pan-African demands being strongly echoed. The formation of the Organization of African Unity (OAU), and the compromises therein made, show to what extent the African nationalist leaders yearned for one form of integration or another.5 The commitment to the more radical approach, namely the political integration among African countries and their people, was most demonstrated by the late Ghanaian leader, President Kwame Nkrumah, when he talked of a 'Union of African States' in the early 1960s.[6] A realistic appraisal of the contemporary situation in Africa makes the achievement of a Union of African states a daunting task. The continent is confronted with the challenges of indebtedness, poverty, political turmoil and insecurity, imbalance in trade relations, lack of access to adequate finance capital and inadequate investment and technology.

It can however be argued that the aspirations for Africans to integrate, and the motivation behind the European integration experience, have some

3 Omar Kabbaj, *The Challenge of African Development,* (New York: Oxford University Press, 2003), p. 67.

4 V. Antwi-Danso, "Regionalism and Economic Integration in Africa: Challenges and Prospects," *Legon Journal of International Affairs (LEJIA),* Vol. 3, No. 2, November 2006, p. 136.

5 Ibid., p. 2.

6 Nkrumah Kwame, *Op. Cit.*, p. 5.

parallels. For instance, it is commonly asserted that many African countries do not have peace, one of the basic conditions for regional integration to succeed. According to Mistry,[7] endemic political instability, exacerbated by debilitating conflict in every region of Africa, will make it impossible for integration to succeed. But the EU (formerly EEC) was founded in the aftermath of the bloodiest war in history, and its primary aim was not to promote trade among member states or institutional convergence, but to prevent further conflict.[8] Another motivation behind the original EEC was to increase its members' bargaining power relative to the United States.[9] The same could be said about African countries; African economies are also too small to negotiate effectively with industrialised countries, other developing countries, or multinational corporations. This explains their motivation to establish first the regional economic communities and eventually the African Economic Community; (AEC) leading ultimately to an integrated Africa.[10] The central issue to these processes and programmes in the integrative effort is the strategy, form and structure envisaged in this Pan-African initiative.

Against this background, this research seeks to analyse the viability or otherwise of the idea of integration in Africa, looking at one of the established sub-regional groupings as a building block. The research will examine the Economic Community of West African States (ECOWAS). It will appraise the challenges facing the sub-regional group, and the efforts being made to address these challenges, in order to enhance its integration effort. It will look at the successes of the organisation, and consider the relevance of the functionalist approach to integration. It will also examine the West African Monetary and Economic Union (UEMOA), a sub-group within ECOWAS and how its existence impinges on ECOWAS. Finally the research will examine the prospects of African integration, using ECOWAS as a yardstick. For the purpose of this research, the term regional integration will be used to demonstrate the features of both economic and political integration in whatever form, as it relates to the desire of African leaders for a continental union.

---

7 Mistry, P. S., *'Africa's Record of Regional Co-Operation'*, African Affairs, 99 (397), 2006, P. 553.

8 UNECA, Paper, 2002, *Institutions and Regional Integration in Africa,* Chapter 2, p.30. www.uneca.org/aria (accessed on 13 April, 2008)

9 *Ibid.*, p. 30.

10 J. Weeks, "Regional Cooperation and Southern African Development," *Southern African Studies, Vol.* 22, No. 1, 1996, p. 99-117.

Clarification of Concepts

Regional Integration: The term regional integration, according to Hans van Ginkel[11] refers to the process by which states within a particular region increase their level of interaction with regard to economic, political, security, and also social and cultural issues. In short, regional integration is the joining of individual states within a region into a larger whole. The degree of integration depends upon the willingness and commitment of the independent sovereign states, to share their sovereignty. Regional integration initiatives should aim to fulfil the objectives of strengthening trade integration in the region, the creation of an appropriate enabling environment, private sector development and the development of infrastructure in support of economic growth. A successful integration should also include the development of strong public sector institutions and governance, the reduction of social exclusion and the development of an inclusive civil society, whilst the integrative process should lead to the contribution of peace and security in the region, and the strengthening of the region's interaction with other regions of the world.[12]

Economic integration: It is "the process by which a group of countries agrees to eliminate barriers between their economies to form a larger economic space. It involves the ceding by member states, of sovereignty over particular economic policies. It devolves activities to a regional authority or institution which exercises its power at the group level. In theory, economic integration arrangements can take a variety of forms, which range from a preferential trade area (PTA), to a free trade area (FTA), a customs union, a common market, and an economic union".[13] The PTA, which is at the lowest end of the spectrum of economic integration, involves the application of lower tariffs by member states to intra-regional rather than to extra-regional trade. In the FTA, there is provision for the tariff-free movement of products between member states. Each member of the group is however free to retain its own tariff against third countries.

---

11 Hans van Ginkel, Julius Court & Luk Van Langenhove, eds., *Integrating Afric:; Perspective on Regional Integration and Development,* (Tokyo: UNU Press, 2003), p. 7.

12 *Ibid.*, p. 9.

13 Olufemi Fajana, "The Economics of Integration," *African Perspective,* Vol. 3, No. 12, May 2000, p. 20.

A customs union is characterised by the abolition of tariff restrictions on trade between the member states, as in the case of the FTA, alongside the adoption of a common external tariff (CET), against products from the rest of the world. In a common market, the basic features of a customs union are present; but in addition, factors of production (labour and capital) can move freely between member states.[14] Thus, this type of grouping provides for not only the integration of product markets, but also for the integration of factor markets. The economic union, which is at the level of economic integration, incorporates the characteristics of a common market, in addition to the harmonisation of fiscal, exchange rate and other economic policies. In a full economic union, there is a unification of these policies, whose formulation and implementation are entrusted to a supra-national organ of the union.[15] Economic integration arrangements, in practice, do not always conform to rigid theoretical classification. For example ECOWAS has yet to attain the status of a FTA, the lowest level of regional economic integration, but it is already implementing a protocol of free movement of persons which is a basic feature of a higher level of integration.

Relevance of Functionalism to Regional Integration: Central to the study of integration is the identification and analysis of forces, both theoretical and empirical, that contribute to the formation and integration of political communities. Functionalism as a theoretical construct, as well as a policy recommendation, began with David Mitrany, a British political scientist, whose writings greatly influenced contemporary integration theorists. Writing, mostly during the interwar years, he termed his collection of ideas as "A Working Peace System."[16] He estimated that the world of the twentieth century was characterised by a growing number of technical issues that could be resolved by cooperative action across state boundaries. The resolution of such technical problems must be addressed by highly trained specialists or technocrats with professional training, instead of politicians who often lack the technical skills. According to Mitrany, such pressing problems, most often having to do with welfare issues, could be addressed outside the politicised

14 *Ibid.*, p. 20.

15 *Ibid.*, p. 21.

16 Mitrany David, *A Working Peace System*, (Chicago: Quadrangle Books, 1966), p. 97. See also Dougherty & Pfalzgraff, *Contending Theories of International Relations: A Comprehensive Survey,* (New York: Longman, 2001), p. 512-513.

context of ideology or nationalism.[17] By placing emphasis on cooperation at technocratic levels, to find solutions to specific needs, the basis would be created for cooperation, leading to the formation and strengthening of international regimes and institutions. The success achieved in one area of endeavour could be replicated in other areas through a cooperative learning process. This condition could lead to the process of 'ramification', that is, the perceived need in one functional task would, contribute to a change in attitudes in favour of even greater cooperation over a wide spectrum of issues. Functional cooperation thus downplays the role of governments and nation states in the direct process of integration, by encouraging multilateralism, and institutional development.[18]

A realistic appraisal of the work and ideas of Mitrany must question the appropriateness of overlooking the role of political elites, political parties and interest groups. Many are of the view that it is doubtful that integration can take place within states and across state boundaries without the involvement of these stakeholders (states, political elites, political parties and pressure groups) who could oppose or accept the decisions to proceed, depending on their expectations of gaining or losing in the process. This led to the revision and adjustment from the earlier position and conclusions of Mitrany, to newer interpretations of neo-functionalism.[19] Essentially it argues that the experts and professionals who collaborate or cooperate to solve functional needs must be answerable to some authority and must be acting within a specificity of identifiable needs, preferably at the regional level.

The practical issues emerging from Mitrany's work, particularly on the question of 'ramification', led to the work of Ernest Haas who investigated the concept of 'spill-over'[20] and its impact on the European integration process. He was of the view that the initial reaction of European elites to the European Coal and Steel Community (ECSC) was one of apathy. It was not until

---

17 *Ibid.*, p. 511.

18 B. Y. Gebe, "In Pursuit of a Union of African States: The State System and Political Integration in Africa," *LEJIA*, Vol. 3, No. 2, November 2006, p. 123-124.

19 Other writers have contributed to the relevance of neo-functionalism in integration including Leon Linberg, Robert Kohane, Phillippe Schmitter.

20 Ernest Haas, "The European and Universal Process," *International Organisations,* 15 Autumn 1961, p. 372.

the practical results of the Community became apparent that the majority of trade unions and political parties decided to support the Community. Similarly, and as a result of the gains from the ECSC, the same group of unions and elites became supportive of the European Common Market.

Relevance of integration theories to Africa: There is no particular theory or model of integration which is universally accepted as an absolute blueprint for a successful integration process. The functionalist school of thought has, as its basic principle the performance of politically neutral, welfare oriented, tasks.[21] It argues that should there be politicisation of issues in integration it is expected to occur much later, as the institutions for cooperation grows and cooperation is intensified. This concept is not applicable to Africa, as the place of politics is right at the inception of the schemes of integration on the continent. Indeed Asante[22] that the treaties establishing these institutions contain such politically impregnated terms as 'consultation', 'collaboration', 'coordination', 'harmonisation' and 'concession'. Even with the EEC, (now EU), which has been used as an example for Africa, this truism could not have been expressed any better than by a former President of the EEC, Walter Hallstein, when he said "we are not in business at all, we are in politics."[23] The political factor has been manifested in the immutable dynamics that underpin all inter-state relations in Africa, including nationalism, ideology or political orientation and leadership idiosyncrasies. For Africa the Eurocentric application of the concept of regional integration seems frustrating, because what pertains is not gradual politicisation but instant politicisation of economic issues. Indeed, issues of economics and politics do not have ramifications on each other, they are completely fused together. Abbas Bundu,[24] says of Africa that the economics of integration and the

---

21 R. J. Lieber, *Theory and World Politics*, (Cambridge Massachusetts: Winthrop, 1972), P. 42.

22 S. K. B. Asante, "The Politics of Regional Economic Integration: The Case of ECOWAS," *Universitas inter Faculty Journal*, May 1978, p. 106.

23 UNECA, *Politics and Policymaking*, Chapter 2 of www.uneca,org/aria, accessed on 11 April 2008.

24 Abbas Bundu, "Sub-Regional Organization and the Promotion of African Economic Integration: The Case of ECOWAS," in Ojomo M. A. and Adewale O., eds., "African Economic Community Treaty: Issues, Problems and Prospects, Nigerian Institute of Advance Legal Studies," 1993, p. 344.

politics of integration are non-separable. Thus Joseph Nye's[25] caution to African integrationists to be conscious of these situations in their attempt at cooperation, rather than to be misled by assumptions natural to developed societies, could not be more appropriate.

It is pertinent to assume that these theories and concepts were developed from economies that have structures and circumstances quite different from what prevails in Africa. Conditions prevailing in Africa are strikingly different from those that exist in the developed world. Thus regional integration in Africa is in many respects a different phenomenon from that of economically advanced Europe. The differences lie in the areas of infrastructure, market mechanism, external dependence, administrative resources, and structure of political groupings, interdependence of social sectors, national consciousness and ideology.[26] Prescribing these theories to the African situation would meet with failures. Focusing on why regional integration in Africa has been painfully slow, a Maastricht World Forum report (1995) attributes it to historical, political, economic and institutional problems.[27] The forum revealed that Africa has neither the favourable international, nor domestic economic environment, which is required to reform economic policies, to enhance any meaningful integration effort. The Maastricht forum is relevant to integrative efforts in Africa as it relates to the theoretical construct, because there are no simple recipes or modalities for regional integration. However, success or failure hinges on the specific context and the environment in which the co-operation operates. Therefore care must be taken not to transplant models from different localities and circumstances, but these must be adapted to meet local needs and circumstances. This underscores the importance of African integrationists, to use the various theories as guides, but to develop integrative processes that would take cognisance of the peculiarities of the African environment.

---

25 Ndongko, W. A., *The Future of Central African Customs and Economic Union,* in R.I. and Sasey A. (eds); The Future of Regionalism in Africa (Macmillan, 1985), p.106.

26 I. Gambari, *Political and Comparative Dimensions of Regional Integration: The Case of ECOWAS*, 1991, p. 2.

27 Maastricht Publications, "Regional Co-operation and Integration," *The World Today*, 1995, p. 68.

The Case for Regional Integration in Africa: The promotion of economic cooperation among developing countries is now a well-accepted part of international development policy. Almost all issues in the field of international economic relations are currently subordinated to the quest for regional economic associations and groupings among more or less contiguous areas. Since the massive movement towards independence in the late 1950s and early 1960s, there was immediate recognition that, while independence had been the primary goal, African countries had been largely artificial by-products of the colonial 'scramble' for the continent.[28] The present fragmentation, and small scale of African markets, emanate from the specific political and economic conditions in which the continent found itself at independence. Africa is a divided continent, with 165 borders demarcating the region into 53 countries – 22 of which have a population of 5 million or less, and 11 of which have a population of less than 1 million.[29] Only the countries of Nigeria, Egypt, Ethiopia, Democratic Republic of Congo (DRC), South Africa and Sudan have populations of more than 30 million.[30] Thirty four of the forty-nine countries currently classified as among the least developed in the world are in Africa, whilst all but six of the thirty five countries, in the 'low human development' category of the 2000, Human Development Report also come from the continent.[31] Roughly half the population of the continent live in absolute poverty, on less than one dollar per day. Average income per capita is lower than at the end of the 1960s.[32] Africa's share in world trade stands at about 2%' having declined from 3.5% in 1980 and 2.7% in 1990. The continent has the lowest rate of investment to GDP among the developing regions of the world. Africa's net direct investment as a proportion of that of Asia declined from 30.6% in 1983-88 to 9.3% in 1996.[33] According to the World Investment Report for 2001, while global foreign investment soars, foreign direct investment in Africa is shrinking. The continent accounts for only 1% of global foreign direct investment. Africa is stuck at the periphery of the global economy

---

28 S. K. B. Asante, *Op. Cit.*, p. 4.

29 K. Y. Amoako, Executive Secretary of UNECA, Speech delivered at 22nd Session of Assembly of ECOWAS, 9 December, 1999. Available from: www.uneca.org/eca, (Accessed on 20 April, 2008).

30 S. K. B. Asante, *Op. Cit.*, p. 4.

31 *Ibid.*

32 Olufemi Fajana, *Op. Cit.*, p. 30.

33 *Ibid.*

and the multilateral trading system. In addition to rising poverty and increasing marginalisation, the continent is beset with other problems that have assumed crisis dimensions to include the HIV/AIDS pandemic and an unsustainable burden of external debt.[34]

Many of the African countries are economically so small, with poor populations, for which domestic production for such small markets will be at extremely high cost if economies of scale are of any importance. Without access to the larger market area that could be created by measures of economic integration, it is impossible to see how the economies of these small countries could be developed and diversified. Without access to a larger market for new productive activities, these countries will remain tied to the world economy, as producers of primary commodities and importers of manufactured goods, with prices which remain beyond the means of many. As noted by Ruth Morgenthau, the typical developing African nation has a sparse population; small internal market, limited infrastructure, new and fragile borders, and economies vulnerable to fluctuating world prices.[35]

Given this background, it was not surprising that integration was seen as a means of helping to overcome the disadvantages of small size, low per capita incomes, small populations, and narrow resource bases, and of enabling a higher rate of economic growth and development. Additionally, it was seen as a means of consolidating the political independence of African countries and thereby strengthening their overall position with respect to developed countries; especially the former metropolitan powers.[36] Through cooperation and integration, regional planning frameworks and trading blocs, the continent could ensure the efficient use of the collective capital, labour and natural resources of its component states. As individual entities, the countries would not be in a position to benefit from such efficiency gains. Even the well-managed ones will remain at risk from the "bad neighbourhood effects" of others.[37]

---

34 *Ibid.*

35 R. S. Morgenthau, "The Developing Status of Africa," *Annals of the American Academy of Political and Social Science*, Vol. 432, July 1977, p. 87.

36 S. K. B. Asante, *Op. Cit.*, p. 6.

37 K. Y. Amoako, *Op. Cit.*

A major step therefore in the evolution of regional integration in Africa was taken in 1963 with the establishment of the Organisation of African Unity (OAU). Although the OAU had, as one of its objectives, the intensification of the cooperation and efforts of the member states "to achieve a better life for the peoples of Africa"; there was a primacy of political over economic goals in the Charter of the organisation.[38] The preponderance of political over economic goals in the initial mandate of the OAU arose from the general belief that once political freedom was achieved and consolidated, the process of sustained and rapid economic growth would automatically be ensured. In this regard, the rich endowment of the continent in human and natural resources gave much room for optimism.[39]

By the 1970s and 80s, however when most African countries had achieved independence, the new states came to the realisation that many were too weak and fragile for any sustainable economic development; the reasons for which have been given earlier. A multiplicity of external and internal factors, both economic and political, accounted for the poor economic performance and marginalisation of African countries in the global economy. In the 1970s, the realities of the second decade of independence forced African leaders to think of integration. This was the decade that saw the emergence of such groupings as, ECOWAS, and the East African Community.[40] It was the decade that saw the demise of the Breton Woods system of fixed-but-adjustable exchange rate regime which was followed by the oil price shocks of 1973/74 and 1979. Indeed, by 1979 African economies were running at minus 1.9% of GDP growth rate. [41]

The recognition of integration resulted in the rapid expansion of regional and sub- regional groupings on the continent. Within fifteen years of independence, over twenty intergovernmental, multi-sectoral integration

38 Olufemi Fajana, *Op. Cit.*, p. 25.

39 *Ibid.*

40 V. Antwi- Danso, *Op. Cit.*, p. 140-141.

41 These were the imperatives that caused the African Governors of the World Bank to appeal to the President of the World Bank to get Africa out of the stagnation, decay, and decline. This led to the inception of the Elliot Berg Commission. The Commission proposed Structural Adjustment, which became the blue print for Africa's development in the 1980's and beyond.

organizations had been established in Africa.[42] In all the regions in Africa, from the north, to south, east to west and central regions of the continent is a multiplicity of regional groupings. Each region contains an average of three to four organizations.

Also pursuing the integration agenda are the sub-sets of some of the above mentioned major regional integration schemes which include the Central African Economic and Monetary Community (CEMAC), and the West African Economic and Monetary Union (UEMOA). These other organizations differ from the major economic communities of which they are components, in terms of geographical and membership coverage, but not in objectives. There is no country on the continent that is not involved in at least one regional integration arrangement. Twenty-seven of the fifty-three Member States of the present AU, belong to two regional or sub-regional integration organization, while eighteen others belong to as many as three of such organizations. The multiplicity and overlapping membership and mandate of the schemes have had significant implications for the effectiveness and performance of Africa's integration initiatives.[43]

The objectives of these communities are all embracing and directed towards the eventual establishment of an African Union, to embrace both economic and political integration. They all broadly aspire to promote and enhance economic development, through close cooperation among the member states, in all fields of economic activity. Specifically, the member states undertook, in the Treaties establishing their communities, to increase their existing transport and communications links and to create new ones, as a means of strengthening the physical integration of the sub-regional groupings and promoting the movement of persons, goods and service within the communities.[44] In the production sector, the member states declared, that they would endeavour to promote autonomous industrialisation within the communities, through the development of the large, intermediate and capital foods industries, promotion of the multinational enterprises, and especially the development of the strategic natural resources of the sub-regions. This they would achieve by establishing metallurgical, chemical and

42 Adedeji Adebayo, '*History and Prospects for Regional Integration in Africa*', African Development Forum III, UNECA, Addis Ababa, 3-8 March, 2002, p. 5.

43 Olufemi Fajana, *Op Cit.*, p. 26.

44 S. K. B. Asante, *Op. Cit.*, p. 9.

petrochemical industries, as well as intermediate and secondary industries such as mechanical, electrical and electronic industries.[45]

To stimulate intra-community trade, the states undertook to gradually reduce and then abolish customs duties and the non-tariff barriers, to which their trade was subjected, so as to build up potential markets for the hundreds of million consumers across the regions of Africa. They also committed themselves to co-operate in the areas of standardization and control of quality of goods, adopt trade facilitation and promote monetary and financial co-operation among themselves. This would be achieved through the establishment of clearing houses, making their national currencies convertible and instituting common monetary zones. Closely related to this was the undertaking to set up financial institutions and development banks or funds to finance projects aimed at increasing the complementarities of the economies of the member states.[46] These elaborate schemes were meant to establish the industrial base to support the development of agriculture and other key sectors. The integration of industry and other sectors was meant to trigger a process of autonomous and self sustained economic development and internal accumulation, and put African economies in a better position to counter international competition, in order to end the economic marginalisation of the continent and to place it among the comity of nations.

A critical appraisal of the achievements of the existing communities must conclude that so far they have not been able to meet their set objectives to transform the socio-economic conditions of the continent and help alleviate mass poverty through sustained economic growth and recovery. In addition, they have so far been unable to mobilise and contribute to the development of underdeveloped resources, which is central to their development effort, and have thus failed to reduce the dependence of members on the outside world and to create conditions that will make self-sustainment and autonomous development possible. In the African Development Report of 2003, for example, African regional groupings had not succeeded in inter-African trade, which has stagnated around 10% of Africa's total trade since the 1990s[47]

45 *Ibid.*
46 *Ibid.*, p. 10.
47 African Development Report 2003: *Globalisation and Africa's Development*, (Oxford: Oxford University Press, 2003), p. 191.

Relationship between the AU, African Economic Community (AEC), and the Regional Economic Communities (RECs).

The institutional transformation of the OAU into the AU began with the adoption of a new treaty; the Constitutive Act, which came into force in May 2001. The AU is the apex institution for political, economic and social integration in Africa. The African Economic Community (AEC), formed in 1994, is the designated continental framework for economic integration. Under Article 6 of the AEC treaty, 6 progressive stages were set for the deepening of integration. The OAU in 1997 designated IGAD, COMESA, ECOWAS, CENSAD, ECCAS, AMU and SADC as the regional economic communities that will be the building blocs for the AEC.[48] According to the Sirte (Libya) Declaration of 1999, the implementation of some elements of the stages was supposed to be expedited; for instance, the Pan African Parliament has already been established.

It is generally felt that the process of economic integration at the continental, the regional and sub-regional levels, form a complicated and resource wasting web, and amount to an institutional waste. The regional and sub-regional economic communities do not neatly fall in line with a co-ordinated and progressive process that systematically evolves into the AEC. The processes of economic integration in Africa, at the continental, regional and sub-regional levels, as constituted in their various areas, in many instances have overlapping membership. Of the 53 African countries, 26 are members of two regional economic communities, and 28 are members of three. The Democratic Republic of Congo belongs to four. Only 6 countries maintain membership in just one regional economic community.[49] This was undesirable to the extent that the process would seem not to reflect the schedule and programme set out in building the AEC as the continental institution for economic integration. Multiplicity of organizations and overlapping membership has institutional and financial implications for members, and if not co-ordinated, may complicate the process of forming the

48 Francis Mangeni, "*Streamlining the Process of Economic Integration in Africa,*" iLEAP Advisory Brief, No. 4, May 2004, Available from: www.ileapinitiative.com (Accessed on 13 April, 2008).

49 50 UNECA Report, 2006, Available from: www.uneca.org/aria. (Accessed on 23 May, 2008).

AEC. It may also complicate the process of strengthening individual regional communities.[50] With these various groupings unable to meet their own set objectives, it would be useful to examine the performance of ECOWAS; one of the designated regional building blocs toward African integration.

The Economic Community of West African States: ECOWA

ECOWAS comprises a geographical zone larger than Western Europe, with a total area of over 6 million square kilometres.[51] With a total population of about 230 million people, it is the most heavily populated of all the sub-regions of Africa. While the size of the population provides a large potential market, the realisation of this is limited by the low per capita income in the region, which is about US $400 in 2006.[52] The ECOWAS region has some of the richest and most populous countries in Africa, with immense mineral resources, such as Nigeria, but also includes most of the poorest nations on the continent, such as Niger.[53] The total per capita income of the region was US $6240m, and the average life expectancy was 50 years.[54] In 1989, the Gross National Product (GNP), of the region was approximately equal to that of Belgium,[55] a country of the size of Togo; one of the smallest countries among the ECOWAS countries.

The Treaty of ECOWAS was signed on 28 May 1975 in Lagos, Nigeria by 11 Heads of State and four Plenipotentiaries representing 15 West African States. The states forming ECOWAS have experienced different external influences, yet many of them share the same ethnic groups and historical and cultural similarities. Five are English speaking, eight are French speaking and two are Portuguese speaking nations.[56] With the successful formation

50 *Ibid.*, p. 6.

51 Emeka Anyaoku, *West Africa: The Politics of the Post-Independence Era*, (Brassey's Defence Yearbook, 1980), p. 2.

52 ECOWAS Commission Annual Report, 2007, p. 29.

53 O. S. Saasa, *Joining the Future: Economic Integration and Cooperation in Africa*, 1991, p. 111.

54 African Development Bank Report, (1995-1998), p. 6.

55 F. Forountan., *Op. Cit.*, p. 1.

56 T. Jaye, *Issues of Sovereignty, Strategy, and Security in the Economic Community of West African States (ECOWAS), Intervention in the Liberian Civil War* (New York: The Edwin Mellers Press, 2003), p. 139.

of the Community there was a unanimous sense of satisfaction among the protagonists of regional integration, particularly those in government at the time and within diplomatic circles in Nigeria and Togo, who were the pioneers of ECOWAS.

Aims and Objectives of ECOWAS

The aims of ECOWAS are to promote co-operation and integration, leading to the ultimate establishment of an economic union in West Africa, in order to raise the living standards of its peoples, and to maintain and enhance economic stability, foster relations among member states and contribute to the progress and development of the African continent.[57] In order to achieve these aims and in accordance with the relevant provisions of the Treaty, the Community is required, among other things to ensure:

a. the harmonization and co-ordination of national policies and the promotion of integration, projects and activities particularly in agriculture and natural resources, industry, food, transport and communications, energy trade, money and finance, taxation economic reform policies, human resources education, information, culture, science, technology, services health, tourism and legal matters;
b. the harmonization and co-ordination of policies for the protection of the environment;
c. the promotion of the establishment of joint production enterprises;
d. the establishment of a common market, through the liberalisation of trade by abolishing among member states, of customs, non-tariff barriers, the adoption of common external tariff and a common trade policy vis-à-vis third countries, removal between member states of obstacles to the free movement of persons, goods, service and capital, and to the right of residence and establishment;
e. the establishment of an economic union through the adoption of common policies in the economic, financial, social and cultural sectors and the creation of a monetary union;

57 Treaty of ECOWAS, (Revised, July 1993), p. 5.

f. the promotion of joint ventures by private sector enterprises and other economic operators through the adoption of a regional agreement on cross-border investments; and
g. the establishment of a fund for co-operation and development.[58]

ECOWAS was inspired by, and deliberately modelled on, the EU. The objective of ECOWAS is to provide the framework for steadily developing economic and political cooperation among member states and to encourage economic development and eventually, political unity. Like the EU, the ECOWAS Treaty calls for the progressive elimination of all customs duties and the development of common trade policies.[59] West Africa is to be turned into a 'common market' for ECOWAS member states. The treaty laid down a fifteen- year timetable for the liberalisation of trade within the Community and the establishment of a full Customs Union. Within the same period, it intends to establish a common customs tariff; free movement of persons, services and capital; and the harmonisation of agricultural, economic, industrial and monetary policies of the member states. The founding fathers of the Community envisaged the emergence, by 1990, of a Common Market, where restrictions not just on trade but also in other areas would be eliminated. [60]

The institutions of ECOWAS are likewise closely patterned on the EU model. The Supreme policy-making body is the Authority of Heads of State and Government, (Article 7), which is made up of the fifteen government leaders. Below that is the 30-person Council of Ministers (two per country), comprising the Ministers of Foreign or Economic Affairs, who meet at regular intervals to coordinate the behaviour of member states.[61] The council is also responsible for the supervision of all subordinate bodies, as well as the development of future policy. To help carry out these functions there is the Executive Secretariat, which is the machinery for the execution of protocols and policies and is headed by an Executive Secretary, which has since 2007 been designated as a Commission headed by a President. Members, unlike

58 *Ibid.*, p. 6.

59 M. Sheenan, "Nigeria and the ECOWAS Defence Pac," *Army Quarterly*, January 1986, p. 9.

60 I. Onwuka, "The ECOWAS Treaty: Inching towards Implementation," *World Today*, February 1980, p. 52.

61 *Ibid.*, p. 53.

UN officials, are supposed to owe their loyalty to the organization rather than to their national countries.[62] There is also the Tribunal, which is responsible for arbitration and mediation of disputes among member states with some limited supra-national powers.

The ECOWAS structure also includes five specialised commissions which were established to perform such functions and act within the limits of powers conferred on them under the Treaty. These are the Transport, Telecommunications and Energy Commission; the Social and Cultural Affairs Commission; the Industry, Agricultural and Natural Resources Commission; the Trade, Customs, Immigration, Monetary and Payments Commission, and of particular importance the Defence Commission.[63] A Protocol relating to Mutual Assistance on Defence (MAD) was signed earlier in 1981. This protocol committed ECOWAS member states to a collective defence treaty, by accepting that armed threat or aggression against one constituted a threat or aggression against the Community, and resolved to give aid and assistance for defence. This protocol was invoked in the outbreak of the Liberian, Sierra-Leone and Guinea Bissau civil conflict, with the deployment of ECOWAS Monitoring Group (ECOMOG) into those countries. In 1993, the Treaty was revised to accelerate the process of integration.

The additions to the original treaty, as a process of furthering the objectives of the organization, include: the Mechanism for Conflict Prevention, Management and Resolution, Peace and Security, which were adopted in 1999. This institution comprises: the Authority, the Executive Secretariat, and a Mediation and Security Council. The Mediation and Security Council serves as the equivalent of the UN Security Council. It oversees the activities of the Defence Security Commission, which comprises the Chiefs of Defence Staff of ECOWAS; the Council of Elders made up of some Eminent Persons from the region that engage in preventive diplomacy, and serve as mediators, conciliators and facilitators. They are appointed by the Executive Secretary. Also included under the Mediation and Security Council, is the Observation and Monitoring Centre, responsible for early warning system within the four Observation and Monitoring Zones designated within the sub-region.

---

62 M. Sheenan., *Op. Cit.*, p. 10.

63 *Ibid.*

As part of the process of furthering integration, ECOWAS also set up the Community Court of Justice in 1999, to address complaints from member states and institutions, as well as issues relating to defaulting nations. The court has a President, a Chief Registrar and seven judges as a panel. The ECOWAS Parliament was also set up in 2002 with a total of 115 Members of Parliament (MPs). Omitted at the time was Cote d' Ivoire, which had no Parliament at the time due to the civil war but was entitled to 7 members. The republics of Togo, Liberia, Cape Verde, Guinea, Guinea Bissau, Benin, the Gambia and Sierra Leone have 5 members each; Burkina Faso, Mali, Niger, and Senegal have 6 members, whilst Ghana and Nigeria have 8 and 35 members respectively. Membership is constituted from the national parliaments of each member state, and a loss of a seat at the national parliament means a loss of seat at the regional parliament. The ECOWAS parliament is situated in Abuja, Nigeria, and at present acts in a consultative and advisory capacity only.

ECOWAS has also set up a series of financial institutions and specialised agencies as part of its reform process. These include ECOWAS Bank for Investment and Development (EBID), ECOWAS Regional Development Fund (ERDF), ECOWAS Regional Investment Bank (ERIB), West African Monetary Agency (WAMA), West African Monetary Institute (WAMI), and ECOWAS Bank (ECOBANK). The other institutions are the West African Health Organization (WAHO), and other Specialised Technical Commissions.

L' Union Economique et Monetaire Ouest Africaine (UEMOA)

The proliferation of Inter-Governmental Organizations (IGOs) remains one of the main obstacles to any integrative effort within the African continent. Within the regional groupings, several of these organizations exist with the same aims and objectives. Within ECOWAS, the major sub-regional group whose activities impinge on its integrative effort and need to be highlighted in this study is the West African Economic and Monetary Union, (UEMOA). When the revised treaty of ECOWAS was adopted in 1991, Article 2 stated that, ECOWAS would "ultimately be the sole economic community in the region for the purpose of integration and the realization of the African Economic Community" and no new IGOs would be formed in the sub-region. It went on to state that the existing IGOs would be progressively renounced in accordance with a pre-established plan of rationalization.[64]

However in January 1994, UEMOA was formed to upgrade and maintain the already existing monetary links between the former French colonies and metropolitan France. The countries originally involved in the UEMOA agreement were Benin, Burkina Faso, Cote d' Ivoire, Mali, Niger, Senegal and Togo. These countries since independence had been linked together by a common currency; the Communaute Financiere Afrcaine (CFA) franc created in 1945, as a means to consolidate French Africa's economies. It is issued by a regional bank located in Dakar, Senegal, and is backed by an external guarantee from the treasury in Paris.[65] The CFA franc has been pegged to the French Franc in convertible terms since 1948 and to the Euro since 1999.[66] This together with their closeness to metropolitan France, account for the strong bond that exists between francophone West Africa as opposed to Anglophone or Lusophone West Africa. In 1997, Guinea Bissau, a Lusophone country, joined this union to become the eighth member.[67] In general terms, UEMOA's striking features are its vast land area, small populations and generally low incomes. The combined total population of UEMOA amounts to 67 million people, representing one-third of ECOWAS' total population of about 230 million people.

Among the reasons given for the establishment of UEMOA is that ECOWAS has not been as effective as expected in fulfilling the aspirations of its member states for the achievement of a sustainable economic development of the sub-region. Other reasons were the close historical relations among the member countries, as well as the apparent need to match monetary union, to build a stronger economic entity which could act as a catalyst for strengthening ECOWAS.[68] The principal objectives of UEMOA are to:

---

64 A. Abankwah, "UEMOA within ECOWAS: Curse or Blessing for Regional Integration," *UNDP Paper*, Accra, 1999, p. 109.

65 S. Kaplan, '*West African Integration: A New development Paradigm*', The Washington Quarterly, 29: 4, Autumn 2006, p. 89.

66 C. Dupont, 'Governance and *Regional Integration: ECOWAS*', 2006, p. 3. Available from www.cdd.org.uk/resources/workingpapers/ecowas (Accessed on 23 April2008).

67 G. K. Bluwey, "*West African Economic Integration, UEMOA and Ghana's National Interest and Options*," UNDP Paper, Accra, 1999, pp. 4-5.

68 Abamkwa., *Op. Cit.*, p. 110.

a. strengthen the competitive economic and financial activities of member states within the context of an open competitive market in a rationalized and harmonized legal environment;
b. ensure the convergence of performance and the economic policies of member states by the creation of a procedure for interstate surveillance;
c. create within member states, a common market based on free movement of persons, goods, services, capital and the right of persons to establish or exercise any activity either independently or paid as well a common external tariff regime and a common commercial policy;
d. institute a coordination of national policies in various sectors , putting in place common actions and eventually, common policies particularly in the areas of human resources, transport and telecommunications, environment, agriculture, energy, industry, mines and territorial development; and
e. harmonize the laws of member states to the extent necessary for the good management of a common market particularly, the fiscal regime.[69]

The interesting irony in the formation of UEMOA is the fact that these laudable objectives had almost the same aims as the provisions of ECOWAS, which in addition allows other West African countries to join as full or associate members. The Treaty provides for an explicit transfer of sovereignty over important areas of national jurisdiction, in particular fiscal policy. "It envisions the establishment of institutions closely related to those of the European Union, including a Conference of Heads of States, a Council of Ministers, a community secretariat, and an inter-parliamentary commission as the first stage toward a fully fledged community parliament, and independent revenue authority and a court of justice."[70] These institutions would be financed through independently determined levies.

At the national and regional levels, UEMOA appears to be far better equipped institutionally than ECOWAS in meeting the complex challenges

69 Treaty of UEMOA,1994, pp. 2-3.

70 J. Fine, J. and S. Yeo, *Regional Integration in a Sub-Saharan Africa: Dead end or Fresh Start?* in Ademola E, Ibrahim Elbadawi, and Collier Paul, eds., "Trade Liberalization in Sub-Saharan Africa, Framework, Issues and Methodological perspectives," Vol. 1, (New York: St. Martins Press Inc., 1997), p. 450.

of West African regionalism. The creation of an eight member Commission has replaced an Executive Secretariat, allowing for greater autonomy, more decentralisation and a less entrenched workforce. The union funds its budget from proceeds from a common external tariff and indirect taxes, to the extent that the problem of non-payment of member's contributions, which has for long bedevilled the ECOWAS integration process, is cleverly side-stepped. Above all, its establishment of a human resources department at the commission has no comparison in ECOWAS.[71] Undoubtedly, UEMOA countries have performed better in terms of intra-regional trade than ECOWAS member states. UEMOA's scheme of trade liberalisation has been better organised, better managed, and implemented. Similarly while ECOWAS countries still struggle with the printing and distribution of documents, UEMOA has geared up its institutions for a customs union. This is intended to eliminate all quantitative tariffs and most of the non-tariff barriers between UEMOA countries. It is also expected to stimulate industrial production within the union, attract more foreign private investments, spur infrastructural development and give a boost to intra-community trade and financial flows.[72] It is being noted also that there is no gainsaying the fact that the member states of UEMOA are demonstrating stronger political commitment to their organization. While, in the case of ECOWAS, absence of political commitment with regard to contributions, data provisions, and implementation of directives are identifiable obstacles, there is in UEMOA, clear evidence of a higher degree of political commitment, reflected in the quick manner in which they are able to implement decisions at the highest level of the Union.

Although the institutional structures of UEMOA are not as elaborate as the EU, from which the former was modelled, UEMOA places a lot of emphasis on the development of adequate institutional machinery as an essential condition for the successful coordination of development policies. In the UEMOA Treaty, member states have surrendered some of their national sovereignty to a central body. However, provision has been made to make sure that matters which may be more effectively handled at the national level are retained at that level. Due to the provision of the supra-nationality clause,

71 S. K. B. Asante, ECOWAS and UEMOA, *Op. Cit.*, p. 7.

72 S. K. B. Asante and A. Abankwah, "Impact of UEMOA on Ghana," UNDP Report, 1999, pp. 20-22.

Union Acts (Acts of the Conference of Heads of State, Regulations, Directives and Decisions of the Council of Ministers and the Commission) become automatically enforceable in member states, irrespective of any contrary national legislation.

Another innovative provision adopted by UEMOA, which other regional groupings on the continent can emulate, concerns the problem of funding. The Union does not depend on annual or periodic contributions from its members, but on a community solidarity levy, called the statistical levy, of 1% taken at source from customs duties levied on third countries' exports to UEMOA member states and credited to the account of the Commission. This does away with the trouble of non-payment of contributions, the bane of many African organizations. The Union has also introduced, at its executive level, the all powerful Commission and endowed it with the institutional authority to accelerate and revitalise its integration process. The Commission is headed by a President, who is assisted by seven Commissioners, each heading a specialised department. The Commission has the power to translate the decisions and acts of the Conference of Heads of State and Government as well as the Council into regulations, which are automatically binding; therefore eliminating the disturbing issue of ratification, which has greatly hampered the rate of implementation of decisions, acts and protocols of the ECOWAS.[73]

The Union has also established regulatory and control institutions like the Court of Justice, Inter-Parliamentary Committee and the Court of Auditors, all of which ensure that member states and the executive bodies effectively implement protocols, decisions, regulations and directives. Besides the UEMOA technical and specialised Commissions, the Union has established a committee of experts, composed of specialists drawn from relevant government and quasi-public institutions of the member states. The function of this committee is to assist the Commission in the preparation of all working documents to be laid before the Council of Ministers. Furthermore, UEMOA has given greater recognition to the private sector by institutionalizing the sectors participation in the planning and implementation of UEMOA's programmes. This is done through the establishment of a Regional Consultative Chamber, which acts as an

---

73 A. Abankwah. *Op. Cit.*, p. 117.

umbrella organization for member states' chamber of Commerce and trader's association. This channel takes the organization closer to a section of the general population for which economic integration is important. [74]

The founders of UEMOA somehow consider its creation as appropriate with the argument that UEMOA was expected to provide the impetus for strengthening ECOWAS. However, the fact that the original seven founding member states were francophone, immediately resurrected the Anglophone/ Francophone divide which had plagued the West African political scene in the past. Indeed there is little doubt that the Anglophone ECOWAS members would find it difficult in joining UEMOA, as it could be considered as a betrayal of their Anglophone solidarity. Secondly, UEMOA within ECOWAS has the potential of splitting the economic front of the sub-region.

The advantages of integration, as reflected in the establishment of UEMOA, are outlined in much the same way as they were in the basic instruments establishing ECOWAS. This involves the creation of large scale economies in the larger market, the emergence of community enterprises and improved circulation of goods, and services.[75] It goes without saying that these advantages are easier to realize in a bigger ECOWAS market of more than 230 million, than the narrow UEMOA market of 67 million people. It should not be forgotten that while a common currency is a powerful instrument for economic integration, it is not sufficient guarantee for rapid economic growth and development. Indeed, after several decades of working for the economic integration of Europe, it is only 1990s that a common currency has been achieved for the use of a greater part of the Union.[76]

UEMOA's operation within ECOWAS, under the current situation where the two bodies are competing for resources, both financial and technical, from the same sources, does not help either. The funds and technical assistance of the two groupings are being dissipated to support similar institutions, with similar aims and objectives, from the same donors. For example under the under the current Lome Convention, the European Development Fund (EDF) within the Regional Indicative Programme (RIP), has provided funding for

---

74 A. Abankwah, *Op. cit.*, p. 117.
75 A. Abankwah, *Op. Cit.*, p. 112.
76 *Ibid.*, p. 113.

both ECOWAS and UEMOA to support their integration efforts. If such funds had been consolidated to provide support to a single organization, it is likely that more could have been achieved.[77]

The other problem with UEMOA's appearance on the West African integration scene is the rivalry it has caused with ECOWAS. The creation of two identical full-fledged organizations, replicating integration activities in the sub-region, can only complicate the process of rationalizing the IGO's in the sub-region. The rivalry has manifested itself in the manner Ministers take decisions for the two bodies. While Ministers from UEMOA have agreed to designate the UEMOA Commission to act on its behalf in presenting and negotiating for funds from the EU, the same Ministers have used their numbers to prevent the ECOWAS Commission, from doing the same for ECOWAS as a whole. Through this process, UEMOA has been able to appropriate a great proportion of EDF resources for its programmes. Again, even though the same offices, and some- times the same officials, in UEMOA capitals were expected to handle both ECOWAS and UEMOA affairs, it was realised that, in most cases, ECOWAS matters were relegated to the background. In short, the UEMOA capitals do not demonstrate the same level of commitment to ECOWAS as they do to UEMOA. Indeed, in a few instances, operational officials had stated that UEMOA regulations took precedence over those of ECOWAS.[78]

The above mentioned problems have not helped UEMOA from the perspectives of non-UEMOA members. It is also the belief that UEMOA was created at the time that the shortcomings within ECOWAS were being addressed, through the revised ECOWAS Treaty, to act as a counterweight to the apparent dominance of Nigeria in the region. It is also the argument, mostly from non-members of UEMOA, in West Africa that its formation contravenes Article 59 of the revised ECOWAS Treaty. Further, Article 59 (4) makes it legally difficult, if not impossible, for UEMOA to co-exist within the framework of ECOWAS. The contention is that UEMOA has carved out 8 members of the ECOWAS who in a separate regime, with separate institutions, has created its free trade zone (1996), and established a common

77 A. Abankwah, *Op. Cit.*, p. 113.
78 *Ibid.*, p. 114.

external tariff (1998), which to all intents and purposes competes with and effectively undermines the ECOWAS.[79]

Article 26 of the Vienna Convention on the Law of Treaties (1969), codifies the principle of '*pacta sunt servanda*'[80] (the rule that treaties in force are binding upon the parties and must be performed in good faith), a rule widely acknowledged as the fundamental principle of the law of treaties. This is enshrined in Article 2(2) of the UN Charter[81], which enjoins Members to a treaty to 'fulfil in good faith the obligations assumed by them'. It is therefore argued that, to the extent that UEMOA is operating its own monetary union, and is inviting non-UEMOA ECOWAS members to become full members or participate in other sector programmes, the activities being pursued within the framework of UEMOA constitute a breach of the ECOWAS Treaty.[82] Thus in accordance with the principle of '*pacta sunt servanda*', the eight countries that formed UEMOA should take the appropriate steps to comply with their obligations under the ECOWAS treaty.[83] Notwithstanding all the criticisms about UEMOA, it has been agreed that it has provided not only ECOWAS, but also all other African regional organizations with the model of a treaty with which they can run their organizations effectively and efficiently.

After the relative success of the UEMOA's monetary scheme, and the need to hasten the ECOWAS integration scheme regarding the use of a single currency in the region, the Authority of Heads of State in 1999 adopted the strategy of a Two-Track ("Fast-Track") approach to economic and monetary integration. This led to the setting up of a second zone, the West African Monetary Zone, WAMZ, in 2000. The aim was to commence a common non-UEMOA currency in zone in 2003, for the eventual merger with the UEMOA zone in 2004. The countries involved in the second monetary zone were Gambia, Ghana, Guinea, Nigeria, Sierra-Leone and Liberia. (Liberia at the time of setting up of the zone, attended WAMZ meetings as an observer

79 K. Gyan, '*ECOWAS Protocols and the Formation of UEMOA: The Legal Implications*', UNDP Paper, Accra, 1999. p. 123.

80 M. Malcom Shaw, *The law of Treaties, in International Law, fifth edition*, (Cambridge: Cambridge University Press, 2003), pp. 811-812.

81 P. Muller Jorg, *The Charter of the UN, A Commentary*, in Bruno Simma, ed., (Oxford: Oxford University Press, 1994), pp. 89-93.

82 E. K. Gyan, *Op.Cit.*, p. 125.

83 *Ibid.*, p. 124.

and had not yet signed the instruments of membership).[84] The arrangement involved the formation of a central bank, and this led to the creation of the West African Monetary Institute (WAMI), in 2001 to commence preparatory work towards the introduction of a single currency and a common central bank in the WAMZ. The operation of WAMI headquartered in Ghana, commenced work in March 2001.[85]

The introduction of the second zone common currency was to become operational in 2005. As monetary unification requires macroeconomic stability, members of the Second Monetary Zone have committed themselves to convergence criteria, focused on price stability, sustainability of fiscal deficit, limiting of deficit financing by the central bank and maintaining sufficient levels of gross official foreign exchange reserves. The Agreement establishing the Zone stipulates convergence criteria to be achieved and sustained within a given time frame. The convergence criteria are classified into primary and secondary.[86] The primary criteria include:

a. single digit inflation rate by 2000 and 5.0% by 2003;
b. fiscal deficit (excluding grant)/GDP ratio equal to or less than 3% by 2000, and 4% by 2002;
c. a ceiling on central bank financing of budget deficit of equal or less than 10% of previous year's tax revenue by 2000; and
d. maintenance of official foreign reserves of equal to or greater than 3 months of imports by 2002; and at least six months by2003.

The secondary criteria were to be observed in support of the primary criteria as follow

a. prohibition of new domestic debt arrears and liquidation of all existing ones by end of 2003;
b. tax revenue to GDP ratio to be equal to or more than 20%;

---

84 G. Simplice Zouhon-Bi and Lynge Nielsen, eds., *ECOWAS- Fiscal Revenue Implications of Economic Partnership Agreement with EU,* Africa Region Working Paper Series, No. 103, April 2007, p. 4.

85 *Ibid.*

86 G. E. Ukpong, *Second Monetary Zone in ECOWAS: Issues, Progress and Prospects,* in Adedoyin Soyibo, ed., *The Challenges of Monetary Integration in West Africa, UN-ECA, Sub-Regional Development Centre for West Africa,* (2000), p. 14.

c. wage bill to tax revenue ratio to be equal to or less than 35%;
d. public investment as ratio of total tax revenue to be greater than 20%;
e. maintenance of exchange stability; and
f. achievement of positive real interest rates.[87]

The general picture of the status of compliance with both the primary and secondary criteria for the countries has been mixed. While some countries have made progress with respect to some of the indicators in one year, slippages have occurred in subsequent years. Others have made little or no progress in any of the criteria. No country has met all the convergence criteria since 2001. Several factors have compounded the inability of the various countries to meet the stipulated convergence criteria. Among these are lax fiscal policies, which have tended to weaken relatively tight monetary policies.[88] Others include falling commodity prices and other external trade shocks, and a general state of poor infrastructure, not conducive to investment and economic growth.

The prevalence of civil disturbances in some of the countries of the zone, i.e. Sierra Leone, and Guinea, has tended to divert resources meant for fiscal consolidation and investments to resolution of conflicts. Politically, the integration of the efforts of the WAMZ have been mainly spearheaded at the executive level by Heads of State and Government, some Ministers (Finance, Planning and Integration, Trade/Commerce, and Foreign Affairs), Central Bank Governors and Senior Government officials. Some National legislatures and Parliaments as well as the general public in the member countries are yet to be brought fully into the picture, to take ownership of the project and lend essential support to the scheme.[89] The compliance for the convergence criteria has remained patchy, and the timeline for the introduction of the common currency within the WAMZ zone has been pushed back on several occasions. The last postponement shifted the introduction of the common currency back from 2005 to December 2009.[90]

87 *Ibid.*, pp.14-15.
88 *Ibid.*, p. 17.
89 *Ibid.*, p. 18.
90 G. Simplice Zouhon-Bi, *Op. Cit.*, p. 4.

Achievements of ECOWAS

Since becoming operational, ECOWAS has devoted attention not only to the establishment of the functional structures of the institutions of the Community. It has also made some significant steps towards building a regional economic community in the principal areas of market, production integration, and infrastructural integration, monetary and financial integration and in the maintenance of regional peace and security. While not much has been achieved in these core areas of regional economic groupings, ECOWAS is not without some impressive accomplishments both tangible and intangible. Some of the key accomplishments include:

Development of Community Spirit

There has been the development of community spirit and regional solidarity among ECOWAS member states. The almost strict and separate existence that Francophone and Anglophone West Africa had been experiencing over the years is gradually becoming a thing of the past, while the concept of a Community citizen, which makes the national of any one Member State a West African and a citizen of the Community, who should enjoy visa-free entry into all Member States and be able to reside and work or establish a business anywhere within the region, has been generally accepted. It should be noted that ECOWAS is the pioneering economic grouping in Africa whose member states have abolished entry visa requirements in order to ease movement of its citizens within the region.[91] Additionally ECOWAS has instituted a travel certificate, which is cheaper and easier to obtain than a national passport, to make travelling within the region less cumbersome. In June 2000, an ECOWAS passport was launched, which now runs alongside national passports of the Community citizens. Also in place within the region is an ECOWAS traveller's cheque, for conducting business within the region, and harmonised immigration and emigration forms at the countries' borders.

---

91 S. K. B. Asante and A. Abankwa, *Op. Cit.*, p. 37.

Infrastructural Development

One of the most significant areas of progresses made by ECOWAS is that of road infrastructural integration. The free and smooth movement of persons, goods and services depends on physical cohesion. ECOWAS therefore made the development of regional infrastructural network an early priority. To meet the challenges of road transport, which remains the most dominant mode of transport in West Africa, accounting for about 90% of the region's passenger and freight transport as well as providing the only form of access to more than 70% of populations in rural communities, ECOWAS, basing itself on the Pan-African highway, adopted a regional road programme. The Organization, in collaboration with member countries, has completed the construction of the Trans-Coastal highway from (Lagos in Nigeria to Nouakchott in Mali), and the Trans-Sahelian highways from (Dakar in Senegal to N'Djamena in Chad), a total of 90,000km of road, in addition to 11,000km of interconnecting roads, to open up landlocked countries in the region.[92] Furthermore, the ECOWAS Brown Card system gives third party vehicle insurance coverage to facilitate cross-border movement, whilst regional conventions have been adopted to enhance inter-state transit operations.

In the area of telecommunications, ECOWAS has completed both the first and second phases of the International Communications (INTELCOM) programme. This is intended to facilitate telephone and fax links between member states. It is also meant to modernise the networks and boost the size, speed and reduce the cost of transaction, and to provide such extra services such as internet facilities for member states. This particular achievement is significant because it eliminated delays in making international calls from the region. Hitherto, a call from Ghana to another African country was routed through London before being connected to a recipient in Nigeria. In similar vein, a call from Benin had to pass through Paris before reaching its destination in Togo.

In the energy sector under the West Africa Power Pool, which defines the framework for energy production, has launched the supply of energy

92 ECOWAS Working Paper: *Genesis and Evolution of ECOWAS*. Available from: www.cdd.org.uk/resources/workingpapers/ecowas/ECOWAS. (Accessed on 18 April, 2008).

at reasonable price meant to member states. ECOWAS has coordinated and completed the construction of the West African Gas Pipeline, the first regional natural gas transmission system in sub-Saharan Africa, consisting of a 569 kilometre long offshore pipeline to ship natural gas from Nigerian oilfields to Benin, Togo, and Ghana. This is primarily for electricity generation and other industrial use. The project estimated at about $700 million was implemented by a consortium comprising Chevron, Shell, the Nigerian National Petroleum Corporation, and the energy providing institutions of the beneficiary countries. All major construction works in Nigeria have been completed and the Natural Gas Export Terminal to the West African Gas pipeline was commissioned in May 2007. The first gas is expected within the first quarter of 2008. ECOWAS has started working in close collaboration with USAID and other development partners to secure further technical assistance to conduct feasibility studies on the extension of the pipeline to other member States.[93]

Institutional Building

ECOWAS has devoted much attention to institution building since its inception. Under the revised treaty of 1993, the Authority of Heads of State and Government had its powers enhanced; making its decisions immediately enforceable in Member States. The other institutions include the ECOWAS Fund, which has been restructured in a fundamental way, with the possibility of non-regional participation. It is now a regional holding Company (ECOWAS Bank for Investment and Development EBID), with two arms: the ECOWAS Regional Development Bank with a commercial orientation, and the ECOWAS Regional Development Fund (ERDF). This institutional framework is meant to enable ECOWAS to attract substantial non-regional capital participation in very viable regional projects, while providing for financial assistance to developmental programmes through the ERDF.[94]

Other institutions include the Executive Commission, restructured to

93 ECOWAS Commission Annual Report, 2007, pp. 69-70.

94 Lansana Kouyate, ECOWAS Executive Secretary's Report, 2000, *Shaping West Africa's Future: Shift from National to Regional Framework* p. 2. Available from: www.sec.ecowas.int/sitecedeao/english, (Accessed on 19 May, 2008).

enhance its dual role of fostering the harmonisation of national economic policies and facilitating the integration of the production base and physical infrastructure through the implementation of regional programmes and projects. In order to further enhance the operational efficiency of ECOWAS and increase its credibility within and outside West Africa, is the establishment and effective functioning of both the Court of Justice and the West African Parliament. This is to assure both Member States and all West Africans involved in the integration process, that their interests and rights will be protected through proper representation in the decision-making process and a regional judicial system.[95]

Peace Keeping

The Community has made commendable interventions at maintaining regional peace and security. There cannot be economic development without political stability and peace. The West African region had been plagued by political instability through military take-overs from the 1960s through to the early 1990s. This was then followed by civil conflicts in Liberia, Sierra-Leone, Guinea Bissau, Guinea, and Cote d' Ivoire. ECOMOG, the first of its kind by a regional body, was deployed and contributed significantly to the restoration of peace in these countries. Perhaps, the military engagement did more to make ECOWAS an internationally known entity than its economic achievements so far. A permanent regional mechanism for conflict prevention and resolution of conflict has been adopted.

In this regard an ECOWAS Standby Force (ESF) was established in 2004. The concept is to develop a military vision, strategy, force structure and the generation and deployment of a force, if necessary, into any part of the region or elsewhere. Training initiatives have been evolved to make the ESF a capable force of mitigating and meeting the challenges of Peace Support Operations (PSO) in the sub-region. Training has been organised for selected officers from member countries in the areas of strategy at the US-Africa Centre for Strategic Studies, and the National War College in Nigeria. At the Operational level, training is conducted at the Kofi Annan International Peace Keeping Centre (KAIPTC), and the Pearson Peacekeeping Centre in

95 *Ibid.*, pp. 3-4.

Canada. At the tactical level, training is conducted at the Ecole de Maintien de la Paix Allioune Blodin Beye (EM-PABB), in Mali, and the Peace Keeping Training School in Zambakro, Cote d' Ivoire. The training is based on the UN Standard Training Modules (1,2&3), developed by the Integrated Training Service of the UNDPKO in order to provide a uniform standard of training for all member troop contribution nations. At present, experts believe ECOWAS can raise troop levels of up to 5000, in any emergency into any part of the sub-region.[96]

Establishment of Free Trade Area

ECOWAS countries have pursued free trade within the framework of the Trade Liberalization Scheme (ELTS). The ELTS divides trade in goods into three categories: (a) unprocessed goods, (b) traditional handicraft products, and (c) industrial goods. The ETLS provided for the immediate and full liberalization of unprocessed and handicraft products, whereas industrial products were to be liberalized over the 2000-2005 period. In 2003 ECOWAS further adopted new rules of origin and a single customs declaration form, and simplified control procedures with a view towards reinvigorating the Trade Liberalization Policy (TLP). The main problem with the free trade area in industrial goods was the need for approval to be sought on a product-by-product and enterprise-by-enterprise basis. Although intra-ECOWAS trade in goods is still subject to many tariff and non-tariff restrictions, trade barriers are coming down and efforts are ongoing to make further progress towards achieving a unified internal market within ECOWAS.[97] Additionally, the share of intra-ECOWAS exports has tripled to 9% by 2004, from just 3% prior to the establishment of ECOWAS. While this development does provide evidence of a deepening of commercial relations among member countries, trade relations deepened faster vis-à-vis other African countries a quadrupling from 1 to 4%. The increase in intra-ECOWAS trade may not have been the result of the political quest for regional economic collaboration, but rather of technological or other developments favouring trade.[98]

---

96 Antwi- Danso V., '*ECOWAS' Unfinished Agenda*', Magazine for Development and Cooperation. Available from: www.inwent.org/E+Z/content/archive-eng/01-2007(Accessed on 19 May 2008).

97 G. Simplice Zouhon-Bi and Lynge Nielsen, *Op. Cit.*, p. 5.

98 *Ibid.*, p. 5.

Challenges that confront ECOWAS

One of the critical challenges facing ECOWAS is the issue of Sovereignty. Sovereignty, in the context of international relations, means the legal authority that a state has to decide and act independently within the system of states in all aspects of policy formulation and implementation. The state in question, therefore, does not answer to any higher authority in the pursuit of its national interest.[99] Even then the state must qualify for recognition under international law based on the criteria of defined territory, recognized population and an effective government. Contemporary interpretations as to where sovereignty resides, whether in the people, the government, the ruler or parliament connotes legalistic or democratic interpretations.[100] Opinions however differ as some recent views associate sovereignty with responsibility on the part of the state towards its people.[101] With regards to the consideration of sovereignty and efforts at achieving a union of African states, the problem has been how much power African governments are willing to forgo to enable central institutions to function effectively. It is noted that the political philosophy of African nations is fundamentally different from Europe where a long tradition of "constitutionalism" makes it easier to accept limits upon the exercise of power. This in turn has made it easier to engineer the sharing of sovereignty with regional levels of government in Europe than in Africa.[102]

It has not been easy to reduce one's sovereignty for community interest in the sub-region. As noted by Senghor, "regional cooperation is an intensely political process and most African governments find it difficult to agree on cooperation that requires sovereignty in certain areas to be handed over for the benefit of the region. No matter the rhetoric, political leaders who jealously guard their sovereignty are unwilling to reduce the power and authority of the state. When governments and politicians do not benefit

---

99 Jackson Robert and Alan James, eds., *States in the Changing World: A Contemporary Analysis*, (Oxford: Clarendon Press, 1993), p. 16.

100 *Ibid.*, p. 23.

101 Francis M. Deng, *Sovereignty as Responsibility: Conflict Management in Africa*, (Washington D.C.: The Brookings Institution, 1996), p. 54.

102 R. Lavergne, *Regional Integration and Cooperation in West Africa: A Multidimensional* Perspective, (Trenton: Africa World Press Inc., 1997), p. 17.

directly from cooperation, they would not seriously pursue its policies.[103] Perhaps with the West African leaders having agreed to transform the ECOWAS Secretariat into a commission, it marked a positive attitude toward ceding part of their sovereignty for the Union.

Economic Dimension

The poor economic health of member states has been a major impediment to integration efforts. Growing, dynamic economies provide a more conducive environment for promoting cooperation and integration than stagnant ones. Severe economic situations have obliged member states to abandon plans for long-term economic development, including regional integration, in pursuit of short-term stabilization. In West Africa, governments are under pressure to prioritise domestic crisis management and, accordingly, to take protective measures as result of economic difficulties. With the limited revenue available to the public sector, this has to be rationed in accordance with short-term priorities that excluded regional integration or gave it only a token recognition.[104] Equally linked to the weak economic issues is that most of the states are dependent on budget substitution; that literally amounts to outsourcing their budgetary needs to donors that use this budgetary support to dictate conditions and influence local policy often detrimental to effective local state policies. Weak and fragile states that have far less links to each other , but rather retain strong links with outside metropolitan powers, have not created the necessary conditions for integration and rebirth on the foundations of democracy, human rights, and good governance, some of the pillars of an effective integration scheme.[105]

In West Africa national economies are only now barely achieving some measure of stabilisation. An analysis of the performance of the economies reveals an expansion of growth on average of 5.7% in 2007. The high growth rate was as a result of macroeconomic management in many of the countries,

---

103 J. C. Senghor, *ECOWAS: Perspectives on Treaty Revision and Reform*, 1993, p. 13.

104 R. Lavergne, *Op. Cit.*, p. 40.

105 Muchie Mammo, Adam Habib, and Padayachee V., *African Integration and Civil Society: The Case of the African Union*, Transformation 61, 2006, p. 17.

and increased demand for key African export commodities resulting in high export prices; especially crude oil, metals and minerals.[106] The establishment of a more stable economic environment, capable of encouraging long-term investment and development, should be one of the preoccupations of the ECOWAS Commission.

Multiplicity of Economic Communities

The other challenge to ECOWAS is the multiplicity of economic communities operating within the region. The phenomenon is well documented in (UNECA 2004; World Bank 2005), and reveals the complex network of regional economic communities in Africa. West Africa, for instance has three integration institutions: ECOWAS, UEMOA, and MRU. In addition, the Community of Sahel-Saharan States (CEN-SAD) covers part of West Africa. With the exception of Ghana and Cape Verde, which belong only to ECOWAS, every West African country belongs to two or three regional economic communities. This complex patchwork resulting from the multiplicity and overlapping membership in regional economic communities raises considerable problems for policy and programme coordination and harmonization. Its drawbacks include: fragmented economic space and approaches to regional integration, increased cost of membership in regional economic communities, unhealthy rivalry for donor funds, and contradictory obligations and loyalties for membership. Others are duplicated efforts, inconsistent objectives and conflicting operational mandates as well as reduced ability for regional economic communities to pursue coherent and effective integration programmes.[107] The emergence of UEMOA, since 1994 in West Africa, has been a source of concern to many observers in the region. It has the potential of threatening the existence of ECOWAS or, at least, constitutes a formidable rival grouping to the community.[108]

---

106 ECOWAS Commission Annual Report, 2007, p. 11.

107 Bjorn Moller, '*The Role of African Regional and Sub-regional organizations in Ensuring Peace and Security in Africa*', Danish Institute for International Studies (DIIS) Working Paper, No. 4, 2005, p. 16.

108 S. K. B. Asante, *Op. Cit.*, p. 28.

Lack of Private Sector

The inability of ECOWAS to actively involve the private sector, which is the engine of economic growth, in the effort to advance the integration process constitutes a challenge to the member states. Meanwhile, the dearth of local private entrepreneurs and their lack of technical management skills is an inhibiting factor to cooperation and/or integration. As a result, the operational management of the economy, including project formulation, project implementation and investment decisions, is left to the public sector, which normally would not be as responsive to opportunities for cross-border investments and joint ventures with businessmen from neighbouring countries and/or from developed countries. In most instances they are not guided by the profitability of projects in economic and financial terms, but by political exigencies. It is the lack of home- grown entrepreneurial capacity and skills which account for the excessive dependence of African economies on imported products. Even though the revised treaty of 1993 provides for the promotion of the private sector in the integration process, the involvement of the private sector remains marginal.

Inability to Incorporate Agreements in National Plans

One of the paramount hurdles to African integration has been the lack of full commitment and disparities in the level of commitment often manifested in the failure to incorporate agreement reached by integration schemes in national plans. This tendency has played down the value of collective agreements to protocols arrived at to expedite trade and harmonise policies at sub-regional levels. In most cases, the failure to integrate the cooperation programmes into the national administrations means that follow-up decisions taken at the sub-regional meetings are left to the Heads of State, or to a few ministers and civil servants in the ministry dealing with cooperation issues, or in the office of the president. The rest of the government and the population of the country are not involved. Indeed they may not even know that there is a treaty establishing cooperation agreement.[109] Treaties or articles of integration become the private property of a few politicians.

109 Nomvette Bax, "Regional Integration in Africa: A path Strewn with Obstacles," *The Eye on Ethiopia and the Horn of Africa*, Vol. 6, No. 39, April-May 1997, p. 26.

Closely linked to this is elitism, which characterises the implementation process of integration. In many of the countries the idea of forming or joining an economic cooperation arrangement is not derived from the wishes of the people, but rather the desire of the leaders. In effect, awareness of the issue of integration has not been promoted at grassroots level and leaders fail to explain to the people the reasons for their participation as well as the advantages that accrue to the majority. The extent that cooperation arrangements are forged without the full participation and knowledge of the population jeopardizes their stability and success in implementation.

Wide Disparity in Economic Size and Fortune

The differentials in the level of development have been a source of fear and suspicion among some member states. The size of individual states is an inheritance from the colonial era, but differences in development stem from resource endowment, conscious effort at development and length of development experience. These differences, however pose the danger of unequal sharing of both the costs and benefits of regional integration; they make for net gainers and losers, if there are no built-in measures to prevent this from occurring. For instance lurking in the political shadows is the unexpressed fear of domination by Nigeria. Nigeria overshadows every other country in the region several times over in terms of population, gross domestic product, and natural resources endowment. An effort has been made to counterbalance this by placing ECOWAS member states on an equal footing in all things except their financial contributions to the Community (which are prorated), but the concern remains.[110] The French tend to provoke and sustain this fear of domination, as they strive to maintain their sphere of influence in the region. It is in the interest of the Community that this issue be carefully dealt with to dispel any remaining fears and promote grater commitment to the regional integration process. The ECOWAS Fund for Cooperation, Compensation and Development was established to play this significant role of working on the need to equalise the benefits and promote balanced development.

110 R. Lavergne, *Op. Cit.*, p. 39.

Lack of Technical Staff

One other area of constraint is staffing; both for general and professional staff. Labour is one of the critical inputs to the success of any regional integration effort. In the case of ECOWAS the technical staffs at the Commission is inadequate; most of them are there for the purpose of maintaining a regional balance or equal representation of member states. On average there are a larger number of employees in the general category than professional staff. The bias towards non-professional staff may have a bearing on the implementation record of the regional community's programme, which tend, to be rather technical. The concentration of non-professional staff may be explained by remuneration levels that are higher than public sector pay at the national level. The premium pay scales might be a disincentive for regional economic communities to hire more professional staff, despite the many technical programmes they have to implement.[111] There is also a high level of professional staff turnover; explained by political appointments. This high turnover has tended to have serious implications for the community's programmes including loss of institutional memory, poor continuity of projects, and limited collaboration with other regional economic communities.

The constraints on operational efficiency coupled with the lack of professional staff have in most cases accounted for some of the gaps in information technology management, law, and accounting. Surprisingly, programmes on agriculture, a prominent feature in the community, are also understaffed, whilst economics and political science, areas that have direct bearing on planning and creating political consensus, are also understaffed. The staffing constraints that limit programme implementation are more linked to budgetary constraint, than to the potential availability of qualified staff. Clearly this shortcoming is linked to member countries' inability to meet the financial needs of the secretariat, one of the consequences of multiple memberships in overlapping regional economic communities.[112]

---

111 UNECA Report 2005;' *The Case for Rationalization*: Chapter 3. p. 59. Available from: www.uneca.org/aria (Accessed on 13 April, 2008).

112 *Ibid.*, p. 61.

The Challenge of Instability

The West African region remains one of the most volatile regions on the continent. From the high frequency of military takeovers in the 1960s through the 1980s, which brought political and economic stagnancy to the region, it has, since the 1990s, been plagued by civil conflict. This has further retarded the political, economic and social development of the region and made the integration effort more difficult in the region. Presently countries like Liberia, Sierra-Leone, and Cote d' Ivoire are recovering from several years of conflict, which to a large extent has not been helpful to ECOWAS, as resources have been channelled into resolving these conflicts. The role of the ECOWAS Standby Force remains critical to the prospects of a better integration effort. Linked to this has been the issue of bad governance which has been the bane of many African countries. It is hopeful that the wind of change in the region now will prevail to enhance ECOWAS' move towards a more stable sub-regional grouping.

Prospects for ECOWAS

Notwithstanding the various daunting challenges that confront ECOWAS, there are some quite positive prospects. The sub-region is experiencing a new wave of democracy with the regional leaders seeming commitment to good governance. The new crop of leadership seems to understand that integration is the only way to emancipate West African economies from the doldrums of stagnation, decay and decline. Instability seems to be subsiding as calm returns to Liberia, Sierra-Leone, and the level of conflict has de-escalated in Cote d' Ivoire. The other crucial aspect is the international community's recognition and support for the integration process.

There has been growing acceptance by both bilateral and multilateral donor agencies to assist with regional initiatives. Notably the EU is placing priority attention on the regional cooperation component of its ACP-EU arrangement. EU and French support had been vital in building UEMOA's in-house macroeconomic and trade capacities in areas such as legal harmonisation, statistics collection, public finance management. Similar assistance would be crucial to developing ECOWAS capabilities with the proposed merger of the two.[113] Already growing rapport between ECOWAS and UEMOA has resulted in a common programme on trade liberalisation and macroeconomic convergence. ECOWAS has agreed to adopt UEMOA's customs declaration forms and compensation mechanisms.[114] In the matter of security of the region which is of crucial interest to the West, the funding by Germany, UK, Italy, Canada and the Netherlands of KAIPTC in Ghana to train ECOWAS soldiers for both UN and local duties underscores the prospects for development of stability.

ECOWAS' prospects are further enhanced by instructional modifications to its mandate thus strengthening the structures, under the revised treaty to make decisions enforceable. The restructuring of the financial institutions with commercial orientation will enable ECOWAS to attract substantial non-regional capital participation in very viable regional projects, while providing financial assistance to development programmes in member states.[115] Additionally if ECOWAS and UEAMOA were to merge and were adequately empowered as envisaged, the resulting organization would improve monetary transaction in the region and facilitate faster economic activity. Its multinational mandate would help it to overcome many of the difficulties that have defeated individual states and play a far greater role in engineering growth in the sub-region.[116] With a concerted effort by the regional leaders with the support of civil society and the people of the sub-region, ECOWAS is poised to be one of the crucial building blocs towards Africa's quest for a greater union.

Conclusion

The promotion of economic cooperation among developing countries is now an accepted part of international development policy, and almost all issues in the field of international economic relations are currently subordinated to the quest for regional economic associations and groupings among more or less contiguous areas. With Africa's share of world trade less than 2%, and classified as the least developed region, with roughly half of its

113 S. Kaplan, *Op. Cit.*, p. 94.
114 UNECA, *Op.Cit.*, p. 42.
115 S. Kaplan, *Op. Cit.*, p. 96.
116 *Ibid.*, p. 82.

population living on less than $1 per day and with declining global foreign direct investment, Africa had major challenges. Integration was seen as a means of overcoming some of these challenges. It can invigorate development prospects by transforming business climates. It is meant to reduce the intensity of inter-group rivalries by the creation of a supranational umbrella, under which all groups are equally represented, with a common agenda.

West African economies have witnessed very little growth since independence, due to the vulnerable nature of the individual economies to external shocks and, in many cases, bad policy choices adopted by member governments. The production of primary commodities for export has tended to marginalise their economies due to fluctuations in the prices of these commodities. The region has witnessed its fair share of political instability through military adventurism and civil conflict. Over time the leaders have come to the realisation that regional cooperation is central to economic growth and prosperity. It was some of these difficulties that saw the formation of ECOWAS in 1975 to harness the potential of the region for its overall development. ECOWAS has come far; restructuring its institutions in 1993 in order to meet some of the emerging challenges after its formation. ECOWAS has made some remarkable progress in terms of institutional building, free movement of persons and goods, development of community spirit and the provision of road infrastructure to ease the movement of goods and services as well as to open up to the landlocked member states. It has improved communication, established financial institutions as well as developing an energy network to distribute power to member states.

In spite of some of these achievements ECOWAS is still saddled with several daunting challenges: the issue of sovereignty and political commitment to the union, lack of civil sector participation in the process and lack of professional staff at the secretariat of the organization. Other challenges include the rationalisation of other unions with similar goals and agenda, such as UEMOA and its monetary union within ECOWAS, which appears to be divisive. The poor level of economic performance of most of the countries and the inability to translate the organization's policies into national programmes of the member countries, along with elitism remain drawbacks to the organizations progress. Conflicts and general instability remains a hurdle for which the leaders, with donor assistance, ECOWAS is striving to make the region stable for development.

Prospects, for the success of the organization remain quite high. With the recognition of the international community of the potential of the organization's ability to be a building block for stability, donor investment assistance and attention especially from the west is being given to ECOWAS to enhance its capability. ECOWAS remains one of the key sub-regional groups in the Africa Union's quest for complete economic and political integration of the continent for the realisation of the vision of the past and present African leaders.

PART III

Ongoing Issues in Africa

Chapter VI

African Genocide: Rwanda as a Case Study

Introduction

Over the course of 100 days between March and July 1994 nearly one million people, mostly Tutsis, were killed in Rwanda. The extermination rates were over five times faster than those achieved by the Nazis during the holocaust of World War II, yet these industrial scale killings were conducted without the technology designed to allow for mass killing. There were no distant concentration camps manned by anonymous uniformed specialists or chambers filled with poisonous gas.[1] In Rwanda, the most common instrument for murder was the machete and, more often than not, it was wielded by the victim's neighbours. To kill using a machete requires extreme effort, which is why there were often multiple killers for each single victim. The Rwandan genocide was carried out by hundreds of thousands and witnessed by millions; it was very much an intimate affair, which involved the direct involvement of the general population.[2]

This essay will examine the reasons behind those killings and explain why they reached the scale they did. It will refute the suggestion that the genocide was an inevitable result of ethnicity and clearly demonstrate the role which colonial policies played in not only setting the conditions for conflict, but also how large-scale Western indifference, inaction and impotence allowed the conflict to escalate into full-blown genocide. Early colonial rule had upset the natural co-existence of tribal Rwanda and caused political and economic inequalities, which would be ruthlessly exploited by ambition and insecurity, to tragic result, years later.[3] A popular misconception is that the

---

1 M. Mamdani, *When Victims Become Killers; Colonialism, Nativism and the Genocide in Rwanda,* (Princeton, Princeton University Press, 2001), p. 5.

2 *Ibid.*, p. 6.

3 E. Braathen, M. Boas & G. Saether, *Ethnicity Kills?* (London: Macmillan, 2000), p. 13.

genocide was a 'simple matter of mutual hatred between tribes erupting into irrational violence'; this is not true - the killings were planned in advance and orchestrated with ruthless efficiency by a tyrannical regime.[4]

The political climate and the international system was important in defining Western opinion and responses; the essay will highlight the lack of political will among Western governments reluctant to become embroiled in yet another African crisis – particularly in a country as seemingly strategically unimportant as Rwanda. This inaction was then further exacerbated by extensive and costly ongoing UN operations in The Former Yugoslavia and the memories of the debacle in Somalia the previous year, when UN and US peacekeepers had been killed. African attention and the global media focus were also further diverted by the adjacent and inaugural post-Apartheid elections in South Africa. UN failings apart, the United States, France, Belgium and the United Kingdom were all individually culpable, to some extent, through inaction and dereliction of moral responsibility in allowing the killings to reach the proportions that they did. This will be examined in greater detail.

Western indifference was ruthlessly exposed by the calamitous failures surrounding the United Nations Assistance Mission for Rwanda (UNAMIR). Undoubtedly well intentioned, the mission was ill-conceived, poorly defined and shamefully unsupported in its execution. The UN's refusal to review the mandate, as the killings escalated, from a Chapter VI (Peacekeeping) to Chapter VII (Peace Enforcement) was instrumental in allowing the genocide to take hold.[5] The reluctance to commit further forces, when the operational situation dictated, undermined the mission and sent out entirely the wrong message to rebel forces who interpreted it as a sign of increasing Western apathy. The early warning signs of the impending genocide, detected and reported by UNAMIR commanders, were continually ignored by the UN Security Council until the situation spiralled out of control. As the killings escalated, Western forces were inserted to recover their entitled personnel (EP), but not given the mandate to remain and prevent the murder of the indigenous population; a situation which nearly broke UNAMIR. General

4 F. Keane, *Season of Blood: A Rwandan Journey*, (London: Penguin, 1995), p. 8.

5 R. Dallaire, *Shake Hands with the Devil, The Failure of Humanity in Rwanda*, (Canada: Random House, 2003), p. 307.

Dallaire wrote: 'I mark that as the day the world moved from disinterest in Rwanda to the abandonment of Rwandans to their fate. The swift evacuation of the foreign nationals was the signal for the genocidaires to move toward the apocalypse.'[6] Further restrictions imposed by the UN prohibited the seizure of rebel weapon hauls and prevented the shutting down of *Radio Television Libre des Milles Collines* (RTLM), a hugely effective Hutu controlled propaganda station that preached hatred and killing, which rapidly became a pervasive influence on Rwandan society. UNAMIR's efforts were consistently thwarted and they lost a large measure of support and the confidence of the population as a result.[7]

Arguably, the biggest single failure was the refusal of the West to acknowledge that genocide was actually occurring in Rwanda. The terms of the Genocide Convention clearly direct a moral obligation to intervene in the event of genocide being declared but the UN repeatedly portrayed the genocide as an ethnic conflict, thereby escaping that directed obligation.[8] All of these factors will be explored in greater detail throughout this essay, to effectively demonstrate how the Rwandan genocide could have been predicted and indeed should have been prevented.

The scope of this part has been designed to provide an essential historical overview, which will give an important insight into the roots of conflict within Rwanda. It will define the consequences of colonialism and highlight the previous disposition towards conflict that has blighted the country. This overview will then lead into a more contemporary assessment of Rwanda in 1994, as it became embroiled in genocide. The crux of the part will explore the complex issue of ethnicity and its particular application to the Hutu and Tutsi and then the wider failures of the West in allowing genocide to take hold in Rwanda.

---

6 *Ibid.*, p. 291.

7 W. A. Dorn & J. Matloff, "Preventing the Bloodbath: Could the UN have Predicted and Prevented the Rwandan Genocide," *The Journal of Conflict Studies*, Spring 2000, p. 36.

8 *Ibid.*, p. 15.

Historical Perspectives and the Impact of Colonialism

Four hundred years ago, a group of people called Tutsi established a feudal kingdom in the land now called Rwanda. Their rule was reinforced by an oral mythology which taught that Tutsi were inherently superior and their dominance was ordained by God. But despite the hierarchical nature of this society it was unusually unified. Tutsi and Hutu lived together, shared the same language and, in most important respects, the same culture.[9]

Despite recent history, Rwanda has not always been a land of conflict; it is a relatively recent phenomenon largely affected by Western influence. With a state history going back to 1500, Rwanda is one of the oldest African countries after Egypt and Ethiopia.[10] It is one of the most densely populated and poorest countries in the world; the eight million Rwandans are comprised of three major ethnic groups: the Hutu (85%), Tutsi (14%) and Twa (1%).[11] Before colonial rule these tribes lived in peaceful co-existence, sharing the same land, diet, religion and values. A self-determined hierarchical society was established with the minority Tutsi exercising control 'over the three main sources of power: the cattle economy, the monarchy and religious life'.[12] Whilst the Tutsis owned the land and cattle, the Hutu were able to service and work the arable farmland. In their study of exile armies Bennett & Latawski concluded, 'the pre-colonial relationship between Hutu and Tutsi was not simply defined in traditional ethnic terms. It was a clientalistic and hierarchical relationship rather than one built upon the more tribal model of parallel existences found in many other African states'.[13] There is no record of any Hutu -Tutsi violence during the pre-colonial period that could be considered as having relevance on later events; tensions were minor and the registered clashes relatively insignificant. Social advancement was possible however, with Hutus often moving strata through marriage, land acquisition and ownership of livestock; this 'created an unusual degree of social cohesion

---

9 G. Vassall-Adams, *Rwanda: An Agenda for International Action*, (Oxford: Oxfam, 1994), p. 7.

10 E. Braathen, M. Boas & G. Saether, *Op. Cit.*, p. 74.

11 G. Vassall-Adams, *Op. Cit.*, p. 8.

12 *Ibid.*, p. 7.

13 M. Bennett & P. Latawski, *Exile Armies*, (London: Palgrave Macmillan, 2005), p. 144.

between the two groups'.[14] In effect, Rwandans were defined by class and clan, not ethnicity.

German colonial rule was established in 1894, which immediately served to upset this established and natural balance of power. Whilst nowhere near as disruptive as the subsequent Belgian rule, the Germans favoured expansion and 'began this process by replacing Rwanda's only Hutu chiefs, in the north-west, with Tutsi chiefs'.[15] This action sparked the first recorded spate of civil unrest, which was subsequently quelled by colonial forces.

Belgian rule commenced after the First World War. It was this period up to Rwandan independence in 1962 that really set the conditions for future conflict, which subsequently spiralled into full-blown genocide. The Belgians adopted an indirect method of colonial rule; exacting Western methods of control that were then executed through the minority Tutsi elite. This form of governance served to reinforce the racial superiority of the Tutsi and elevate their dominance even further, whilst simultaneously highlighting the inferiority and serf-like status of the majority Hutu.[16] Belgium effectively shattered the natural social order and prevented any social mobility or power retention by the Hutu; thus being Tutsi became synonymous with affluence and superiority. Public endorsement and legal empowerment of Tutsi superiority further alienated Hutu support and by formally introducing ethnic classification, Belgium effectively sanctioned a form of apartheid by elevating one group over another. The humiliation of the basic methods used for racial classification, such as the measurement of facial features and ownership of cattle, were not lost on either side. The Tutsi, encouraged by Western sponsorship, exploited their positions of power by exerting influence over the seemingly inferior majority, whilst Hutu resentment and anger smouldered. Ironically, it was this Western system of social classification and the introduction of identity cards as tools of social control in suppressing Hutus, which served to aid the mass scale killings that occurred decades later. They provided an exact and readily available target list for Hutu extremists intent on murder.

14 Ibid.
15 G. Vassall-Adams, *Op. Cit.*, p. 8.
16 Brumell, History Channel (2006).

It would be naive to claim that the harmonious co-existence of pre-colonial rule in Rwanda would have continued indefinitely, particularly as Western influence spread into Africa in the 20th Century. However, the divisive nature and exploitation exacted by indirect Belgian rule proved instrumental in creating ethnic division, tension and distrust between Hutu and Tutsi. Vassall-Adams observes, 'People classified as Tutsi were systematically favoured in the education system and the colonial administration. The Hutu majority were, in effect, assigned the status of permanent underclass, excluded from the power structures of their country'.[17]

The next key milestone in Rwandan history was the perceptible shift that was enabled through the movement toward eventual independence; this transfer of authority sparked an era of almost continuous conflict. After the Second World War Rwanda-Urundi became a Trustee Territory of the UN and pressure was applied for Belgium to grant independence and implement democratic election processes.[18] In preparation Belgium began to strip the Tutsi of a significant number of positions to provide a more representative ruling class, asserting that minority rule was no longer acceptable. The Hutu, on gaining increased levels of power, exacted quick revenge for what they perceived as years of discrimination and exploitation by Western sponsored Tutsi rule. The increased social tension escalated into violence and the subsequent persecution of Tutsis resulted in significant internal displacement causing thousands to flee to neighbouring Uganda, Burundi, Zaire and Tanzania. In effect, the Tutsi became the persecuted minority. These Diasporas quickly formed militias and exile armies in the hope of returning by force and restoring Tutsi rule.[19]

Rwanda achieved Independence in July 1962 and the first government was comprised entirely of Hutus, who considered the Tutsi 'as the eternal enemy'. [20] This was a significant period in the history of Rwanda – for the first time, there was a democratically elected government providing legitimacy to the persecution of Tutsis.

---

17 G. Vassall-Adams, *Op. Cit.*, p. 8.

18 *Ibid.*

19 *Ibid.*, p. 9.

20 L. Melvern, *Conspiracy to Murder: The Rwandan Genocide*, (London: Verso, 2004), p. 8.

The first recorded post-independence mass killing was in 1963, when 14,000 Tutsi were murdered after an attempt to remove Hutu President Kayibanda following an invasion from Burundi. The West was shocked by the savagery of the murders but significantly no-one was held accountable and the incident was quickly forgotten. The Tutsi then committed genocide of their own, by murdering 200,000 Hutus in neighbouring Burundi in 1972; again no-one was charged with responsibility, which fuelled the perception that the West was just not concerned. Kayibanda exploited the killings in Burundi to launch an offensive against the Tutsi in Rwanda and commissioned a campaign to 'purify' the country.[21] This sparked another process of intimidation, murder and violence, which resulted in the further displacement of thousands of Tutsi to neighbouring countries. President Kayibanda was eventually ousted in a coup in 1973 when the Hutu controlled MRND party, under Juvenal Habyarimana, seized control and there followed a period of relative stability. The MRND actually encouraged some of the understandably reluctant Tutsi to make a return to Rwanda.

The 1980s saw a worsening economic crisis, exacerbated by famine and over-population that caused the ruling Hutu regime to seal the borders against returning Tutsis.[22] This caused a new uprising in tension and the organisation of large numbers of armed Tutsi on the Rwandan border, in the form of the Rwandan Patriotic Front (RPF). In turn, this further undermined Hutu insecurities and provoked retaliatory killings of Tutsi civilians still living in Rwanda.[23] Deep seated Tutsi bitterness and 'statelessness' provoked the RPF to conduct numerous incursions into Rwanda, which culminated in a large-scale invasion and brutal fighting in October 1990; as Bennett & Latawski observed, 'this resulted in 800,000 Hutus fleeing south, further legitimizing and substantiating Hutu fears of Tutsi rule'.[24]

This whole sequence of exploitation and persecution, by both Hutu and Tutsi, was initiated and enabled by Western interference and the impact of this specific form of colonial rule. Other African states, including those in the Great Lakes Region, have recovered from colonialism without any

21 *Ibid.*, p. 10.
22 Brumell, *Op. Cit.*
23 G. Vassall-Adams, *Op. Cit.*, p. 9.
24 M. Bennett & P. Latawski, *Op. Cit.*, p. 146.

enduring tension between ethnic groups; but, significantly, they were not subject to the 'divide and rule' form of governance, with one group socially and economically elevated above the other through a direct result of Western intervention.

Rwanda, 1990 – 1994: Staring into the Abyss

In the early 1990s, Rwanda was a country ravaged by civil war. An atmosphere of hate, suspicion and fear had been cultivated by the ruling Hutu regime, under President Habyarimana, by exploiting the security anxieties held by the general population. Rumours of violent Tutsi reprisals against Hutu communities were propagated in an attempt to recruit wider Hutu support and thereby retain political control and legitimacy. The formation of the Democratic Republican Movement (MDR) in 1991 represented another genuine and more adjacent threat to Habyarimana than the RPF. Comprised predominantly of moderate Hutu, the MDR presented Habyarimana with a credible opposition from within his 'own people' and he increasingly feared a loss of power. Internal pressure on the ruling Government was accompanied by increasing external pressure. As Kehoe wrote, 'the international pressure was by now mounting for the democratisation of Rwanda and this was making the Hutu elites nervous', as they realised that any change in government would end the fiscal advantages that they had been receiving through regime sponsorship.[25] As Melvern and other leading analysts have concluded, it was this period, in late 1991, when a Presidential appointed commission began to plan the killings.[26] This is an extremely important observation: that the notion of genocide in Rwanda was awakened through the internal struggle for political power, status and money. It also supports the thesis that the Rwandan genocide was a pre-meditated and carefully planned operation, rather than an unforeseen explosion of unpredictable violence.

The sheer scale, brutality and relentlessness of the civil war eventually forced the international community to intervene. A peace agreement was

---

25 *Ibid.*, p. 8.

26 L. Melvern, *Conspiracy to Murder: The Rwandan Genocide*, (London: Verso, 2004), p. 61.

brokered by emissaries from the United Nations and the Organisation of African Unity (OAU) in August 1993, which detailed an immediate ceasefire and outlined the timelines for power-sharing negotiations.[27] Critically, the MRND were not included in these negotiations, which were then imposed. As Bennett and Latawski observed, 'these Arusha Accords represented, at best, enormous constitutional change, at worst, surrender for the Habyarimana regime and they acceded to the settlement from a position of profound weakness'.[28] The Hutu power base was thus significantly undermined and faced with loss of power and social prestige the ruling MRND party subsequently stalled on every opportunity to implement the terms of Arusha. As the status of the ruling Hutus was gradually devalued, the role of the RPF increased commensurately with a greater allocation of ministerial positions and command posts.[29] Hard-line politicians fuelled the perceived injustices by empowering and encouraging Hutu extremist groups, under the guise of self-defence, to ultimately prevent this transfer of power to the Tutsi. As Fergal Keane wrote,'while publicly proclaiming himself to reform, the president was privately financing and helping to organise the Hutu extremist.'[30] It was Western insistence on coercive diplomacy, to enforce democratisation in Rwanda, which forced the Hutu into a corner from where violence was the only escape: 'the political instability unleashed by democratisation and the Arusha process was translated into genocide through the endeavours of hard-line politicians. As such, Rwanda's genocide was a means of maintaining political power in a state where the ruling party had been forced to relinquish its grip'.[31]

The terms of the ceasefire saw the initial deployment of UN Peacekeepers, under the auspices of UNAMIR, with a mandate to oversee the implementation of the Arusha Agreement. The wider failings of Western military efforts will be examined in greater detail later in this essay, but it is important to highlight the initial shortcomings particularly in force disposition, which ultimately set the tone for the entire mission. The troop composition of the first UNAMIR deployment was weak. Belgium, because

27 M. Leitenberg, "Rwanda, 1994: International Incompetence Produces Genocide," *Peacekeeping & International Relations*, Vol. 23, No. 6, Nov/Dec 1994, p. 6.

28 M. Bennett & P. Latawski, *Op. Cit.*, p. 149.

29 *Ibid.*

30 F. Keane, *Op. Cit.*, p. 25.

31 M. Bennett & P. Latawski, *Op. Cit.*, p. 149.

of historical connections, was the only developed nation to commit forces; thus an inexperienced, poorly trained force of limited capability was deployed into an area of significant tension with a recent history of extended conflict and extreme violence.

The UNAMIR commander was unequivocal as to the reasons for this reluctance to become involved. As Dallaire commented, 'Rwanda was on nobody's radar as a place of strategic interest, it had no natural resources, no geographical significance and was dependent on foreign aid. Even if the mission were to succeed the only real beneficiary internationally would be the UN'.[32] Traditional contributing nations were also claiming that they were over-committed because of larger operations in the Balkans and Somalia. Either way, this lacklustre deployment was not lost on either the Hutu or Tutsi leadership, who interpreted it as a lack of genuine Western commitment to Rwanda. This was further example of poor judgement by the UN, as the perceived lack of purpose was critical in its timing. As Melvern observed, 'In peacekeeping, the transition from dictatorship to democracy is the most dangerous time. It is used by extremists to make the most of a vacuum. Any delay or hint of a lack of commitment serves only to encourage the hardliners who do not want peace'.[33] This message was clearly demonstrated by the activities of extremist groups, on both sides, who exploited the shortcomings of the UN deployment.

Despite his continued stalling, President Habyarimana still managed to anger Hutu hardliners with his apparent willingness to entertain the power-sharing arrangements detailed by the Arusha agreements. Conversely, his obstinate resistance to reform provoked both Western disapproval and RPF fury and threatened the legitimacy of the ceasefire. On returning from Arusha, on 6 April 1994, Habyarimana's aircraft was shot down over Kigali. [34] The proponents of his murder have never been confirmed, but it is widely believed that Hutu extremists were responsible for the attack in an attempt to prevent any further advancement at the peace accords. However, the Tutsi led RPF were immediately blamed for the shooting, which signalled the beginning of the killings that quickly escalated into genocide; 'the violence

32 R. Dallaire, *Op. Cit.*, p. 89.
33 L. Melvern, *Op. cit.*, p. 82.
34 M. Bennett & P. Latawski, *Op. Cit.*, p. 150.

was aimed at exterminating any that supported the RPF or the process of democratisation; in effect anything and anyone who undermined Hutu supremacy'.[35]

Ethnicity Kills

'To describe 6.5 million Hutus as a tribe and 265,000 Icelanders as a nation is ethnocentric bias. Ethnicity in Rwanda does not explain genocide, but ethnic solidarity and the asymmetric relationship in size between the Hutu and Tutsi might explain why so many were killed'.[36]

Ethnic conflict is a global phenomenon; it is not just an African affliction and is certainly not applicable to just the Great Lakes region. What is unique about Rwanda however, is the sheer number of ordinary citizens who became embroiled in large scale killing and extreme violence. This essay has already examined how the inspiration for planning the killings was born from the fear of loss of power, status and political control, but that does not explain the mass complicity of the general population in active participation. Why did the killings reach the proportions they did and what caused the complicity of so many to commit genocide so freely?

This section will aim to demonstrate that the key motivating factor amongst the populous was fear. This fear was evident on distinct and separate levels. Firstly, it was a primordial fear of persecution by the seemingly increasingly powerful and revengeful Tutsi; but, it was also an acute fear of the Hutu extremists and the consequences of retribution that could have resulted from non-compliance or participation. Hutus have subsequently claimed that they committed murder in order to simply preserve their own survival. This fear, on both levels, was exacerbated by the consequences of over-population, poverty, debt and social injustice. The sense of belonging, associated with ethnicity, was ruthlessly exploited by extremists, in uniting the masses. This proved particularly effective in a society where the role of authority was paramount and there was no effective rule of law or legal accountability.

---

35 *Ibid.*

36 Braathen et al, p. 72.

The term 'ethnic conflict' has become central to the considerations of many commentators when attempting to provide a rationale for people killing each other, particularly in Africa. However, this can be a label that is too easily applied. In his study of ethnicity, Sadowski dismisses these 'simplistic notions' and argues that since the high profile ethnic conflicts which marked the dissolution of Yugoslavia and the Soviet Union, it has become *de rigueur* to reclassify any conflict as ethnic, even when it is clearly a power struggle or ideological conflicts such as in Nicaragua or Somalia.[37] To label such struggles as ethnic conflict have more far-reaching consequences than a simple misnomer. Braathen in his book '*Ethnicity Kills*', observes that the 'preoccupation with the ethnic component in contemporary Sub-Saharan civil wars leads to the neglect of other crucial variables'.[38] Politics, power and economics are instrumental in setting the roots for conflict and whilst ethnic differences are a vehicle for exploiting these insecurities, an often cause for conflict lies outside of racial or ethnic classification. Braathen amplifies the argument: 'Whilst ethnic affiliations often structure the constitution of armed factions it is too easy to characterise war in Africa as tribal conflict; the various conflicting groups must be understood in the light of the socio-economic context in which they operate and ethnicity is just one of the variables.'[39] It is evident therefore that these modern forms of ethnic conflict are not primarily derived from ancient hatred but are sparked by more contemporary socio-cultural and political agendas. Indeed Sadowski writes: 'the claim that ethnic conflicts have deep roots has long been a standard argument for not getting involved, but the reality is that most ethnic conflicts are expressions of modern hate and largely products of the twentieth century.'[40]

One of the many failings within the international media, which will be examined in detail later, was to describe the Rwandan genocide as tribal anarchy; this unwittingly provided Western governments with ammunition for not wishing to become embroiled in an 'orgy of ethnic violence'.[41] The importance of a clear understanding as to the origins, cause and nature of any conflict is therefore vital in evolving a strategy for its successful prevention or

37 Y. Sadowski, "Ethnic Conflict, Foreign Policy," Summer 1998, p. 12.
38 Braathen et al, *Op. Cit.*, p. 19.
39 *Ibid.*, p. 4.
40 Y. Sadowski, *Op. Cit.*, p. 13.
41 L. Melvern, *Op. Cit.*, pp. 137-8.

cessation – an area in which the West failed in its appreciation of Rwanda.

As Braathen concludes, 'societal inequality is a vital dimension of conflict and violence in Sub-Saharan Africa.'[42] This was especially true in Rwanda, in the early 90s, when economic hardships were so severe that individual survival was often threatened as a result. This observation must be evaluated within the context of those conditions; what might seem irrelevant or inconsiderable to a Westerner could prove the difference between life and death in Rwanda. Trivial inequalities therefore, assumed huge importance and perceived injustices were easily exploited by subversive propaganda and behaviour. Extreme levels of social inequality are, more often that not, created by the state. In the case of Rwanda these divisions were the result of Belgian colonial policy and the subsequent Tutsi pursuit of political and economical hegemony. Hutu rule was biased towards increasing the status of its relatively recently established ruling elite, at the expense of removing the deep seated inequalities and hardships afflicting the majority of the population. By aligning the economic power to political status the masses were marginalised, impoverished and embittered, which resulted in a highly unstable and volatile population that was susceptible to exploitation. Because of the economic advantages attached to the Hutu elite, largely based in Kigali, and the historical socio-cultural differences between the Hutu and Tutsi, the Rwandan inequalities quickly became both rurally based and inter-ethnic.[43] This country-wide dispersion of tension and mistrust was to prove instrumental in ensuring that the killings were conducted on a national scale and that the genocide was able to take hold in even the most remote rural areas in Rwanda.

It is important to appreciate the definition of genocide in attempting to apply the context to the killings in Rwanda. Article 2 of the United Nation's Convention defines it as follows:

Genocide means any of the following acts committed with intent to destroy, in whole or in part, a national, ethnical, racial or religious group as such: (a) killing members of the group; (b) causing serious bodily or mental harm to the group; (c) deliberately inflicting upon the group conditions of

42 E. Braathen, M. Boas & G. Saether, *Op. Cit.*, p. 13.
43 *Ibid.*, p. 16.

life calculated to bring about its physical destruction in whole or in part; (d) imposing measures intended to prevent births within the group; (e) forcibly transferring children of the group to another group.[44]

Interestingly, this definition does not include politicide, which is recognised as 'government sponsored or accepted murders of political dissidents or class enemies or others who are killed for political purposes'.[45] The first murders committed in the immediate hours after Habyarimana's death were of moderate Hutu politicians – those whom posed the most immediate threat to the ruling regime. Thus politicide was a key component of the overall strategy of genocide devised by the extremist Hutus. This often overlooked factor adds further evidence to the hypothesis that the genocide in Rwanda was not only planned, but that it was conducted in order to consolidate political power and status.

A key enabler in spreading fear and preparing the country for genocide was the Hutu controlled RTLM, which became notorious by transmitting extreme anti-Tutsi propaganda. This highly popular radio station, which was considered to be the voice of the nation, openly broadcast messages containing incitement to murder, rape and subjugation. These transmissions were made with impunity and there was no attempt by the West to intervene. An equally sinister function was RTLM's role in dehumanising and demonising the Tutsi. Robin Williams, in his studies of genocide, recognises this process as key in convincing the masses to take up arms against any enemy: 'they do this by numerous and diverse tactics: dramatising historical wrongs, stressing contradictory religious beliefs, spreading allegations of atrocities and asserting inherent evil in the other'.[46] The Tutsi were further devalued by invariably being referred to as *Inyenzi*, meaning cockroach, whilst the superiority and virtues of the Hutu were consistently exalted.[47] Another method of dehumanisation, which RTLM effectively preached was the assertion that the Tutsi were outsiders, not Rwandans, but an invasion force to be feared from Uganda, Zaire and Tanzania. This process of devaluation

---

44 R. M. Williams, *The Wars Within, People and States in Conflict*, (New York: Cornell University Press, 2003), p. 194.

45 *Ibid.*

46 *Ibid.*, p. 199.

47 *Ibid.*, p. 197.

and insecurity resulted in an increasingly fearful Hutu population that was completely ostracised from any meaningful connection with the Tutsi and thus more susceptible to coercion to commit murder. Once the killings began, the extremists made open use of the radio to encourage the population 'to seek out the enemy and those who do not share our opinion'.[48] The effectiveness of the radio should not be under-estimated; it rapidly turned into a vital propaganda tool in spreading fear and extremist bigotry to even the most remote parts of Rwanda, thereby priming the Hutu to kill.[49]

It is a natural tendency, particularly in times of tension and fear, for people to seek security in the solidarity of ethnicity. As Braathen observed: 'as wars mount and fear and hate spread, people do not choose to support their armed community companions out of persuasion. Instead, their place of birth or family relationships decide which group of people they belong to – under these circumstances ethnicity becomes the only safe haven, when things fall apart people are often left with no protection but the solidarity of their ethnic kinsmen.'[50] This enforced polarity reached extreme levels in the immediate run-up to the genocide. Both Hutu and Tutsi took refuge in numbers, thereby exacerbating the divisions that were already evident. It was this mass grouping of Tutsi, gathered to seek refuge, which presented the extremists with obvious and congregated targets in the early days of the genocide. Ironically, if they had remained dispersed their chances of survival would have been greater, particularly in rural areas. Conversely, the large numbers of Hutu allowed easy access for the extremist leaders to spread further insecurity and anxiety and encourage their active participation in the killing.

Fear of retribution, through non-participation was very real for the Hutu majority. It very quickly became an issue of self-preservation. Berkeley, in his study of ethnic Africa, interviewed a Hutu accused of murdering his Tutsi brother-in-law: 'I killed because I was forced to. I either had to do it or I would die myself, many were killed for refusing to kill.'[51] Some, who had initially refrained from participation, became active when it became evident

---

48 L. Melvern, *Op. Cit.*, p. 160.

49 Bill Berkeley, *The Graves are not yet Full: Race, Tribe and Power in the Heart of Africa*, (New York: Basic, 2001), p. 261.

50 E. Braathen, M. Boas & G. Saether, *Op. Cit.*, p. 18.

51 Bill Berkeley, *Op. Cit.*, p. 1.

that full-scale genocide would take hold and they believed that domination over the Tutsi was inevitable. This, they believed, would ensure their share of the victory spoils when the promised re-distribution of Tutsi land was conducted; thus greed and fear of losing out became a motivating factor.

Another aspect which contributed to mass participation was the structured and authoritarian society to which the majority of Hutu had become accustomed. Appointed *bourgmestres*, prefects and figures of authority commanded instant respect and were rarely disobeyed. Once the killings commenced the interim government appointed 'pacification ministers' whose purpose was to co-ordinate the 'cleansing' strategy applicable to their area of responsibility.[52] As Berkeley observed, 'when these authorities attached a rational motive such as self-defence to an ingrained inclination to obey the results were inevitable'.[53] As such the authorities were able to exploit the obedience and inherent complicity within the Hutus' natural psyche. Combined with the absence of possible legal retribution, which had marked all previous conflict in Rwanda, the motivating factors for Hutu participation were substantially increased.

There is not one single factor that causes genocide in itself. A combination of events and conditions will however certainly increase the probability. Williams highlights a number of these key factors; 'strong ethnic cleavages and past discrimination, economic distress, war and revolution, political threat to ruling groups, rapid change in political alignments and ideologies of group superiority and group threat.'[54] Nearly all of these afflictions could be aligned to Rwanda, but they require a more personal and tangible effect if they are to manipulate a people to commit genocide; in the case of the Hutu, fear was clearly the stimulus that triggered those insecurities.

The Failure of the West: Preventative Measures

Western efforts in Rwanda lacked conviction from the very start. This lack of commitment was obvious to both Hutu and Tutsi, who rapidly became

52 L. Melvern, *Op. Cit.*, p. 160.
53 Bill Berkeley, *Op. Cit.*, p. 255.
54 R. M. Williams, *Op. Cit.*, p. 198.

contemptuous of UNAMIR and actively encouraged by ongoing Western inaction. Rebel leaders did not believe that the West possessed either the collective political will, or resources, to fund a meaningful deployment that would guarantee their individual interests in the application of the Arusha accords.

The peace agreement was a complex and detailed document that had been overseen by the Tanzanian President, Ali Hassan Mwinyi, at Arusha during eighteen months of acrimonious negotiation.[55] The accords prescribed an ambitious schedule of reforms that were to be introduced into Rwandan society over a period of nearly two years. It set the agenda for the formation of a shared transitional government, democratic elections, the restoration of economic confidence and public services, the re-integration of refugees and the demobilisation of the armed factions on both sides.[56] The UN mission to Rwanda was designed as a traditional Chapter VI deployment to 'guarantee the shaky ceasefire on which the peace accords rested' and assist in the execution of the reforms.[57] Greater analysis of the specifics of the accords would however have revealed significant short-comings in key areas of negotiation. Firstly, there were no detailed plans on how the proposed power-sharing was going to be implemented between the two warring factions, additionally there were no proposals for the controversial issue of land-share, specifically for returning refugees. It was, therefore, dangerously short on detail in areas that had the most potential for further violent confrontation and this should have been evident to the UN in New York.

The UNAMIR reconnaissance to Rwanda set the tone for the entire mission. Planning teams were forced to conduct their assessments on tourist maps, due to a lack of proper resources and their ambitious initial deployment was limited to a small team, who had less than two weeks to consider all aspects of an UN peacekeeping mission. This incorporated the political, humanitarian, administrative, logistical and military perspectives that were then used to define and scope the requirements for the overall mission.[58] Dallaire was advised by Maurice Baril, a leader at the UN Department of Peacekeeping Operations, before the reconnaissance to 'keep the overall mission small and

55 R. Dallaire, *Op. Cit.*, p. 54.
56 *Ibid.*
57 *Ibid.*, p. 53.
58 *Ibid.*, p. 58.

inexpensive, otherwise it will never get approved by the Security Council'. As Dallaire observed, he was being told to 'situate the estimate' and design the mission to fit resources, rather than to respond to the actual demands of the situation they were being sent to assess.[59] It was obvious that the UN would not sponsor a resource-heavy and financially burdening operation similar to their ongoing commitments in the Balkans and Somalia. This was certainly not the most effective manner either to prepare, or define, a deployment of troops into a volatile, inhospitable country that had been ravaged by violent conflict for nearly half a century.

The lead elements of UNAMIR deployed into Rwanda on the 22nd of October 1993. By late December, there were 1,260 UN troops on the ground from Belgian, Tunisian, Ghanaian and Canadian (staff officer) contingents, which increased to its maximum of 2,548 in early 1994.[60] The force strength of these troops was markedly limited, as Dallaire himself noted in an interview with RUSI, 'except for the Belgians, I did not have troops with the right skills nor the weapons to back up even the self protection requirement, let alone the offensive capability.' Only this single contingent was self-sufficient, thus a large proportion of the initial Command effort was afforded to logistical and administrative procedures. The mission consequently lost critical impetus in the important early days and weeks of the deployment; rather than being seen as a meaningful, committed and dynamic force for good, they appeared unorganised and half-hearted, thus losing vital early credibility. By this stage, the Chapter VI mandate had still not been ratified and no Rules of Engagement had yet been authorised, despite troops being deployed. The overall effect of these uncertainties was significant because it denied UNAMIR the ability to effectively conduct the preventative measures, which would have aided both the implementation of the Arusha agreements and combated the early planning processes behind the genocide.

In their study of the UN in Rwanda, Dorn and Matloff observed that UNAMIR 'failed to create any form of preventative diplomacy, demonstrations of resolve, political lobbying or even moderate shows of force'.[61]

59 *Ibid.*, p. 56.

60 Bruce D. Jones, *Peacemaking in Rwanda, The Dynamics of Failure*, (Colorado: Lynne Riener Publishers, 2001), p. 108.

61 W. A. Dorn & J. Matloff, "Preventing the Bloodbath: Could the UN have Predicted and Prevented the Rwandan Genocide," *The Journal of Conflict Studies*, Spring 2000, p. 33.

These preventative measures should have been allied to a robust intelligence capability, which could have allowed for specific focus of effort to achieve maximum effect. At this stage, there were clear warning signals of impending violence which even a rudimentary intelligence organisation would have detected. Unfortunately, UNAMIR force structures did not allow for an intelligence section; this proved to be a key weakness. As Dorn & Matloff concluded, 'information led operations could have directed the preventive actions to counter people (plotters and resistors), the genocide structures (networks) and the tools (weapons) of the genocide'.[62] None of these key components were effectively targeted, until it became too late to prevent the killings.

The most significant diplomatic failures were at the strategic level. Jacques-Roger Booh-Booh, the former Foreign Minister of Cameroon, was the first appointed Special Representative of the UN Secretary General (SRSG). As such, he was the senior UN diplomat assigned to Rwanda and held a key role in negotiating with both Hutu and Tutsi and in aiding the implementation of the peace agreement. Booh-Booh was not a particularly experienced or dynamic diplomat, appeared reluctant to engage with political leaders and was an openly declared Francophile. The Tutsi were consequently increasingly suspicious of his personal motives, due to the close links between France and the ruling Hutu (France had for generations been directly involved in the military training and supply of weapons to Hutu forces). A perceptible rift quickly developed between UNAMIR and the SRSG, which detracted from the unity of effort that was required for mission credibility. As Dallaire observed, 'he seemed to bring nothing new to the table in the way of expertise on Rwanda, knowledge of the conflict, familiarity with the Arusha accords, or skill at identifying and dealing with the political intrigues of the nation. He was not inclined to take the lead on the international political effort and had no strategy to engage effectively'.[63] This inability to understand and integrate with the 'plotters and resistors' ensured that the extreme intentions of the political elite were never effectively exposed. In short, the preventative actions to counter the personal element of genocide, as prescribed by Dorn and Matloff, failed markedly.[64] As the genocide spread, Booh-Booh left Kigali

62 *Ibid.*, p. 34.
63 R. Dallaire, *Op. Cit.*, p. 118.
64 W. A. Dorn & J. Matloff, *Op. Cit.*, p. 34.

permanently and based himself in Nairobi, thereby effectively severing what little political influence he still had. Booh-Booh was eventually replaced as the SRSG by Shararaya Khan, who proved more effective at political negotiation and provided greater strategic credibility to the mission, albeit too late to prevent the killings.

Parallel to this lack of higher level engagement were the ongoing challenges being presented to UNAMIR, courtesy of New York and the wider international community. A key component of the mission was to oversee the demobilisation of the Hutu and Tutsi armed forces, which was integral to the overall success of the peace accords. Central to this demobilisation was the IMF and World Bank funding, which underpinned the ability to sponsor the short-term basic needs of the troops and permit their gradual integration back into society. In February 1993, UNAMIR learnt that this money was to be withdrawn, which resulted in them having to manage the release of nearly 40,000 men without any degree of financial support. This set-back was viewed with even greater disdain by the Hutu and Tutsi hierarchy, who interpreted the decision as symbolic of yet another indication of Western apathy. Dallaire was also prohibited from actively engaging with the moderate political leadership in order to re-ignite the impetus behind the stalling peace agreements. The UN declared that the mandate was simply to oversee the implementation of Arusha, not to become involved in the actual negotiation process, which could be viewed as a violation of impartiality. Again, this inability to interact contributed toward the ultimate failure of Arusha and crucially the marginalisation of moderate leaders, at a time when their influence was needed to quell the growing tension amongst the general population.

So what exactly were these warning signs of impending disaster that the West consistently failed to notice? Firstly, there were the structures of genocide – those elements that Dorn & Matloff referred to as the 'networks'. The Interahamwe and other ethnic based militias were openly recruiting and mobilising large groups of disaffected Hutu youths, under the auspice of training for self-defence operations. As early as March 1992, the Rwandan press had described the group as 'military killers' and later the journal Le Flam Beau, claimed that leaders within the MRND and CDR were 'seeking a final solution where political adversaries and defenceless populations would be targeted and slaughtered'.[65] Human Rights Organisations had been active in Rwanda since the start of the decade and had witnessed the Interahamwe at close quarters, reporting their sinister activities at regular intervals. The muted International response to these repeated appraisals was characterised by a lack of collective will to intervene in internal ethnic tensions and crucially the early warning signs were continually ignored. The subversive nature and impact of the Hutu controlled RTLM has already been analysed. Despite openly declaring support for the genocide and actively encouraging the killings, RTLM was immune from UNAMIR intervention. Dallaire reported the severity and viciousness of the propaganda and requested permission either to destroy or electronically jam the radio station to prevent the transmissions. The UN again refused these requests on the basis that they did not fit the mandate and could be viewed as discriminatory. UNAMIR's subsequent recommendation to establish their own form of Information Operations capability, through a UN sponsored radio to counter RTLM, was denied on budgetary grounds.[66]

The next significant preventative failing was the inability to deal effectively with the 'tools' of genocide.[67] Western arms supplies were readily available in Rwanda, with large quantities stockpiled by extremist groups such as the Interahamwe. Civilians had been armed – under the pretext of self-defence and weapons were being sold alongside fruit on the market stalls in Kigali.[68] UNAMIR even discovered a plane load of illegal arms with manifests from Western companies in the United Kingdom, Belgium and France as late as January 1993. The UN mandate authorised the troops to monitor illegal arms but did not allow for the 'conduct of searches, raids or to confiscate weapons from civilians and militia members'.[69] Despite continued warnings about the associated dangers of the weapon proliferations, UNAMIR were consistently refused permission to seize or confiscate the weapons. Later in January, an Interahamwe informant approached UNAMIR and detailed the exact nature and violent intentions of the Hutu extremists, including death-lists, the intention to target Belgian peacekeepers and the location of weapon

---

65 W. A. Dorn & J. Matloff, *Op. Cit.*, p. 25.
66 www.ambarwanda.org.uk accessed 31 January, 2014.
67 W. A. Dorn & J. Matloff, *Op. Cit.*, p. 34.
68 *Ibid.*, p. 16.
69 *Ibid.*, p. 17.

stockpiles. Realising the significance of the arms caches, Dallaire immediately planned an offensive operation to seize the initiative and confiscate the weapons.[70] He consequently received a swift prohibitive order from New York, and a sharp rebuke for planning outside the allowances of the Chapter VI mandate, which did not permit deterrent operations. Despite repeated attempts, Dallaire failed to get the UN to act on the intelligence supplied. He believes that this was due to the UN's nervousness surrounding offensive peacekeeping operations, which emanated from the deaths in Somalia and also the possibility of escalation.[71]

As Dorn & Matloff concluded, what was needed for genocide prevention was an intelligence capability, preventative measures and the political will to exploit them.[72]

The UN in Rwanda, as has been demonstrated, failed on all three counts. The killings were predictable but the warning signals were not accurately assessed or effectively processed: militia groups with proven links to previous outbreaks of extreme violence were openly training, illegal weapons were being stockpiled, extremists preached the propaganda of hate and killing, there was a history of massacre and informants were revealing detailed plans of death lists and imminent slaughter. The UN had, unwittingly, permitted the preparations for genocide to reach the stage of inevitability.

Failure of the West: The Dereliction of Moral Responsibility

President Habyarimana's plane was shot down at 8.23pm on 6 April 1994. Within an hour RTLM had reported his death, blaming it on Tutsi forces thus sparking the Hutu consciousness.[73] By midnight the killing and looting had started, with the main focus of effort being the systematic targeting and murder of all opposition politicians. The majority of these initial killings were conducted by the Presidential Guard, adhering to an orchestrated and pre-planned 'execution list'. One of the first to be murdered was the moderate Hutu Prime Minister Uwilingiyimana, who was the legal successor to the President. Her Belgian bodyguards had also been captured by the

70 R. Dallaire, *Op. Cit.*, p. 146.
71 *Ibid.*, p. 147.
72 W. A. Dorn & J. Matloff, *Op. Cit.*, p. 10.
73 L. Melvern, *Op. Cit.*, p. 116.

Presidential Guard, taken to a military compound in Kigali and macheted to death – their bodies were not recovered for over 2 days. The Interahamwe informant's intelligence, dismissed lightly by the UN, had proven accurate. The extremists were also deliberately exploiting the West's recognised aversion to casualties, particularly during peace-keeping operations.

The first large scale massacre was discovered shortly afterwards; the Interahamwe had forcibly entered a mission church in a suburb of Kigali and hacked, kicked and beaten to death over 500 Tutsi men, women and children. Over the next three months, massacres like this became commonplace.[74] Meanwhile, Dallaire was urgently pressing New York for a revision of the mandate as it became obvious that UNAMIR was being drawn into a peace enforcement scenario for humanitarian reasons.[75] He reported: 'If this mission is to be changed into a peace enforcement scenario to stop the massacres and rescue threatened civilians, then a change in mandate will be required and the mission must be reinforced with men, weapons and equipment. The force cannot continue to sit on the fence in the face of all these morally legitimate demands for assistance and protection.'[76] Predictably, it was the murder of the UN peacekeepers that had the greatest strategic impact in the West. The immediate reaction within the UN, led by the UK and US, was not to urgently review the existing mandate in order to increase the powers of UNAMIR, but rather to lobby for an immediate withdrawal of all UN forces from Rwanda. The political will was diminishing further.

Almost immediately the major Western nations announced the closure of their embassies in Rwanda. To facilitate the withdrawal of entitled personnel (EP) Belgium, France and Italy sent troops with orders to rescue only Westerners. Dallaire was given instructions from New York to support the evacuation operation: 'You should make every effort not to compromise your impartiality or to act beyond your mandate, but you may exercise your discretion to do [*sic*] should this be essential for the evacuation of foreign nationals'.[77] It became evident that the UN would break the Chapter VI mandate to ensure the safe evacuation of the EP, but they were not prepared

74 *Ibid.*, p. 132/3
75 R. Dallaire, *Op. Cit.*, p 307.
76 Ibid.
77 L. Melvern, *Op. Cit.*, p. 140-1.

to extend the scope of the mission to protect the general population.

The evacuation took just over 4 days to complete. Despite their pleas Rwandan embassy staffs were left behind, often to the mercy of the Interahamwe death squads, who moved in as the EP trucks departed. Throughout the evacuation, the killings continued unabated, with foreign troops, under national command, unable to intervene. With just over 2000 poorly trained and ill-equipped UNAMIR troops, Dallaire did not have sufficient resources to protect the general population. He is adamant however, that if the evacuation force of nearly 1000 highly trained para-commandos and armoured vehicles had not been withdrawn, then the killings would have been prevented. There were also 500 Belgian commandos in Kenya and over 250 US Rangers in Burundi which could also easily have been committed. As Fergal Keane observes in his book, 'this was not Somalia where the Americans encountered a well-armed and trained opposition, the Interahamwe were by and large cowards armed with machetes and axes, who fled when faced by superior firepower'.[78] Dallaire complained, 'even though Kigali was crawling with elite foreign forces, no nation was interested in reinforcing us.'[79] This observation was not lost on the Tutsi, who believed the West had simply abandoned them, whilst the Hutu were encouraged by the West's apparent indifference to the massacres of Rwandans. The extent of Western apathy was openly demonstrated by Robert Dole, the US Republican Leader of the Senate on CBS television, the day after the evacuations: 'I don't think we have any national interest here, I hope we don't get involved there. I don't think we will. The Americans are out. As far as I'm concerned, in Rwanda that ought to be the end of it.'[80] As the killings escalated into genocide and the massacres continued, the Belgian government succumbed to national pressure and withdrew their peace keepers from UNAMIR. This had an immediate effect: the Interahamwe murdered two thousand Tutsi taking refuge in a school that had been under the direct protection of a Belgian contingent. The troops had simply abandoned their task in order to make the plane at Kigali.

But why was Western indifference so marked? As already demonstrated,

---

78 F. Keane, *Op. Cit.*, p. 108.
79 R. Dallaire, *Op. Cit.*, p. 284.
80 L. Melvern, *Op. Cit.*, p. 148.

the initial reluctance was caused by the lead nations claiming over-commitment to ongoing peace support operations in Yugoslavia. The Balkans, situated on Europe's doorstep, were of greater strategic importance and commanded greater resources. The US had been humiliated by offensive peace operations in Somalia and it was instrumental in influencing the reluctance to commit money and resources to what it viewed as an 'age-old ethnic hatred'.[81] President Clinton, in an address to the UN in September 1993, said that 'the UN must learn to say no', 'ask hard questions' before deploying peace keepers and realise that it 'cannot become engaged in every one of the world's conflicts'.[82] Shortly thereafter, the US issued Presidential Decision Directive 25 (PDD-25) which formally detailed sixteen stringent factors that the US government would consider if required either to vote on peace operations in the UN Security Council or commit US Forces to participation in operations.[83] This PDD was constructed as a direct result of public opinion after the deaths of US servicemen in Mogadishu. As the situation in Rwanda worsened, the reluctance of Western nations to become involved increased commensurately because the physical risks to troops and financial commitment became greater, the withdrawal strategy became more uncertain and the military task increasingly blurred.

Running parallel to this aversion to getting involved were the misconstrued messages being portrayed by the media. The perception that the Rwandan killings were the direct result of an ethnic conflict, seemingly gave credence to the Western reluctance to commit. Roger Winter, the director of the US Committee for Refugees, recently returned from Rwanda, desperate to change this perception wrote an article 'outlining the political nature of the violence, a plot by extremists devised to retain power, using ethnicity to achieve its aims'. The report was rejected by all the major US part of researchs, including the Washington Post and New York Times.[84] Dallaire desperately tried to generate greater media interest on the ground but was largely thwarted; the number of reporters in Rwanda during the genocide never increased above 15, yet in South Africa, in early May, there were 2500.[85] An international investigation into media activities after the genocide, criticised the press for

81 Bill Berkeley, *Op. Cit.*, p. 8.
82 M. Leitenberg, *Op. Cit.*, p. 7/8.
83 *Ibid.*
84 L. Melvern, *Op. Cit.*, p. 138.
85 *Ibid.*, p. 178.

'being fundamentally irresponsible by failing to report that genocide was taking place, and thereby generate public pressure for something to be done to stop it, [and thus] contributing to international indifference and inaction, and possibly to the crime itself'.[86]

The crux of responsibility for denying that genocide was occurring however must rest with the UN. By consistently avoiding the issue of mass killings by concentrating on the issue of civil war and the means of restoring the Rwandan ceasefire, they abdicated their moral responsibility to respond on humanitarian grounds. The Czech ambassador to the UN observed, 'It was scandalous that the UN spent 80% of council efforts discussing the withdrawal of peacekeepers and 20% trying to get a ceasefire in the civil war. It was rather like wanting Hitler to reach a ceasefire with the Jews'.[87] Despite the obvious humanitarian crisis, the first time that the UN High Commissioner of Human Rights visited Rwanda was not until early May – nearly three months into the killings.

Inevitably, the genocide continued unabated. The UN, despite stirrings of interest, remained largely impotent. UNAMIR was not reinforced: troop levels at one stage fell to 503 when the mandate had detailed for 4600. The remaining peace keepers made valiant attempts to protect the general population but, despite individual acts of heroism, they were unable to prevent the mass killings from spreading. The Tutsi led RPF had by now managed to move into Rwanda, many units conducting revenge killings as they advanced, and they gradually forced the Hutu forces into Kigali. The UN, seemingly paralysed by inaction, eventually approved the national deployment of a French intervention force known as Operation Turquoise. This operation was not without controversy, with suspicions being raised over France's motives and her strong patronage of the (now losing) Hutu; nevertheless the deployment was ultimately welcomed, as it would stop the killing. Operating, ironically, under a Chapter VII (Peace Enforcement) mandate the 2500 strong force was comprised of elite Legionnaires, Commandos and Special Forces. They were accompanied by armoured vehicles, helicopters, communications and fighter aircraft. As Dallaire observed, if UNAMIR had been provided with a fraction of those resources

86 *Ibid.*, p. 138.
87 *Ibid.*, p. 179.

in the first place the Rwandan genocide might never have happened.[88]

Conclusion

The genocide in Rwanda was a humanitarian tragedy of immense proportion. In an era of mass communication and instantaneous news, it remains almost unbelievable that so many people could be killed, so violently and so quickly, whilst the International system's most powerful organisations did nothing and the majority of the world's population remained unaware of what was happening. As this essay has proven, the genocide was planned, in careful detail, in order to retain political control and status. It was not an ancient tribal conflict, but a bitter and violent power struggle that used ethnicity as a tool for murder to achieve that power. The West failed both to predict and prevent the genocide. Its belated acceptance of culpability disguises the extent to which the UN ignored its moral responsibility to the people of Rwanda.

The form of apartheid introduced by colonialism elevated the supposed superiority of the Tutsi and created a Hutu permanent underclass, based on ethnic classification. Western apathy in confronting the perpetrators of subsequent violence and the lack of legal accountability did nothing to discourage the killings. Anger and resentment grew and when the ruling elite were faced with the loss of their autonomy, through Western style democratisation, the planning for genocide commenced. Increased ethnic tension was therefore a consequence of political conflict, not its cause.[89] Fear was used as a tool of control to exploit the insecurity of the masses, provide political legitimacy and create hate, which was eventually expressed through genocide. On an individual level, this fear was manifested on three separate levels: fear of Tutsi persecution, fear of extremist retribution and fear of losing out.

Western responses were poorly scoped, lacklustre and largely inadequate. As Dallaire himself observed, 'In UN terms, the mission was to be small,

88 R. Dallaire, *Op. Cit.*, p. 449.
89 Bill Berkeley, *Op. Cit.*, p. 15.

cheap, short and sweet'.[90] The original mandate was quickly proven to be insufficient but, almost inexplicably, never revised despite repeated attempts by the UNAMIR Commander. The void of strategic leadership within the UN and lack of International political will ensured that, despite valiant tactical level endeavours, the operation was bound to failure as extremists became emboldened by Western apathy.

Lack of resources and mandate constraints prohibited any meaningful form of preventative action and the warning signs of impending disaster were repeatedly missed. The fear and anxiety that permeated through Rwandan society were never acknowledged or challenged, despite years of conflict neither the structure, nor the tools of genocide, were effectively targeted or neutralised before it was too late. There were sufficient numbers of well trained and fully resourced Western troops in Rwanda to stop the genocide during the evacuation process, but shamefully they were extracted once Western interests were satisfied. These troops could have prevented further killings, but they were withdrawn because the lead member countries, motivated by self-interest, would not sanction any further UN commitment to a marginal ranking African state.

One of the greatest failings of the West was the denial of genocide by the media and more importantly by the UN. This ultimately relieved the West of the obligation to intervene and allowed it to avoid its responsibilities under International law. These renunciations of genocide were orchestrated by the lead 5 nations who, pre-occupied with their notions of civil war, repeatedly influenced the assessments of the Security Council - the US and the UK even insisted on the removal of the word 'genocide' from intelligence reports. The continued Western indifference at the strategic level and the ongoing failings of UNAMIR in Rwanda, ultimately allowed the genocide to escalate into one of the worst crimes against humanity in modern history.

---

90 R. Dallaire, *Op. Cit.*, p. 89.

Chapter VII
Challenges in Rebuilding Military in a Post Conflict State

Introduction

Since the end of the Cold War, the world has been confronted with new threats to international peace and security which have disrupted national institutions in some countries. These threats which are closely linked to human security are associated with poverty, population explosion, environmental degradation, infectious disease and intra-state civil wars. This has created new challenges of peace building across the globe. Throughout the twentieth century, the concept of world security had been influenced by the realistic thinking which equated it to state security.[1] In the new context, security issues have to be tackled beyond the confines of the state. One commentator has observed that the ending of the Cold War has created "a remarkable fluidity and openness whereby security concerns transcend geographical labels".[2] Unlike in the past where emphasis was put on military security, today's security is taken to be about "the pursuit of freedom from threat and the ability of states and societies to maintain their independent identity and their functional integrity against forces of change".[3]

These changes in global security have adversely affected poor nations, especially in Sub-Saharan Africa. African states have been weakened further by the forces of globalization that have swept the entire globe. According to Mittelman, "Contemporary globalization is a world wide phenomenon which is a coalescence of varied transnational processes and domestic structures, allowing the economy, politics, culture and ideology of one

---

1 Laurent Goetschel, "Globalization and Security: the challenge of collective action in a politically fragmented world," *Global society*, Vol. 14, No. 2, 2000, p. 262.

2 Barry Buzan, "New Patterns of Global security in the Twenty–First Century," *International Affairs*, Vol. 67, 1991, p. 432.

3 *Ibid.*

country to penetrate another".[4] This rapid spread of globalization has had some catastrophic effects on some African states resulting from increasing levels of poverty and violent conflict. Robert Orr is right to observe that "Violent internal conflict often lead to a sudden collapse of state institutions, sometimes accompanied by dissolution of a stable political consensus".[5] The military institution which has been a key player in these internal conflicts in Africa has emerged weaker or even in worse cases disintegrated.

The purpose of this essay is to discuss the challenges of rebuilding military institutions in a post conflict situation in Sub Saharan Africa. The essay shall identify common factors in African states which have affected institution building in general which shall give it a theoretical framework. Then, a comparative study of Uganda, Namibia and Mozambique shall be made in order to illustrate the similarities and differences of the challenges faced while rebuilding their military institutions. These three countries have been selected for two reasons; the first one is the level of external support they got mainly from the international community. Whereas Namibia and Mozambique were heavily supported by the international community while rebuilding their militaries, Uganda did not get the same support, at least in the initial period. This could be attributed to the Cold War which was still raging when Uganda embarked on rebuilding her military in 1986. The second reason is based on the nature of the conflicts that these countries were involved which culminated in the break down of their military institutions. Whereas Namibia's conflict was an anti-colonial struggle that resulted in gaining political independence, Uganda's and Mozambique's conflicts were internal civil wars that broke out during the post independence period.

The essay is divided into four sections. Section one is concerned with theoretical framework of challenges of institution re-building. Section two discusses the sources of violent conflict in Sub Saharan Africa. In section three, a comparison has been made of the experiences of rebuilding military institutions in the three countries. Section four is the conclusion

---

4 James H. Mittelman, "The globalization challenge: Surviving at the margins," *Third World Quarterly*, Vol. 15, No. 3, 1994, p. 428.

5 Robert C. Orr, *The United States as Nation Builder: Facing the challenge of post – conflict Reconstruction*, in Robert C. Orr, ed., Winning the peace, An American Strategy for post conflict Reconstruction, Washington D.C. ,Joint CSIS/AUSA, project publishers, 2004, p. 8.

which will show the differences and similarities of the challenges faced by the three countries. The interplay of both local and international players in contemporary post conflict reconstruction in today's globalized world has become a reality. An analysis of this interaction in the countries under study has been made in order to assess its impact on rebuilding the military institution.

Actions Taken

Huntington believes that some institutions in Africa are illegitimate to the political process they claim to support. He singled out the military and argued that,

> The legitimate exercise of political power by elected politicians is a chief feature of the Western model. Colonial rule was, on the other hand, characterized by the forceful exercise of illegitimate power. In this context, the colonial military was merely the armed wing of the colonial state.... European colonialists' claims that they groomed an apolitical military for the Successor post-colonial states of Africa were insincere protestations.[6]

John M. Mbaku has put the blame for these failed institutions on colonial rulers. He has argued that;

> .... colonial laws and institutions were not the results of voluntary agreements entered into by the people of the colonies, but structures designed by the Europeans and imposed on the African peoples..... Basically, colonial institutional arrangements were designed to maximize European entrepreneurial activities and severely restrict African participation in economic and political markets.[7]

Much as it is true that colonialism distorted the development of institutions in Africa, African leaders could have made an effort to reconstruct them. Mbaku has equally not spared them the blame when he describes them as,

---

6 S. P. Huntington, *The Soldier and the state*, (Massachusetts: The Belknap Press of Harvard University, 1967), p. 232.

7 John M. Mbaku, *A balance sheet of structural adjustment in Africa: Towards a sustainable development agenda*, in J. M. Mbaku, ed., preparing Africa for the twenty first Century, Ashgate publishing company, p. 120.

"The opportunistic post-independence elites who turned these governance structures into instruments of plunder for their own benefit."[8] The blame for the inappropriate institutions in Africa lies with initially the European colonialists and then the African leaders after attaining independence.

The failure of African institutions can be traced from the nature and character of the nation state that Sub Saharan African countries inherited at Independence. Almost without exception, all the boundaries of African states were arbitrarily drawn following geographical features. This resulted in bringing together under one administration people of different ethnic background, history, as well as levels of political and economic development. This resulted in disjointedness and lack of political, economic and cultural harmony. Unless this arbitrariness of the nation states is addressed, there is not much progress expected in reconstructing post conflict institutions. This is because, as Caroline Thomas has correctly observed, "the growth of the nation and the state in Africa did not coincide in the way they had come to do in Europe".[9] She goes ahead to illustrate the European experience;

> The coincidence of nation and state in Europe is generally regarded as providing the model for statehood, since it assumes bounded territories, social homogeneity and the monopolization of violence by a single centre....The European pattern developed over several centuries in a conflictual and competitive international environment .The process was slow, and the vast majority of states disappeared.[10]

In light of Thomas's observation, it is high time Africa started addressing this disjointedness. They do not have to take the same path which Europe took in order to work out appropriate models for statehood. For example there is need to redraw some of the colonial boundaries. This is going to be an uphill task given that the contemporary international system does not support the redrawing of boundaries except in very rare cases.

Liberal democracy which has been prescribed to most of the third world countries by western governments as a necessary condition for development

---

8 *Ibid.*, p. 119.

9 Thomas C., *New directions in thinking about security in the Third World*, in Thomas Caroline and K. Booth, eds., *New Thinking about Strategy and international security*, (London: Harpen Colline, 1991), p. 269.

10 *Ibid.*

may not solve some of the pressing problems in Sub Saharan Africa because of different historical experiences. That is why Buzan has noted that, "Experience strongly suggests that state-building is a tricky, difficult, long term and violent business under any circumstances – especially so for poorly placed and poorly endowed late comers under pressure to conform naturally by more powerful states in the international system".[11]

Following the end of Cold War, the restructured international system which is now multipolar with United States retaining military superiority is advocating for reforms in all national institutions of developing nations. This has posed a number of challenges to many African institutions because of the demands put to them. For instance, the requirement to restructure their institutions so that they can enhance citizens' participation in national development is new to them. This calls for among other things the adoption of new security sector reforms which are aimed at changing the pattern of civil-military relations which for a long time had been shaped by the Cold War ideological rivalry, among other things. They also call for cutting military expenditures in order to utilize the saved funds for social and economic development. Some of these reforms have not adequately addressed security concerns of young nations.

Sources of Violent Conflict in Sub-Saharan Africa

The widespread poverty that has affected all Sub Saharan African countries is associated with violent conflict. Recent studies have shown that there is a close relationship between poverty and armed conflict. A World Bank study has revealed that in Sub Saharan Africa, where most of the devastating conflicts have occurred, more than 250 million people were living below the poverty line in the mid- 1990s.[12] World Bank data showed the regional growth rate in gross national product (GNP) per capita as -1.1 percent between the period 1985 and 1995. Earlier in 1981, the same bank had issued a report highlighting Africa's deteriorating economic conditions.[13]

---

11 Barry Buzan, "New Patterns of Global security in the Twenty–First Century," *International Affairs,* Vol. 67, 1991, p. 440.

12 M. J. Mbaku, *Op. Cit.*, p. 126.

13 *Ibid.*, P 126

Ethnicity is also another major cause of conflict in different states in Africa. European colonial rule brought within the fold of one country peoples at different levels of social development. They also split nationalities into or among several countries as we have mentioned. The incorporation of different ethnic groups under the same rule would not have been a problem in itself had it not been for the antagonisms that were exploited by the Europeans. In the 1960s, the newly independent African states inherited these boundaries. The conflicts which have erupted as a result of this arbitrary arrangement have been more widespread in the early 1990s. Examples include wars in the following countries: Northern Uganda, Rwanda, Sudan, the Democratic Republic of Congo just to mention a few.

Ethnic tensions have permeated government institutions including the military sometimes on the instigation of political elites. This has resulted in the military being violent and brutal toward civilians. It should be recalled that the military training that the colonial authorities gave to Africans was to prepare them to deal with fellow citizens who would rebel against the colonial set up. Parsons has brought this out clearly in the case of the British when he noted that,

> ...for Kenya and Uganda, the colonial army's primary mission was internal security. Yet the regiment was not a police force; its paramount peacetime function was to intimidate potential African opponents of the colonial regime.[14]

That is why they emphasized that certain areas should be reserved as recruitment zones for the military. Upon completion of training, they would be deployed in areas outside their home areas.[15] In Ghana, 60% of the colonial army at the time of independence had to be recruited from the northern nationalities. In Nigeria, the Hausa dominated the colonial army; in Sierra Leone, it was the Northern Karankos, the Mandingos, the Fula and the Limbe. In Uganda, the Nubian, the Acholi and the Langi.[16] This factor has had a negative impact in almost all the above mentioned countries.

---

14 Timonthy Parsons, *The African Rank-And-File, Social Implications of Colonial Military Service in the King's African Riflle, 1902-1964*, (Portsmouth: Hienemann, 1999), p. 2.

15 A. Omara-Otunnu, *Politics and The Military in Uganda, 1890 – 1979*, (London: McMillan Press LTD, 1987), p. 24.

16 L. Kuper and Smith M. G. (1969), p. 28.

During the immediate post colonial period, some of the ruling elites used the military to acquire and retain power undemocratically. They found it easy to do this because most of the African militaries which were inherited from the former colonial powers were dominated by uneducated people. Parsons does not put total blame on the British for this anomaly of recruiting only illiterates into the army especially given that men with proper educational qualifications were not easy to find. He argues that the few educated men would be attracted to private employers who offered higher pay and more comfortable working conditions.[17] At the risk of contradicting himself, he adds that "Many officers believed education and affluence spoilt potential soldiers and were unequivocal in their preference for 'illiterate savages' "[18] This was deliberately designed so that this institution could play a repressive role against the local people as we have observed.

Abuse of human rights by dictatorial and repressive governments in Sub Saharan Africa has also been a major cause of conflict. The Cold War period was conducive for the rise of a number of dictators in the Third World. Within the first ten years of attainment of political independence, a number of African states witnessed the rise to power of dictators, such as Idi Amin of Uganda, Bokassa of Central African Republic, Mobutu of former Zaire, Siadi Barre of Somalia. All these dictators and many others grossly violated their citizens' rights and freedoms with impunity. Apart from the extra judicial killings that were rampant, there was no respect of civil liberties and there was lack of freedom of association and assembly. The rule of law and democratic governance were totally lacking. In Southern Africa, the situation was made worse by the apartheid system in South Africa which brutalized the black Africans in the whole region.

From the 1960s to the late 1980s, it became South Africa's policy to destabilize all the neighbouring independent African states either by supporting insurgent groups or by outright invasion as in Namibia. By so doing, they hoped to deny military and political bases to different groups that were opposed to apartheid rule. Some of the violent conflicts that have erupted in most of the states that were under dictatorial rule during and after

17 Timothy Parsons, *Op. Cit.*, p. 87.

18 *Ibid.*, p. 54.

the Cold War were liberation struggles aimed at overthrowing dictatorships and establishment of democratic rule.[19]

Most of the wars that have erupted in Sub Sahara Africa since the end of the Cold War have been intra state in nature. They have had a negative impact not only on institutions of the state but also on innocent civilians. For example in 1996 alone, 14 of the 53 countries of Africa were afflicted by armed conflicts, which accounted for more than half of all war related death world wide.[20] There has also been destruction of property, displacement of persons resulting in refugee outflows and massive immigrations. All these have resulted in severe disruption of economic and political progress.

Uganda, Namibia, and Mozambique: Their Experiences

Like almost all African armies, Uganda's was a colonial inheritance which has been refashioned from the British officered King's African Rifles (K.A.R.). Immediately after the British established a colonial foothold in Uganda, they embarked on the 'pacification' of all tribes that did not cooperate with their administration. To accomplish this job, they first used the Swahili and Indian soldiers whom they had brought from the East African coast. They also utilized Sudanese soldiers left behind by Emin Pasha. These soldiers proved to be unreliable because of the mutiny of 1897. Thereafter, a decision was made to disband these forces and recruit the local people. In the early period of colonial rule in Uganda, the Baganda played a leading role in pacifying the rest of Uganda. Their performance in combat impressed the head of the British colonial administration so much so that in one of his dispatches to London he recommended to his superiors thus, "I have much pleasure in adding my personal testimony as to their excellent work, which is deserving of substantial recognition. I have accordingly included in the medal rolls the names of certain chiefs and others who have most distinguished themselves, as deserving the medal, a mark of approval which they greatly appreciate".[21]

---

19 *Ibid.*, p. 430.

20 K. Annan, *The Causes of Conflict and the promotion of durable peace and sustainable development in Africa*, Report of the Secretary General, 1998.

21 W. Lloyd-Jones, *K.A.R. Being an un official account of the origin and activities of the Kings African Rifles*, (London: J.W. Arrow Smith Ltd., 1926).

Initially, it had been envisaged that the operations of the K.A.R would only be limited to fighting and subduing the 'stubborn' tribes that were resisting colonial rule. The outbreak of the first World War in 1914 forced the Colonialists to deploy them against the German Imperial forces in Eastern Africa as Lloyd- Jones has observed

> Although the K.A.R. were certainly never intended or expected to take part in anything but localized operations against a savage, or at most a Semi – Savage, enemy, Fate called upon them to play a leading role in the defense of the British Dependencies and the offensive movements which finally led to the surrender of the German Imperial forces in Eastern Africa.[22]

Bartlett has contested this view by saying that "the provisional regulations contained a warning that battalions of the K.A.R. could be called upon to serve anywhere, and might meet an enemy more sophiscated than the 'native' tribes".[23] In fact, he goes ahead to point out that the regulations of the K.A.R. which were issued in 1905 were very clear on the relationship between the military and civil authorities. He wrote,

> The separation of civil and military authority and the subordination of the latter were emphasized. As Commanders –in- Chief, H. M. Commissioners were responsible for defining the object and scope of military operations, but not for undertaking their immediate direction. Military authority was never to be exercised in opposition to, or in competition with, that of the civil power.[24]

Volten's recent study has revealed that "The military institutions of any society are shaped by two forces: a functional imperative stemming from the threats to the society's security and a societal imperative arising from the social forces, ideologies and institutions dominant within the society..."[25] Arguably, we can say that the function of the colonial Army in Uganda and

---

22 *Ibid.*, p. 171.

23 Moyse Bartlett, *The King's African Rifles*, (London: Gale and Polden, 1956), p. 130.

24 *Ibid.*

25 Peter M. E. Volten, *New approaches to Security Studies, implications for Civil – Military Relations in Theory and Practice*, in George Cristian Maior and Larry Watts, eds., *Globalization of Civil – Military Relations: Democratization,Rreform and Security*, (Bucharest: Enciclopeca Publishing House, 2002), pp. 315-316.

beyond was to defend British colonial interests. These interests included raw materials for British industries and a market for their finished products. Anything that threatened these interests had to be confronted with maximum force. During colonial rule, the character of the Ugandan Army was shaped by the defence of these interests. This also, shaped the pattern of civil-military relations which made the army subordinated to the colonial authorities.

Following the mutiny of 1897, it became a colonial policy to draft troops from ethnic, geographical and religious backgrounds different from those of the people among whom they were to be deployed. The practice of recruiting troops on ethnic and linguistic criteria thus became entrenched in the process of building the Ugandan Army. The Baganda who had replaced the Indian, Sudanese and Swahili troops eventually were to be replaced by the Northern tribes of Acholi, Langi and Lugbara of West Nile region because the British colonial masters thought that they possessed the required "martial qualities".[26] As a result, the majority of the troops who were enlisted from the northern peripheral areas, where formal education was almost non existent, were illiterates.

When political independence was fast approaching, the colonial administration saw the need for africanisation of the Officer Corps in the Ugandan Army. All along, it had been a policy for the K.A.R. to be officered by the British in East Africa. When the africanisation of the Officer Corps started, promotion was based on seniority. Naturally, it was the long serving but poorly educated men who became officers. Those people who were commissioned to officer ranks prior to independence in 1962 rapidly rose in ranks and occupied senior positions in the army within a period of less than ten years. For instance, Shaban Opolot and Idi Amin who were commissioned as lieutenants on 11 August 1961, were already Generals by 1966 and the former was the Army Commander while the latter was his deputy. Until the advent of the National Resistance Army (NRA) in 1986, the Ugandan Army had remained largely rooted in the traditions of the colonial experience

Those who took over power from the British in 1962 had the opportunity

26 Samwiri Lwanga Lunyigo, *The Colonial Roots of Internal Conflict,* in Kuper L. and Smith M. G., eds., *Pluralism in Africa*, (Berkeley and Los Angeles : University of Carlifornia Press, 1969), p. 30.

of reversing this trend but they did not. This was after the army mutinied in 1964, demanding an increase in pay. Similar incidents also happened in Kenya and Tanzania but the response of these administrations were different to that of Uganda. President Nyerere decided to dismiss the leaders and ordered the arrest of all those who were involved in the mutiny, as did his counter part in Kenya whereas in Uganda the leadership decided to appease the men in uniform by increasing their pay. As if this was not bad enough, in 1966 Prime Minister Milton Obote decided to use the army to suppress his political opponents. The 1966 Buganda crisis was a result of a disagreement between Obote and Sir Edward Mutesa who was the King of Buganda and at the same time the President of the Republic of Uganda. Obote responded by deploying troops to attack the King of Buganda at his palace in Kampala. This incident was a turning point in the political history of Uganda for it marked the beginning of the military's involvement in civil – Political matters. Right from that period, the civil–military relations in Uganda deteriorated very fast and this is blamed on Uganda's national leaders.

The climax of this deterioration was Idi Amin's take over of power in January 1971.The forces that brought Amin to power were both internal and external. The internal ones were due to the political tensions which had led to the political leadership to use the army to solve purely political problems. There was also tension between the small number of Sandhurst– trained men, mostly young officers and educated southerners and the majority of the Northerners with little or no education, promoted to senior ranks.

The external forces behind the coup were linked to the Cold War which was prevailing at the time. The Obote government had decided to adopt a socialist/communist economic programme after abrogating the 1962 independence constitution. His programme was contained in a document entitled "First steps for Uganda to move to the left", and it proposed to strengthen the public and cooperative sectors of the economy. This explains why Idi Amin's coming to power was welcomed in Western circles.

The gross violation of human rights by Idi Amin's regime has been well documented. During his period in power the military was dominated by people who hailed from his home area, particularly from Kakwa, Lugbara and the Nubian tribes. His regime was eventually overthrown by a combined force of Tanzanian Military and Ugandan exiles in 1979. The Ugandan Army disintegrated and a new one had to be rebuilt starting from scratch. The leadership of the new army which was called Uganda National Liberation Army (UNLA) was dominated by the Luo speakers from Northern Uganda.

The period following the overthrow of Idi Amin's regime was characterized by political instability which was not conducive for building a viable military institution. After the disputed elections of 1980, Obote became president again. To consolidate his rule, he enforced a monopoly of the armed forces by the ruling political party. The military got involved in violations of human rights which involved killing innocent civilians especially in the southern part of the country where Obote was unpopular. Around the same time, Yoweri Museveni launched a guerrilla war against the Obote government which was based in central Uganda using the National Resistance Army (NRA).This guerrilla struggle culminated in the capture of state power in January 1986. Museveni's army, the NRA was also biased in favour of Southern and Western Uganda and most of the combatants who captured power in 1986 were not professional soldiers.

From 1986 onwards attempts have been made to rebuild the military institution so that it becomes national in character and outlook. This is the post conflict period that has witnessed the amalgamation of different fighting forces, downsizing of that force involving demobilization; reintegration of forces in civilian life; and recruitment, training and equipping of a new force.

Before the NRA captured power in 1986, it had started absorbing the forces that were on the opposite side which included government forces and rebels that had been fighting the Obote government. It should be remembered that it was not only the NRA which was fighting the Obote government. Other groups included Uganda Freedom Movement (UFM), Former Uganda National Army (FUNA), and Uganda National Rescue Front (UNRF). After retraining, all these groups were merged with NRA to form the new national army. The training and educational programmes that were conducted were designed to instill patriotic and nationalistic feelings which helped to bring the required *espirit de corps*. Right from 1986, political education has been emphasized along side the teaching of other military science subjects like field craft and skills at arms while training raw recruits and officers.

Another factor which made the Ugandan situation peculiar was that the

NRA which had succeeded in defeating government forces was the one responsible for integrating the other forces. They therefore made sure that anybody who wanted to join them must do so on their terms. Right from its inception, the NRA was a guerrilla force fighting for political objectives, which they continued upholding even after the capture of power in 1986. Farley was partly right to observe that:

> NRA was itself in some senses a 'democratic' movement: it was not an army of soldiers drawn from previous Ugandan armies (at least before 1986); it was composed of volunteers from civilian life and recruited more numbers as it progressed through the country. Its 'officers' did not hold ranks or have badges of office.[27]

It is true that many men and women who joined NRA did not have a professional military background, but it is erroneous to say that there was nobody who joined NRA having served in the previous Ugandan army. Quite a big number defected from the government forces (UNLA) and joined the NRA and these were the ones who took up command positions.

The biggest challenge has been the professionalization of this force by ensuring that it becomes neutral and non partisan after capturing power and reintegrating other forces from different backgrounds. From 1986 up to 1995, the NRA was heavily involved in national political work which even required the appointment of serving army officers to cabinet ministerial positions and other public service jobs. Up to now the army has representatives in the National Parliament. This has always been a point of contention among the opposition groups who feel that this compromises its neutrality. The government position has been that the Army should continue to be in parliament because it is good for civil-military relations given the country's history. This was more so during the period of transition when national reconciliation, reconstruction and constitution making were the priority tasks. Political party activities were suspended in order to form a broad based government which would heal the past divisions. In one of his first public addresses to the army after capturing state power in 1986, President Museveni defended its involvement in politics thus;

---

27 Oliver Furley, *Democratisation in Uganda*, (London: Research Institute for the Study of Conflict and Terrorism), 1998, p. 1.

> Yesterday, I was talking to some elders, some of them UPC supporters, and I explained to them that our line is to take all Ugandans as one, and to regard every Ugandan as equal to all other Ugandans. The largest part of the political work was done by you. If you had made errors, my words would have been meaningless.[28]

This involvement of the Army in politics was given a legal backing which was contained in the legal notice No.1 of 1986 which established the National Resistance Movement government. It provided that "The National Resistance Council and the National Resistance Army shall participate in the discussion, adoption and promulgation of the Constitution". This provision was vehemently opposed by other political groups who felt that the Army was not impartial and so did not have the right to participate in the deliberations of the constitution making exercise. One of the opposition parties stated its position thus:

> The Uganda Peoples Congress (UPC) does not recognize or accept that the NRC and the NRA are the legitimate and impartial organs to deliberate, adopt and promulgate a National Constitution for the people of Uganda. The UPC shall only recognize and accept a constitution deliberated upon, adopted and promulgated by a constituent assembly: Composed of representatives who have been freely elected from all parts of Uganda.[29]

However, after the promulgation of the 1995 Uganda Constitution, the roles of the Ugandan Army which had changed its name from NRA to Uganda Peoples' Defense Forces (UPDF) were clearly spelt out as follows:

> Preserve and defend the sovereignty and territorial integrity of Uganda.
> Cooperate with civil authority in emergency situations and in case of natural disasters.
> Foster harmony and understanding between the defence forces and civilians.
> Engage in productive activities for the development of Uganda.

These constitutional provisions helped to focus the Ugandan military on its path to professionalism. Since the promulgation of the 1995 Constitution the UPDF has taken a number of steps which have transformed it from a

28 Y. K. Museveni, *The path of Liberation: A selection of President Yoweri,* Museveni's Speeches, Kampala, 1989 p. 49.

29 Oliver Furley and James Katalikawe, (1999), p. 3.

predominantly guerrilla force to a modern professional army. The Uganda Defence Reform Program (UDRP) which was launched in 2001, The Comprehensive Defence Bill of 2002 which became an Act of Parliament in 2005, and the UK-funded Uganda Defense Efficiency Study (UDES) are some of the milestones that have transformed the UPDF.

The demobilization of the Ugandan force which was commonly known as Reduction in Force (RIF) in 1993 was a big challenge that the government had to cope with. This program was imposed on the Ugandan Government by the donors, led by the World Bank (WB). This was aimed at making savings which were used to support other sectors of the economy. According to the World Bank analysis,[30] military expenditure as a proportion of recurrent expenditure peaked at 46.3% in 1991 financial year. This was seen as an astronomical figure which had to be reduced. 30,000 soldiers were demobilized and resettled in civilian life with financial support from the WB. The exercise of resettlement was spread out for a period of four years and initially it appeared to be working. No sooner had the international donors started applauding the Ugandan experience which they recommended to other African governments, than the security situation in Western and Northern Uganda deteriorated. These security concerns forced the government to remobilize the ex – combatants and they were quickly deployed to fight insurgency.

Another challenge that confronted the Ugandan Military Force as it emerged from conflict was the spread of the killer disease HIV/AIDS. This deadly disease greatly devastated the army in the late 1980s when most of the top commanders started dying at an alarming rate. This disease equally affected the rank and file. The Government had to respond by launching a public campaign that sensitized not only the soldiers but the general public as well. Uganda has made significant progress in the fight against AIDS to the extent that it is no longer as big a threat to the force as ten years ago.

The problem of lack of adequate resources to support the military forces in the execution of their constitutional duties has consistently hampered service delivery. Since 1987, the Government of Uganda has embraced the IMF and WB's structural adjustment programme. Through this program, the donors

30 World Bank Discussion Part of research No.331.

have insisted on the government's reduction of public expenditure if it is to continue benefiting from donor funding. The Ministry of Defense has been among those ministries that have been forced not to spend beyond the ceiling of two percent of GDP. Much as this donor supported structural adjustment program has led to Uganda's rapid growth in certain sectors, it has affected the security sector negatively. The unending insurgency situation in the north of the country and the increased small arms trafficking in north-eastern Uganda can partly be blamed on it.

The challenge of small arms proliferation in the Great Lakes Region affects the UPDF directly and requires a lot of resources to combat it. A lot of stockpiles of weapons that found their way to this part of Africa during the Cold War are still controlled by non state actors who use them to cause insecurity. Kathi is correct to observe that;

> Since the end of the Cold War, the Great Lakes region of Africa – an area that includes Rwanda, Burundi, Uganda, Tanzania and Democratic Republic of Congo has experienced an unstoppable flow of small arms and light weapons. This has contributed to the rising tide of militarization and conflict with a corresponding decrease in human security.[31]

Regional and international efforts which have been put in place to address this problem are beginning to produce positive results like the ending of three major conflicts in Burundi, DRC and the Sudan. A lasting solution to this problem lies in concerted efforts to tackle the underlying causes of armed conflicts which make the acquisition of small arms an attractive option. Poverty eradication will contribute greatly in addressing this challenge.

Efforts for UPDF to join hands with the rest of the Eastern African forces to address these challenges are already in place. The instruments establishing the East African Standby Brigade have already been endorsed by Uganda. UPDF will be contributing troops very soon which will be deployed in Peace Support Operations. UPDF has also been active in regional integration efforts to address security issues. Prominent among these has been the East African

---

31 Kathi Austin, *Light Weapons and Conflict in the Great Lakes Region of Africa*, in Jeffrey Boutwell and Michael T. Klare, eds., *Light Weapons and Civil Conflict, Controlling the tools of Violence*, (Boston: Rowman and Littlefield Publishers, 1999), p. 29.

Community (EAC) and the Inter Governmental Authority on Development (IGAD) whose efforts are geared towards conflict prevention and promoting economic development. These regional organizations are also addressing conflicts emanating from environmental degradation. Uganda has had to grapple with this security threat especially in the north-eastern part of the country among the Karimajong pastoral communities. The decrease in grazing grounds and watering places for their animals has resulted in violent inter tribal conflicts which spill across the Uganda-Kenya and Uganda-Sudan borders.

The changing roles and missions of the military in Uganda have come with big challenges to the UPDF. There is now an urgent need to attract and recruit educated men and women who will be trained with a different mind set that encompasses the broader spectrum of security. Higher management of the military will require people with higher education and advanced military training to be able to deal with issues related to accountability, planning and allocation of resources. To retain and develop the quality of manpower required has continued to be a challenge because of the need to absorb former rebel groups who in most cases lack the necessary qualifications. Some times this is done at the expense of quality because failure to do it may result in more conflicts. There are no incentives to attract educated people into the military because of low pay and poor terms and conditions of service. If UPDF is to be transformed into a modern and professional force, attracting people with advanced education and technical skills will be a prerequisite.

Namibia became a German colony following the Berlin Conference of 1884-85. The advent of colonial conquest heralded an era of land confiscation from Africans and the imposition of the capitalist mode of production by force. The cruel and brutal methods adopted by the Germans and their collaborators soon provoked African resistance. The period of German rule of Namibia was short lived because of the outbreak of World War I in 1914. After the war South Africa got a formal authorization from the League of Nations to administer it. South African control of South West Africa which later came to be called Namibia increased the number of white settlers and introduced there the apartheid system. This system continued even after World War II although most UN members condemned it.

This state of affairs attracted renewed resistance starting in 1950s. Some of the militant resistance groups which were formed around this time to fight South African rule included South West African National Union (SWANU), South West African People's Organization (SWAPO) and Ovambo land people's organization. Eventually, SWAPO launched an armed struggle which attracted a lot of sympathy and support both locally and internationally. SWAPO's protracted struggle lasted for almost thirty years before the South African government would grant them independence. Pisani has correctly observed that "The Namibian State took shape against the background of a triple inheritance; colonialism, apartheid and liberation".[32] In the same vein, the Namibian military was shaped by a diversity of historical and political factors stemming from the above triple inheritance. Prior to attainment of political independence, a decision was made by the UN Security Council to demobilize all armed groups. Thus, the Namibian Defense Force (NDF) was formed immediately after independence by carrying out a fresh recruitment exercise of both civilians and former soldiers.

The support that Namibia received from the international community and some western countries in rebuilding her institutions was very crucial. The rebuilding of the military benefited immensely from this external support. The United Nations mission for Namibia (UNTAG) oversaw the demobilization, reintegration and resettlement of former combatants before the recruitment could start. In addition to this, the UN provided funds and other resources which facilitated the training of the new force as well as providing infrastructure to receive, process, and resettle returnees.

The biggest challenge that Namibia faced in rebuilding its military institution at the end of the conflict was a fragile political climate. The different political groups which had participated in the armed struggle were interested in contributing forces that would form the new military. These very groups were at the same time interested in participating in the electoral process that resulted in the formation of the new government. Some of them actually politicized the military building exercise during the campaigns. For instance the 1989 Swapo Election manifesto proposed an armed force based on national conscription but with the Peoples Liberation Army of Namibia (PLAN) forming the backbone. SWAPO saw PLAN as being unquestionably loyal to it and this would help it to control the entire force.

---

32 Andre du Pisani, *Op. Cit.*, p. 63.

Another challenge related to the above was that some of former soldiers who joined the NDF were from groups that had been trained by the racist South Africa to fight SWAPO. The process of integrating former combatants from different cultural, political and military backgrounds into one force was very problematic. From the very start, there was suspicions and mistrust because the wounds of the liberation war were still fresh. One of these groups was South West Africa Territorial Force (SWATF). These challenges were quickly overcome by the presence of international actors who supervised the entire exercise with impartiality and professionalism. The first Battalion was selected and trained by the Kenyan contingent of the UNTAG. Subsequently the British Military Advisory Training Team (BMATT) assumed the responsibility of training the new force. This early intervention of a foreign and neutral force to conduct the training of the NDF was very instrumental in instilling military professional values as observed by Pisan,

> Standardized military training and a common military doctrine fed into the project of national reconciliation and of nation-building. These provided the new state with values and practices around which the members of the NDF could draw together.[33]

The subordination of the new military institution to civilian authorities was another challenge. New military institutions that are built with the support of United Nations like Namibia are required normally to conform to the Western civil-military relations model. This model is drawn along Huntington's theory of "Objective civilian control of the military", as opposed to what he calls "Subjective civilian control".[34] According to this theory, objective civilian control makes the military a tool of the state and it is opposed to the military participation in politics. Subjective civilian control on the other hand presupposes the military's involvement in politics. Most of the liberation forces in Africa have had a tendency of identifying themselves with the political leadership. This was the case in Namibia where the military struggle was tied to the political objectives. Different forces that had joined NDF continued to be loyal to their old political organization even after the government had been set up. This undermined the principle of neutrality that is required of a professional military especially in a multiparty political environment.

---

33 *Ibid.*

34 S. P. Huntington, *Op. Cit.*, p. 83.

The Namibian military was formed at a time when there were serious military threats emanating from Angola due to the conflict between the Movement for the Popular Liberation of Angola (MPLA) and the National Union for the Total Independence of Angola (UNITA). The proliferation of small arms was one form of spill over from this conflict which posed a serious challenge. These arms increased the level of violent crime inside Namibia which the civil police could not manage alone. The young military institution had to support the civil police to deal with this problem. Also related to this, was the increase of the number of displaced people and refugees who would cross the border fleeing the war situation. The military had also to lend a hand to other government departments to settle big numbers of refugees.

Inadequate resources were yet another challenge faced while building the NDF. Much as the international community was willing to provide resources for building the military institution, they had other commitments inside Namibia that required immediate attention. Issues such as education, public health, building of physical infrastructure as well as supporting the democratic process were competing for the same resources. At a very early stage a decision was taken by the donors and the international community that Namibia should have a small military which should be well trained and equipped. This proved to be a challenge because the new threats that emerged after attainment of independence required a bigger force. The political crisis in neighboring Zimbabwe, the problems emanating from Angola as well as the territorial dispute with Botswana are some of the problems that created new security threats to the new nation.

The young military that has been created has had to deal with new security threats that confronted the world in the wake of the post Cold War period. The problem of HIV/AIDS has had a devastating effect on the Namibian nation affecting the military as well. This required the Namibian Government to take immediate measures to address this problem. Preventive measures which included public education and encouraging the use of condoms were put in place. The new force is also getting prepared to play a role on peace support operations in the Southern African Development Community (SADC). This is in line with the current thinking that African problems should get African solutions. Namibia as a member of SADC will be required to contribute troops to the Southern Africa stand by brigade. This brigade will be one of the five, from the different regions of the continent of Africa which will make up the African standby force. This is a new approach of solving regional problems as envisaged by the African Union (AU) Peace and Security Council (PSC).

Portugal who was Mozambique's colonial power lacked a strong industrial base. Unlike the other European powers that participated in the colonial race with an aim of getting raw materials for their industries and market for finished products, Portugal was the odd man out with its predominantly pre-industrial economy. Therefore, the relationship between Portugal as a colonizing power and Mozambique as a colonized people was dictated by the nature and character of the Portuguese State. It was this economic weakness of the colonizing power which paved way for South Africa's economic dominance of Mozambique. The discovery of minerals in South Africa and the growth of industries forced her to search for cheap labour from the neighboring colonies. Mozambique, like the rest of the Southern African countries became a source of cheap labour. This labour was provided by African blacks and was sold to South Africa by the Portuguese colonialists and settlers.

The military institutions which the Portuguese recruited and trained in Mozambique were to ensure that there was a constant supply of cheap labour to South Africa and also to enforce the forced labour policy of Africans who were to work on the white owned farms of the Portuguese settlers. Another role that was played by the military in Mozambique during the colonial period was to drive away Africans from the fertile and productive land for the Europeans to occupy.

These injustices forced the Africans to organize themselves and struggle for Independence. In 1962, the "Frente de Libertacão Mocambique" (FRELIMO) was formed under the leadership of Mondlane and it launched an armed struggle against Portuguese colonialism. Right from the very start, the military was fused with the political leadership. This idea was well articulated during Frelimo's second congress which was held in1968 and it was stated;

> Our war is essentially a political war, and its direction is defined by the party. The people's army is part and parcel of the party, and its strategic plans are made by the top leadership of the party.[35]

---

35 Carrie L. Manning, *Op. Cit.*, p. 46.

The fusion of the military and political leadership which is a characteristic of most of African liberation movements has greatly affected Mozambique while it rebuilt its military institution after the Frelimo liberation war. During the negotiations that led to the granting of independence, the Portuguese delegation proposed that all Mozambicans that had served in the colonial army should be integrated into the post independence military. Frelimo rejected out rightly this proposal on the ground that they were part of the colonial machinery to be dismantled. Everyone in the Frelimo organization that had participated in the liberation struggle felt that he should be rewarded with a political appointment. This was practically impossible because the available jobs were limited and most of the people who had participated in the armed struggle did not have the academic qualifications needed for responsibilities at the national level.

The above situation of dissatisfaction produced a large number of discontented people who felt marginalized. Soon, they took up arms and decided to fight the new government under an organization called "Reisistencia Nacional Mocambicana" (Renamo). In an attempt to explain this organisation's political support, Cahen has described it as "a coalition of the marginalized and those social, cultural and ethnic groups that were historically excluded from the modern state; the Portuguese colonial state and then later the independence nationalist state".[36] Another factor that favoured the formation of Ranamo was external. Rhodesia and South Africa were interested in destabilizing Mozambique and so, they heavily supported Ranamo. The bloody conflict that broke out 1976 lasted until 1992.

Like Namibia, the military in Mozambique has been rebuilt from the background of liberation struggle and international intervention after the end of the Cold War. The signing of the General Peace Agreement (GPA) in Rome on 4 October 1992 brought to an end a long conflict between the Frelimo government and Ranamo rebels. This agreement provided for among other things the creation of a new force which was to be known as "The Mozambican Defense Force" (FADM). Its role was to safeguard the countries sovereignty, independence and territory. It was made clear right from the very start that this force shall be made up of Mozambican citizens drawn from the two protagonist forces. It was also emphasized in the agreement that

36 Quoted by Carrie L. Manning, *Op. Cit.*, p. 66.

the new force should be non partisan, career oriented, professionally trained and above all competent.

The creation of this new force had to be preceded by the United Nations (UNOMOZ) supervised demobilization and reintegration program (DRP) for ex-combatants. The demobilization of an estimated 100,000 government and guerrilla forces was a key component that preceded the exercise of building a national military institution. The conduct of this exercise posed challenges which seriously affected the next phase of military building. First of all, there was lack of mutual trust between the parties. This resulted in failure to disclose the exact figures of combatants and weapons. Secondly, the resources which were required to conduct the exercise were slow in forthcoming. This created some snags in the implementation of the whole program. The above challenges were mitigated by the establishment of a joint political-military coordination committee. The political commitment of the parties to the conflict played a large role in the success of the demobilization and reintegration program.

The problem of lack of resources to support the exercise was solved by the commitment of the international community and some international non governmental organization. The active involvement of Western Governments with the US playing a lead role as well as the efforts of an Italian Catholic NGO called "community of Sant'Egidion", helped to supplement the resources supplied by UN. The demobilization was finally completed in 1994 which marked the beginning of building a new force. Although it had been agreed that the parties to the Peace Agreement would contribute towards a figure of 30,000 troops to join the new national army, by 1995, they managed to raise only 12,195.

The immediate problem which faced the government in selecting people to join FADM was the lack of personnel with the basic education and skills required to occupy certain positions. Most of the guerrilla ex-combatants who were presented for selection had low education levels. This proved to be a great challenge because the new force would have to play new roles in a changing and complex environment. The leadership of the new force would be required to have an understanding of such concepts as the rule of law, observance of human rights and the tenets of good governance if they were to operate within the parameters of the constitution.

At the same time, the composition of the new force had to reflect the multi ethnic nature of the Mozambican nation–state. Failure to recognize this, would lead to more instability. At independence in 1975, Frelimo had proclaimed that for the nation to survive, they had to do away with tribal considerations. They were mistaken because this created discontent amongst some tribes which felt left out in power sharing, and so had to resort to armed conflict. This time they had to give it serious consideration in order to remove this discontentment. Most of the Renamo military commanders who hailed from the Manica, Zambezia, Nampula and Tete tribes could not take up political posts and so they ended up joining the army. This compromised on the quality of the force as some of them were given higher positions and ranks which they were not fit to hold.

Another post-conflict military challenge that faced Mozambique was the rapid increase in violent crime. The end of the armed conflict had left large numbers of redundant weapons in the hands of demobilized soldiers and civilians. Returning refugees, displaced people and thousands of decommissioned soldiers who were unemployed easily got involved in violent crime. The government did not have enough resources to provide for their needs. So the military was forced to work along side the police to ensure internal security. But soon they realized that the solution to this problem lay beyond the military and police. The root cause of this violent crime was poverty and if not addressed early, it could easily degenerate to a bigger conflict.

Economic related problems increased the challenges faced by the military in the first decade of post-conflict period. These problems could be traced right from the colonial period and the post independence period whereby the continuation of the state of war disrupted most of the economic infrastructure. To overcome these problems, the World Bank and the International Monetary Fund prescribed the structural adjustment program. This program required Mozambique to reduce its public expenditure and cut on defence spending. It was argued that the saved funds would be channeled to other sectors like education and health. Even the disarmament and demobilization exercises were implemented in this spirit. The share of the national budget allocated to defence during the mid 1980s had reached fourty percent, but it had to drop to three percent by the end of 1990s.[37] As

37 Joao Paulo, Borges Coelho and Paulino Macaringue, *Op. Cit.*, p.50.

a consequence of this policy measure, economic growth figures in the late 1990s have been impressive although there are still big imbalances in the distribution of national wealth.

The new security forces that have emerged at the end of the conflict have to come to terms with the new understanding of security. Volten has rightly observed that, "Security and defense policy is more than just fielding tanks and soldiers and has to address economics, finance, foreign affairs, trade and the like".[38] This means that, much as the traditional approaches to security are still relevant and deserve our continued attention, the post Cold War situation demands that the military institution has to broaden the scope of its roles.

Environmental security is one of the non traditional concepts that have confronted the new force in Mozambique. Conflict over environmental resources are caused by high population growth of both human beings and animals which puts pressure on scarce resources, like water, land and food. Competition of man over these finite resources has led to environmental scarcities. This has resulted in deprivation, ethnic conflict and rural urban migration. The military has had to come in to support police in the enforcement of law and order. People living adjacent to conservation areas normally have access to grazing land, firewood and building materials. Military and Para military groups have to make sure that these protected areas are properly conserved. Water is another resource that has a potential for causing conflict because it tends to be transboundary. At the same time it can increase chances for cooperation between different states. All these issues have got to be grasped by the Mozambican military especially when it comes to regional cooperation in security matters.

Security arrangements to address some of these new security threats transcend national borders and involve new actors apart from the state. Defense diplomacy is one area that contemporary militaries have to be involved in. In the post Cold War era, the military is increasingly getting involved in conflict preventive measures that tend to address the root causes of war. Peace Support Operations, conferences, and joint training exercises are becoming very common. This increasing interaction of the local/domestic actors and international actors to address security problems has changed

38 Peter M. E. Volten, *Op. Cit.*, , p. 317.

the mind-set of current militaries including Mozambique. That is why some commentators have said,

> The military has to take into account the societal and international changes arriving from social forces, ideologies and institutions. The latter ultimately define the outcome of civil–military relations and these have to be addressed actively, not passively in our rapidly changing political environment.[39]

Mozambique is faced with the challenge of contributing troops to the African Standby Force of Southern African which has been discussed above. The problem with poor countries like Mozambique which have just emerged from a conflict situation, is they are required to contribute troops who are at the same level of training and equipment as say South Africa or Botswana. There is a need to harmonise the military doctrine, at least in peace support operations and standardize the equipment. Otherwise, mere ambitious dreams may not be realized.

The last challenge that the Mozambican military has faced is on how to conduct civil – military relations in a changed environment. The redefinition of the new military roles as contained in the National Defense and Armed Forces Act stress the strict subordination of military forces to civil authorities. This was not easy to achieve because of the institutional reforms that were effected alongside the democratic transition. The realization that the military institution had a potential as a power base to influence political reforms made it essential that no one faction either dominated or controlled it. However, it was very hard to get a neutral force after the restructuring exercise because of the problem of making the armed forces politically and ethnically representative. Even with the above mentioned challenges, Mozambique has managed to transform its military into a modern professional force that is subordinated to an elected civilian government.

Conclusion

Countries emerging from Conflict situations face several challenges which affect their institution building capacity. This is more so in some Sub Sahara

---

39 *Ibid.*, p. 320.

African countries where the long periods of violent conflict have left national institutions severely disrupted in the post Cold War period. This essay has argued that the changed international environment at the end of the Cold War has brought new variables which affect nation building. These new variables which include the spread of Western liberal democracy, poverty, demographic trends, infectious diseases, environmental protection and globalization have posed challenges to the rebuilding of military institutions in all the three countries we have compared. There are also some challenges which have been identified that are peculiar to some states.

The Ugandan experience of post-conflict rebuilding of the military institution is different from that of Mozambique and Namibia because of the limited involvement of the international community at the beginning. This led to the development of the unique civil-military relations that allowed the army to participate in politics. The British supported Defence Reform Unit which has resulted in the restructuring of the forces has helped to focus the Ugandan Military on the professional path. However, even the other two countries that got external support from United Nations and other donor countries have not found it easy to transition from a guerrilla force to a modern professional military force. This has been due to the political interference of former guerrilla leaders who opted to join politics.

It has been found out that lack of adequate resources was a common challenge to all the three African states when it came to rebuilding their militaries. This was because of reduction in military expenditure which had been dictated by the donor countries and the international financial institutions. The requirement that all the three countries should contribute troops to the African standby force challenged them to develop a common doctrine and standardise their equipment. The need to restructure their military forces so that they adjust to the new roles of peace support operations is yet another challenge. All these required extra funding which their governments did not have.

Problems associated with internal insecurity have brought new challenges, especially after the implementation of the disarmament and demobilization exercises. The economic pressures which these nations have had to face after the implementation of the IMF and WB structural adjustment programmes have led to increased levels of poverty, which has contributed to violent crime. The availability of small arms due to the fragile security situation has made the situation more difficult. There is no doubt that both the colonial legacy and the Cold War impacted on the character of all these militaries.

Chapter VIII
War on Terror in Africa

Introduction

The events of 11th September 2001 and the following 'war on terrorism' put Africa into a new light. Africa is now seen as a potential security risk for the United States (US) and Europe in terms of the size of the continent, population and ineffective borders, making the continent a possible recruiting ground for terrorists. Regardless of the facts that one third of Africa's population is Muslim living in poor conditions, Osama bin Laden was hiding in Sudan and allegedly Moroccans are suspected of Madrid bombing, there are other important factors which could lead to this conclusion. Africa has the potential to fund terrorist activities through the smuggling of diamonds and precious metals, money laundering, drugs and other criminal motion.[1] This essay will examine the fundamental reasons and causes of possible African 'domestic' terrorism and will also explain why international terrorists can benefit when nestling in or operating from African territory.

Africa and especially Sub-Saharan Africa, is already struggling a lot in terms of its economical problems, weak and failing states, suffering from HIV/AIDS, malaria and other diseases and for many other reasons. Anyone of them is definitely the question for security. Several conflicts and wars showed that the drivers and causes are mainly political, economic and social exclusion; poor governance and huge corruption; manipulation with and of ethnicity; abuse of human rights; ineffective regional security structures; poverty itself and the lack of conflict prevention from regional and inevitably the international community. A combination of those factors could easily result in an aggravation to terrorism. However, it is necessary to strictly distinguish between international terrorism based on radical, mostly Islamic fundamentalism and African domestic terrorism, which is driven by greed

1 Cobbold & Mills, *Op. Cit.*, p.164.

and the temptation of power. Both types of them could be of course, finally combined or be unified, but roots are definitely separate. African warlords and/or leaders directed their effort to control mineral resources and terrorise local populations by spreading their power by fear. Throughout these mineral resources were used by the warlords to finance and back up their operations. Despite the fact that some African countries are committed to the Algiers Convention on the Prevention and Combating of Terrorism, one has to note that the same countries have been plagued by periods of domestic terrorism, with devastating effect on human life, stability and development. This situation in Africa is created by the absence of effective local authority and it enables such terrorist activities to be conducted by external and mainly internal actors.

When answering the title's question, then yes. Africa could be a breeding ground for terrorists. There are examples which prove this statement. Nevertheless, this part will try to explain what the international community is doing and should do towards Africa in the future. Conditions which allow back up and support of terrorists should be tackled by combined and coordinated effort. Initiatives are focused on African development, fighting against poverty, as well as HIV/AIDS, malaria and other diseases. This effort, according to various experts, should relieve the current situation in Africa and further development will bring security and stability to the continent. This stable and secure environment should exclude or at least minimise the possibility for terrorists to find any kind of shelter or support. Successfully combating African domestic terrorism should result in security guarantees and it should also introduce Africa's new peaceful face. Regional inter-state cooperation should also contribute to enhancing stable conditions across Africa which would allow further development of the continent, required for most of the countries.

This part will try to evaluate and compare several approaches by national and international institutions and organisations to Africa's problems. Many discussions are held about which initiative could be the best for Africa. The United Nations (UN), the European Union (EU), France, the United Kingdom (UK) and US initiatives, as well as other open African programmes, in particular the New Partnership for Africa's Development (NEPAD), will be compared. Evaluation will be driven by political and economical factors which are influencing the development of the continent. Analysis of these approaches shows that all of them have a lot of common. Nevertheless, coordination at all levels, as well as between recipient and donor of any kind of aid or assistance has to be improved. It is also fair to say that different actors have different interests in Africa; and one has to carefully select or decide which initiative would be the most effective and proper one in order to provide relief to Africa. This relief combined with proper governance could sketch positive examples for the future of Africa without terrorism. Only combined and coordinated efforts by the international community should be more successful in the future assistance to Africa.

Meaning of Terrorism in Africa

The current, as well as previous situation in the Democratic Republic of Congo(DRC) in particular, will be elaborated from the author's personal experience.[2] The DRC as the second biggest country in the continent went through a remarkable and bloody history whilst the country starved for years under different rulers. Their ineffectiveness in the post-colonial era made scars on the country's face. Finally, the focus on Africa's needs and necessary structural changes will be also sketched. The necessity of regional partnership and cooperation among African states in solving potential future conflicts, as well as further African development and shape of the states and leadership will be also examined. These mentioned factors, as well as eradication of poverty, are parts of the fundamental background which should exclude such conditions where terrorist can find any kind of support or favourable conditions.

What does terrorism actually mean and what is hidden behind that word? One could find plenty of definitions of terrorism. But the most accurate one comes from Sun-Tzu, 2,500 years ago: "*Kill one – frighten ten thousand!*" This technique of intimidation has been used by governments to discipline their people and by dissidents and religious sects to weaken and overturn the established authority since the dawn of civilisation.[3] Terrorism is, nevertheless, a multi-faceted phenomenon involving both a systematic and sporadic use of terror by governments and other social actors, with a view to

2 MONUC, May 2000 – May 2001
3 Clutterbuck, *Op. Cit.*, p. 4.

forcing some specific or general political and related objectives.[4] For much of the West, terrorism is little more than a totalitarian ideology and a barbaric political enterprise by religious zealots.[5] It is seen as multiple manifestations of anti-systemic forces in order to destroy western civilisation. Western analysts frequently put terrorism into a group along with economic crimes, ethnic conflicts, civil wars and state collapses. Those factors usually appear within borders of weak or failing states as seen in Africa.

Is this grouping also valid for Africa? Was the aggravation of movements such as terrorism inevitable? The answer is not a simple one. There is a lot of room where weak states offer sanctuary and succour to terrorist movements. This was visible in Sudan with the National Islamic Front (NIF) in the lead, which covered Osama bin Laden for various reasons in the 1990s. His presence in Sudan, where he moved after being disillusioned with the Saudi royal family who had allowed the US deployment in Saudi Arabia in 1990, was a clear example of state terrorist support. Bin Laden financed the training of terrorist groups like Eritrea's Islamic Jihad and Uganda's Lord's Resistance Army in camps in Sudanese territory. He allegedly spent US $15 million on a single shipment of weapons and explosives, suspected of being used in (at least) the US embassy bombing in Nairobi.[6] His ties with the NIF were even more strengthened when the NIF was trying to expand Islam towards the Great Lakes Region and to the Horn. Despite the fact that Bin Laden was one of the main backers of the NIF, its leaders probably never fully trusted him. His radicalism was so extreme that it might have become a threat to them. Bin Laden was finally ousted from the country in 1996 partially also as a result of US and Saudi political pressure on the Sudanese government. The question of what links he still has to Sudan remains unanswered.

On the other hand, the absence of local authority or effective security power could lead to the situation when paramilitaries terrorising local population or tribal entities start to fight each other. Most of the African states, especially the twenty-four countries partly or wholly south of the Sahara Desert, suffer from two deeply rooted problems: their tribal structure does not coincide with their frontiers, which are based on the boundaries

---

4 Amuwo, *Op. Cit.*, pp .205-6.

5 *Ibid.*, p. 274.

6 Clutterbuck, *Op. Cit.*, p. 4.

thrashed out between their former colonial masters; and, in many of them, advances in medicine and hygiene are resulting in their populations growing faster than their national Gross Domestic Products (GDPs), and faster than they can provide and distribute enough food for them.[7] This was clearly seen for example in Sierra Leone, Liberia or the Great Lakes Region in the late 1990's, and in the beginning of the new century respectively. Tribal conflict between Hutu and Tutsi has evolved to the genocide in the eastern Congo, resulting in fatal outcomes – hundreds of thousands killed and millions displaced.

Terrorists could also easily find a breeding ground and support in conditions of poverty or in conflict situations, both of which are already widespread in Africa. This thought was clearly expressed by Tony Blair, the UK Prime Minister, at the October 2001 Labour Party Conference stating that: *"The state of Africa is a scar on the conscience of the world. But if the world as a community focused on it, we could heal it. And if we do not, it will become deeper and angrier"*.[8] This suggestion was doubtlessly linked to the events of 11th September 2001. The terrorist attack against the USA has provoked a concern that those who oppose the West may take advantage of relative lawlessness in Africa to seek sanctuary and to establish operational bases. Whether this is true or not is unclear, but as previously mentioned the stay of Bin Laden in Sudan pointed out that the issue is serious enough to interest some Western security agencies.[9] This kind of depressive African environment, in concert with frustration and radicalism which appears among lots of Africa's failing or weak states, is another fundamental reason for terrorist escalation. Finally, African history, as well as liberation movements in several states, where armed groups, regardless if legitimate or not, gain the power and create situations when opposition could also use terror as a tool of their dissatisfaction with the regime, tribal or political leadership, and security or economic starvation. This we can find for example in the history of the DRC, the Central African Republic (CAR) and even South Africa. On the other hand it is fair to say that the DRC, for example, failed not only because of the economical situation or that it had bad leaders, but also because its large size and multi-ethnic composition made it difficult, if not impossible, to rule the country successfully.

---

7 Fullerton, *Op. Cit.*, p. 10.
8 http://web.mit.edu/jeremyp/www/blair.html
9 Herbst & Mills, *Op. Cit.*, p. 30.

History shows that local or regional African organisations are unable to effectively deal with security problems in the long term. Institutions and organisations like the Organisation of African Unity (OAU) were almost helpless in the past and it would not be capable of working alone in the future. Crisis in the Great Lakes Region showed that Africa itself cannot effectively manage such situations. Nevertheless, African countries also recognised that their previous practice to not interfere in each other's internal affairs has not been satisfactory in terms of preventing conflicts or when conflicts spilt over boundaries and afflicted even more countries. Thus, they asked for change, when the situation had become a collective responsibility. Furthermore, in 1999 the OAU took a further step by agreeing to exclude countries whose governments came to power by unconstitutional means, as a result of which the Ivory Coast was excluded from OAU meetings after its military coup.[10] More successful and more promising for the future should be the NEPAD programme. It is actually an African-led strategy for sustainable development and poverty reduction in Africa. African leaders are trying to involve Western countries (preferably G8) and get all the spectrum of support within this framework. The programme itself seeks to Africa's responsibility for establishing stable secure conditions without conflict and for improvement of economic and political governance, as well as better regional integration. The NEPAD main activity is represented by following goals:

- eradicate poverty
- place African countries, both individually and collectively, on a path of sustainable growth and development
- halt the marginalisation of Africa in the globalisation process and enhance its full and beneficial integration into the global economy
- accelerate the empowerment of women[11]

The NEPAD is definitely a long term initiative and it will require a lot of effort, compromises, and last but not least money. The programme will also try to involve all of the already existing African institutions and organisations, namely the Economic Community of West African States (ECOWAS) and Southern African Development Community (SADC). Close cooperation with the UN Economic Commission for Africa (ECA) and the

10 www.fco.gov.uk
11 www.fco.gov.uk

Africa Development Bank (AfDB) should be fruitful and should also assist to achieve the Millennium Development Goals (MDGs), introduced as a main UN Africa initiative described later in this part of research.

Some of the African countries still suffer after years under 'Marxist' governments which were even more inefficient than those in Europe, Asia or Latin America, since they lacked the depth of education, administrative experience and infrastructures to run their theoretically centralised command economies. For many of these countries, the Cold War simply represented a black and white view on the world. But what unexpectedly (to them) happened at the end of the Cold War? It has changed their priorities, policies and often also leaderships, and also removed political barriers to globalisation, while demonstrating the ascendancy of Western values. Some of the African states may disintegrate into anarchy, with rival warlords holding sway over their fiefdoms, as in Somalia. Some may face sporadic bursts of civil war with thousands of casualties in a week, as Angola and the DRC have. Some, in desperation, may rally to authoritarian governments. Others, with a façade of democracy, may sink more and more deeply into corruption and organised crime.[12] What happened in Angola in the late 1980's and early 1990's showed that the country could not be run well without communist support. The withdrawal of Cuban troops and Soviet support from the Angolan Government side caused the situation that they could not control the whole country and the National Union for the Total Independence of Angola (UNITA), still allegedly being supplied by the US, was still effectively fighting against the Angolan Army, which was unable to achieve outright victory against UNITA. But what interestingly happened was that Jonas Savimbi, the UNITA leader, became seen more as a local African warlord rather than a leader of an anti-communist fraction. He was a clear example of an African domestic terrorist. His effort was financed by sales of diamonds and other minerals which had being mined in areas he controlled. A new concept of domestic terrorism or rebel movement based on the rise of warlords, private security or military companies was introduced in Africa. A situation very similar to Angola's was observed in Sierra Leone in the late 1990's, when Ferde Sankoh, the Revolutionary United Front (RUF) leader, also used diamonds to finance his fighting to terrorise and destabilise the country. The fact is that if warlords or any armed group leader physically

12 Clutterbuck, *Op. Cit.*, p. 10.

controlled diamond or other mineral sources and could profit from them, they could effectively conduct their operations. Wars in Africa are not fought for real victories, but rather to engage in profitable crime under the pretext of terrorism or war. Diamonds were first discovered in Sierra Leone in the 1930's and have been a major cause of political conflict fuelling the decade-old war.[13] This shows once again that the background of African domestic terrorism is based on greed and on temptation to get at least regional power. This security problem should not be solved by external actors alone. African countries themselves have to deal with that whilst organisations like the UN could effectively contribute in peacekeeping or humanitarian assistance.

Problems Ahead

What could, should or have the Western world done to at least relieve Africa's problems? Despite the security threats, the Sub-Saharan population is severely devastated by HIV/AIDS, malaria and other diseases. Here is the highest number of HIV/AIDS and malaria cases reported in the region. There are 24 million people suffering from HIV/AIDS. Malaria allegedly kills more than two million people each year, 90 per cent of them in Africa. Furthermore, the *Lancet* Medical Journal released information, based on scientific study in Sub-Sahara, that people with HIV are twice as likely to catch malaria as those without the virus. This was the latest news which links both of the worlds' biggest killer diseases. There is no doubt that HIV/AIDS represents one of the greatest challenges of our time. Its defeat will require constant and concerted commitment from the entire world.[14] George W. Bush, the President of the USA, already announced the Emergency Plan for AIDS Relief. When introducing this plan he stated: "*in the face of preventable death and suffering, we have a moral duty to act, and we are acting*". The USA allocated US $15 billion for a five-year initiative, which would target millions already suffering, as well as prevention programmes. Nevertheless, it should be presented as a joint effort. The USA could not achieve the required impact on its own. Further appeals to other countries and leaders from government, community, religion and private sector are really essential. They have to be ready and willing to confront HIV/AIDS not in terms of words, but in terms

13 Abiodun, *Op. Cit.*, p. 21.
14 Campbell, *Op. Cit.*, p. 1.

of action. The virus does not know boundaries; it discriminates against no religion or ethnicity.

One has to look primarily at what is the real threat for the West. Figures about migration of African population are noticeably overwhelming and should be in high consideration of any Western state. On the other hand, any refugee crisis could pose an actual threat to state security. Therefore it is doubtless that the movement of peoples fuels civil conflict and regional instability.[15] This has been remarkably seen in the Great Lakes Region genocide in 1994, when involved parties failed to respond adequately to the crisis in order to separate the militants from the general population. The migration of population for whatever reason seems to be one of the main African problems. For example, 750,000 people enter Libya from the south, Sub-Saharan Africa every year and the country is not a final destination for them. They are heading further north towards Europe and the West. Why is this happening? One can offer a couple of reasons for that huge migration. Poverty and general dissatisfaction with the economic situation, lack of opportunity, security concerns and incomparable incomprehensible standards of living conditions force people to leave their homes and move. The widespread growth of the internet around the globe did not avoid Africa. Africans could now easily find out and understand what is 'the abyss' between themselves and the West. Western pro-active policy towards further African economic and security development should at least stop the increasing migration of Africans to the West.

One other reason or cause of this situation could be the rapid rate of population increase in Africa. Africa at predicted levels could represent around 22 per cent of the world's population in 2050 compared to 9 per cent in 1950. Much younger than Europe's population, it is not difficult to imagine a rapid rise in the number of Africans seeking work in the labour-starved economies of the North.[16] Not only the UN but also the EU should start to deal with this growing problem. It was already presented by Barry Buzan and at various security forums that understanding of security has changed since the end of the Cold War. A remarkable fact is that the large-scale displacement of a civilian population could become a deliberate conflict strategy.[17] It is

15 Mills & Norton, *Op. Cit.*, p. 1.
16 Herbst & Mills, *Op. Cit.*, p. 31.
17 Loescher & Milner, *Op. Cit.*, p. 24.

necessary to understand that refugees would create an insecure environment in the state of conflict, in the state hosting them and in the region of origin. It is also a threat to wider international peace and security. As a result of which, international organisations like the UN, NATO and the EU should take it into deep consideration. This is usually followed by a number of actions taken against the country of origin. Diplomatic pressure, economic sanctions, humanitarian aid and often armed intervention usually under Chapter VII of the UN Charter are those which are imposed if required. All of them were necessary and used in the Great Lakes Region in 1990s, however, a little late. But it is fair to say that this avoided further genocide in the area after 1994. But what is more hidden, on the other hand, is the indirect security threat. It is this threat, which is more difficult to identify - possible impact of refugees on the host state, especially where limitations of resources already exist on their own. Just the simple presence of them could cause grievances among local populations. The aggravation of the situation is usually observed when refugees compete with the locals for jobs and local services. They are also often prioritised and it could cause another social instability. Clash of cultures has to be also discussed in similar situations, as well as the aspect of different religion. The international community is, in most examples, blamed for lack of solidarity and understanding. How to deal with the refugee situation in the long term view? There is not an easy answer on that question. However, the policy response should be very comprehensive and complex. It has to include measures like suppression of armed elements within refugee locality, various UN embargos, disarmament and many others. The UN High Commission for Refugees (UNHCR) is a main actor and has already introduced a framework for formulating and implementing a comprehensive solution for Africa. This, however, would not be applicable in Western Europe, where strict terms like asylum and temporary protection are used. Nevertheless, as already mentioned the number of illegal refugees/emigrants arriving to Europe is continuously increasing and only pro-active policy by the West towards hot spots in Africa could somehow be fruitful in the future. Otherwise the Western countries, like Italy and France, would have to continue dealing with a situation similar to the one when emigrants from the communist block and colonies were seeking asylum in the West during the Cold War era.

The number of terrorist attacks against the West which occurred in Africa is also alarming. Africa recorded 6,177 casualties from 296 acts of terrorism between 1990 and 2002, making the continent with the second most casualties in the world, after Asia. There has been a marked increase in the number of attacks and their intensity since 1998 (reflected in the figures of casualties).[18] It is fair to mention at least a few of the main ones from the last period. Two of them occurred in 2002: car bombing attack against a synagogue in Tunisia and an attack against an airliner and a hotel in Mombassa, Kenya. Another was simultaneous attack against restaurant and hotel in Casablanca, Morocco. And finally the last one in Sharm-el-Shaikh, Egypt where terrorist-suicide bombers initiated an explosion in the hotel restaurant and at the market place in very popular tourist area. All the mentioned attacks clearly show that Africa's territory is a reasonably successful playground for extreme international and Islamic terrorist for various political reasons. Those carefully selected targets are particularly Western centres and the Western life style, present in Africa, itself. It is, nevertheless, important to stress that these figures and events only reflect the number of international terrorist attacks on African soil. Additionally, African domestic terrorism was devastating several not only Sub-Saharan countries for years.

Another extremely valid point when discussing Africa and its involvement in terrorism would be the rise of Islam, especially in the Sub-Saharan region. Why? According to several experts, poverty is the main cause of terrorism. However, terrorism is a more complex phenomenon. It is based on interaction of social depression, a loss of cultural identity, lack of economic perspective, a dysfunctional state and political repression. In this case plenty of African countries could successfully breed terrorists and the Sub-Saharan region would be full of those. Nevertheless, international terrorism requires two additional factors: a mobilising, unifying idea, such as that offered by Islamic fundamentalism; and appropriate agitators, who abuse this idea in order to organise powerful terrorist force against a common external enemy.[19] There are numbers of centres of Islam, described by experts: the zone along the Gulf of Guinea, the West African Sahel zone, the Nile region in Sudan, Ethiopia and the East African coastal area. There were different developments of the religion reported across the regions, mostly because of different historical and social context. Despite all the facts, Islam in Sub-Saharan Africa did not become an exclusive state religion, but it still keeps its ideological and political power. The interpretation of Islam seems to be

18 www.state.gov

19 Mair, *Op. Cit.*, p. 1.

less fundamental or militant and it is presented in "moderate" way in the area. Nevertheless, there are no guarantees that it could not be changed somehow in the future. But the situation that African terrorism would become integral and organic part of such network like al-Qaeda seems to be very unlikely. There is still the possibility, however, that such African variations of terrorism could run independently. All previously mentioned factors needed are present in Sub-Saharan Africa. In the DRC, for example, blaming the West for the country's misery became very common. People in Kinshasa and elsewhere in the country showed a tendency to believe in conspiracy theories that industrialised countries keep the level of prices of common products (like raw materials, oil, food etc.) extremely high and the only way for the Congolese to ensure free access to all the necessary resources is to use force.[20] In this situation a mobilising idea and specific interpretation could be easily misused for any kind of violence. An interesting fact is that Africa is becoming a battlespace in the war between terrorists and the West, but it must not be that interesting for Africans. They are increasingly going to wonder if the war on terrorism is really "their" war. Their basic needs like drinking water, enough food and stable/secure conditions for agriculture activities are far distant from the Western ideas of a peaceful and prosperous globalised world where freedom of religion, movement, speech and trade are the fundamentals.

The USA is putting a lot of efforts to control and supervise the African problem. Their approach in the long term programme seems to be really comprehensive. They also divided African countries or regions according to terrorist threat risk and consequently threat to security and stability.[21] In the group marked as high risk we can find obviously the Great Lakes Region, Sudan, Algeria and may be surprisingly, Kenya. Several incidents and the inability of the local government to deal with these threats in the northeast part of the country shifted Kenya to the high risk category. Safe travel in this part of the country is only possible in military protected convoys. Somali warlords and gangs control the area, as Kenyan security forces have moved to isolated forts. But the US again, cynically or not, concentrates their prioritised effort to countries where they easily control, influence or

---

20 Author's personal experience – MONUC, Kinshasa and Goma (May 2000 – May 2001)

21 US GAO, *Op. Cit.*, p. 65.

supervise the mining of oil, and it is currently the Gulf of Guinea and off shoring countries. Nevertheless, not only the US military is embarking on the long-term push into Africa to counter what it considers growing inroads by al-Qaeda and other terrorist networks in poor, lawless and predominantly Muslim expanses of the continent.[22] The US engaged African countries by many ways to enhance their anti-terrorist activities and capabilities. The Pan Sahel Initiative (PSI), one of them, is an US programme to assist Mali, Niger, Chad and Mauritania in protecting borders, countering and combating terrorism, monitoring movement of suspected persons and generally to enhance regional stability. Nevertheless, this is again connected to the increase of stability in and around the vicinity of the Gulf of Guinea, where significant oilfields lie.

One has to ask if there is any priority for the West-European powers like France or the UK. French interests are predominantly orientated to the north, Mediterranean Africa from the historically-colonial reasons and traditions. However, France is also actively involved in some Sub-Saharan countries to engage herself politically, economically and if necessary, also militarily. There are four garrisons permanently positioned in Senegal, Gabon, Chad and the Ivory Coast.[23] France is also maintaining a connection to the CAR, one of the poorest countries in the region keeping airline connections with the country and investing heavily in the national CAR airways the Air Afrique. They have also identified 'Solidarity Action Zones', which includes states such as Liberia, Nigeria and Angola, to show that their aid has a more ethical basis, similar to the British 'ethical dimension' to foreign policy.[24]

The UK position seems to be far more streamed and focused on current or previous Commonwealth members. But the reality is far different. The UK is heavily involved in projects, particularly in the NEPAD, which is the latest African recovery plan launched in 2001. One could find official UK priorities in this programme, namely to help African leaders to achieve their goals on conflict resolution and better governance. G8 activity, on the other hand, is mainly focused on achievement of greater policy coherence to improve the quality and the quantity of the aid Africa receives, and on the prospects

22 Scott-Tyson (2005), p. 1.
23 Fullerton (2001), p. 9.
24 *ibid.*, p. 9.

of further foreign investments. However, the situation in various countries did not allow, to date, taking any specific measures regarding the aid. The previous aim of British policy towards Africa was to promote positive change across the entire continent. Goals were (and probably still are) to build peace, prosperity and democracy in Africa. The 'ethical dimension' so widely talked about in the 2000 elections manifesto has recently been put to one side but in its place the Government appears to be ending its indifference towards Africa and extending its influence on the continent.[25] Operations in Sierra Leone and the Ivory Coast, as well as military presence in the DRC, are clear examples that Africa is gaining more and more importance within UK foreign policy. Nevertheless, the announcement of the UK Prime Minister, Tony Blair, as part of building new partnerships to rise the UK bilateral aid to Africa to £1 billion by 2006[26] is in light of common EU budget cuts (16th December 2005) which are likely to be debatable. Is there a real interest and political consensus to help Africa or will the Live8 and Make Poverty History and other activities be once again effectless in the long term view? But when judging the ethic it is fair to follow the behaviour of some UK citizens. When the ticket lottery for the Live8 concert in the London Hyde Park in 2005 was launched, first lucky ticket winner-holders put those tickets on eBay website for bids. Making profit on these beneficiary or solidarity performances should be publicly denounced. So, if the society asking for ethic, where was one in London that time?

Meanwhile, Gordon Brown, the British Chancellor of the Exchequer, stated that 2005 will be a milestone in Britain's campaign to meet the UN Millennium Development Goals to reduce poverty, illiteracy and disease across the world.[27] The entire world is full of those ridiculous situations. Anyway, Brown focused his statement mainly on problems of primary education, halving poverty and on the elimination of preventable infant deaths. All of these follow establishment of the Blair Commission for Africa in 2004 and also previous trends which started at G8 meetings 2002 and 2003, where Africa was placed on the G8 agenda. Brown's project is based on the increase of the G8's development aid to Africa. There are institutions like the International Monetary Found (IMF) and the World Bank (WB) also

25 The UK's policy towards Africa (2000), pp. 1-3.
26 Website: www.fco.gov.uk
27 Brown (2004), p. 127.

involved. Brown's goal is to boost the capital which flows to the continent, primarily direct to the humanitarian aid. There are, however, voices and arguments which would argue with him. Richard Dowden of the Royal African Society for example mentioned that Africa has had a trillion dollars in aid in the last 50 years, roughly US $5,000 for every African living today if distributed evenly at today's prices. If aid were the solution to Africa's problems, it would be a rich continent by now.[28] In some African countries the aid definitely could help and make a difference, therefore humanitarian aid should continue. Nevertheless, how is this fact addressing structural problems of Africa? The issue clearly is how to change political structures in the best way, not just fuel existing dysfunctional formations.[29] History has shown that aid was very often used as a political tool for local African leaders to enhance their positions and those who really need the aid continued suffering.

Brown's effort to target education programmes especially in Sub-Saharan Africa is also facing difficulties. It is basically a very clever idea. Nevertheless, the misallocation of funds, lack of prioritisation, corruption and wastage are not obstacles but huge barriers. Kenya is a clear example of this situation. According to the Transparency International, Kenyan Ministry of Education heavily mismanages its accounts every year and is the third most mismanaged ministry in the government.[30] Similar situation could be easily found in various countries in Africa, and in the Sub-Saharan region in particular

Another important actor dealing with Africa on the British political scene is the Department for International Development (DFID). The institution, which is part of the UK Government, is responsible for managing Britain's aid to poor countries and it is also involved in tackling of extreme poverty. The reason why the UK is so interested in problems like Africa is simple. Anything like war or conflict, international crime, refugees, international drug trade or spread of diseases such as HIV/AIDS are caused or made worse by poverty in developing countries directly or indirectly affect the UK. Reduction or elimination of poverty would make the world better for everybody. The DFID in close cooperation with the WB created the Africa

28 Dowden, *Op. Cit.*, p. 1.
29 Taylor, *Op. Cit.*, p. 4.
30 Parajuli, *Op. Cit.*, p. 1.

Catalytic Fund to help African countries make faster progress on their priorities for improving health, education, infrastructure and access to water. The UK Government already allocated £200 million to the Fund. The use of the Fund would be supervised by the Africa Partnership Forum, which was established in the Evian G8 Summit in 2003. All the main international actors as the African Union (AU), the NEPAD, the UN, the IMF, the WB, the Organisation for Economic Co-operation and Development (OECD), the World Trade Organisation (WTO), the AfDB as well as African governments are represented in the Forum.[31] So, this activity and projection its ideas on the ground, supported, of course by sufficient funding and proper coordination among all the actors should bring very positive outcomes and mainly it should relieve weak African states or regions.

Position of West Toward Africa

The UK position towards Africa more or less corresponds with the policy of the European Community / European Union (EC/EU). Nevertheless, it is necessary to look back how the EC/EU approach has developed, especially towards the Sub-Saharan region. It is doubtless that Africa, and particularly the Sub-Saharan area has changed significantly since the end of the Cold War, and that the process of changes has not finished yet. Previously, the Africa case was not among high priorities of EC/EU leaders in Brussels. But the situation evolved and the Common Foreign and Security Policy (CFSP) was developed. Sub-Saharan Africa was carefully chosen as a region where the EC/EU could become a significant international player. Despite the fact that the percentage of European development assistance received by Sub-Saharan Africa dramatically decreased from 59.4 per cent in 1990-91 to 33.6 per cent in 2000-01[32], the EC/EU aid had a number of new goals and purposes added to the original aid aims. One of the architects of new CFSP was Andrew Moravcsik, who successfully managed to combine bilateral and multilateral foreign and security policies of individual member states. He named it 'liberal intergovernmentalism'.[33] According to him, new 'European

31 www.dfid.gov.uk

32 OECD, *Development Cooperation Report, The Development Assistance Committee*, Paris: OECD, 2003, p. 305.

33 Moravcsik, *Op. Cit.*, pp. 611-628.

interests' could be different from the national one of any member state. The European Commission represents such common interests and has responsibility for day-to-day policy towards Sub-Saharan Africa.[34] Although giving aid to Africa was reduced it continues to be a significant tool for the EC/EU. Nevertheless, it becomes increasingly important to react to the threats from insecurity and instability in Sub-Sahara. The development of CFSP was one answer to these new security threats.[35] As a result, the EU launched its first initiative on conflict prevention and resolution in Africa in 1993. It was followed by sending a special envoy to the Great Lakes Region, when the world was shocked by genocide in Rwanda in 1994. Aldo Ajello, the EU representative was appointed to help the countries in the region to resolve the crisis affecting them.[36] Although his activity was not particularly effective, the EU did not give up. Finally, the EU launched a military operation *Artemis* in 2003. 1,800 EU troops were deployed in the Ituri province in Congo under the UN Security Council Resolution 1484.[37] Their main task was to stabilise the security conditions and improve the humanitarian situation in the area. This was a remarkable step forward for the EU to send troops outside of Europe for the first time. When elaborating on the mission it is fair to say that operation Artemis was very successful and opened new doors of collaboration between the EU and the UN. This could be an example of the EU responsibility to maintain peace in areas where NATO has not enough will or intent to react. The EU has clearly showed its interests in managing conflicts in Africa in the future. Its main goal seems to be in promotion of democracy and respect for human rights in the Sub-Saharan region. There are, however, various limitations for any security initiative. Not every member state of the EU shares 'European security ambitions' as they are still thinking nationally. A future agreement among the three big European powers: the UK, France and Germany would be essential and crucial for further intensified collaboration on European defence in relation to Africa.[38]

G8 approach towards Africa is also getting very valuable. It is definitely due to the fact that the most powerful countries in the world could, and

34 Olsen, *Op. Cit.*, p. 427.
35 *Ibid.*, p. 428.
36 *Ibid.*, p. 432.
37 www.un.org/sc/resolutions.shtml
38 Olsen, *Op. Cit.*, p. 433.

should deliver the most noticeable effects to Africa. G8 already affirmed their commitment to the Heavily Indebted Poor Countries (HIPC) initiative. This initiative is primarily determined to debt reduction and freeing up resources for spending on poverty reduction. Debt relief was agreed for 23 African countries, out of 27 poorest in the world. The G8 also supports African activity to restore peace and security in Sub-Sahara and particularly in Angola, the DRC, Sierra Leone, Sudan, Burundi, the CAR and the Ivory Coast.

Projects financed by the G8 were and are closely connected to the security situation in the area. Institutional capacity-building for peace and security, development of an effective network of peace training centres for both military and civilian personnel are just some of them.[39] One of the key elements of the G8 agenda in terms of African peace and security is the Joint Africa – G8 plan, introduced in the Evian G8 Summit, to enhance African capabilities to conduct peace support operations. Furthermore, at the G8 Gleneagles Summit in 2005, Tony Blair appealed for an African approach and the summit was again focused on Africa, as well as climate changes. Kofi Annan, the UN Secretary General called this G8 Summit "*the greatest summit for Africa ever*". The leaders finally agreed to completely eliminate debts of the poorest countries and also promised to increase support for African peacekeeping forces to help to deter, prevent and resolve conflicts in Africa. Additional investment in education and the fight against HIV/AIDS and malaria was also announced at Gleneagles. The G8 also fully support the UN Millennium Development Goals (MDGs) programme and all the activity is coordinated and fully corresponds with this programme. Just before the Summit, remarkable events were set up by musicians, lead by Sir Bob (Robert) Geldof. The Live8 concerts, exactly 20 years after premier Live Aid, was not to raise money for Africa primarily, but mainly to send a message to the G8 leaders that international community and ordinary people simply care. This was a remarkable display of solidarity and sympathy with Africa. Their motto – "*Make Poverty History*" was clearly heard around the globe. Their contribution was anything but weak. Live8 did not finish its activity and Sir Geldof publicly promised to follow all the African cases up. The website and other notions prove that the job is not done yet.[40]

---

39 www.fco.gov.uk
40 www.makepovertyhistory.org

The UN approach to Africa's problems is generally very comprehensive. The organisation clearly expressed its effort to find a practical solution to the situation in Africa. The UN secretariat together with the specialised agencies of the UN structure, as well as representatives of the IMF, the WB and the OECD defined a set of time-bound and measurable goals, the MDGs. They are aimed at halving poverty and hunger, achieving universal primary education and gender equality, reducing children under-5 mortality by two thirds and maternal mortality by three-quarters, reversing the spread of HIV/AIDS, halving the proportion of people without access to safe drinking water, ensuring environmental sustainability, and promoting a global partnership for development.[41] Such a project was and still is very welcomed especially by Sub-Saharan African countries. Despite the fact that remarkable progress has been observed in some of these countries, this is the only region where poverty has been increasing during the 1990s. Current estimates, which were also mentioned by Gordon Brown in his project, are operating with figures for the 22nd century, when MDGs targets would be achieved. Therefore any acceleration of the programme is really needed. The unrealistic prospect of such development forced the international community to put Africa on the global agenda. One of the UK initiatives was an establishment of the Commission for Africa, by Tony Blair in 2004. The Commission's task is to define the challenges facing Africa, and to provide clear recommendations on how to support successful and faster African development.[42] It is doubtless that this was a great UK contribution but it has to be followed up by other western countries. Delivering and achieving physical objectives would be another step forward. Changes for example, have to be made such that any kind of aid should be firstly agreed between Africa and its donors, it should address priority challenges and it should also be derived from the country's development strategy. Any further help to this may not necessarily have immediate, social and economic impacts. The proposed doubling of aid to Sub-Saharan Africa to US $50 million in 2010, and US $75 million in 2015 should be considered as a positive development in this direction.[43] Finally, it is necessary to say that the MDGs represent an unprecedented opportunity for Africa and the entire world to reduce poverty.

41 www.un.org/millenniumgoals/index.asp
42 Report of the Commission for Africa (2005), p. 321.
43 *Ibid.*, p. 327.

When comparing and elaborating different policies and approaches towards Africa, it would be fair to look more deeply inside at least one of the Sub-Saharan countries. The DRC, formerly known as Zaire and the Belgian Congo is located in the heart of Africa and is as big as two third of Europe. The DRC borders nine African countries, most of which are politically and/or economically weak, and it is geopolitically important to Central Africa because of its geographical position in the continent. Excluding the DRC conflict, described by many commentators as *'Africa's first world war'*[44], the downfall of regimes in neighbouring countries could itself easily result in the regional instability, insecurity and further conflict. The DRC has for a long time been one of the most strategically important countries on the African continent. It is probably the richest country in the world in terms of mineral and natural resources. Natural reserves of industrial diamonds, uranium and copper-cobalt were a mainstay of Allied (NATO) strategic mineral production during the Cold War, for instance. The DRC also has offshore petroleum deposits that are produced by a consortium of foreign companies led by Chevron.[45] But what was behind the country's instability for years - greed and efforts to control the wealth of the country – diamonds, gold and other lucrative mineral resources. The country faced security problems for generations. Belgian King Leopold, who ruled Congo from the beginning of the colonial era, was responsible for killing allegedly ten million people when producing and trading with African natural white gold – the rubber. The country has never been unified. More than 70 ethnic groups subdivided into tribes forming social coalitions for survival. However, this grouping inclined to preserve it from outside influence. Any interaction between societies was almost excluded as a very small percentage of the population had formal education, which was restricted by the colonial power. As a result the population was not cohesive enough to form a united nation when the independence was granted to the country in 1960s. Also the assassination of Patrice Lummumba did not introduce Belgium to the world in the right light either. Tribal dispute between Hutu and Tutsi has scared the Congo, as well as other countries like Rwanda, Uganda or Burundi. The DRC has had three successive leaders, who could be called 'accidental', in the last 40 years.

44 K. H. Butts, K. H. & A. L. Bradshaw Jr, *Central African Security: Conflict in the Congo, The Center for Strategic Leadership*, Carlisle: U.S. Army War College, 2002, p. 11

45 *Ibid.*, pp. 4-5.

Joseph Mobutu Sese Seko, Laurent Desire Kabila and Joseph Kabila were in large part designated, selected, or given the qualifications for office by outside actors.[46] They did not appear as capable leaders, who could successfully run the country. They, except the later one, were autocratic, corrupted and unable to even simply provide security for the Congolese people. There were also main five warlords who terrorised the population for the last decade. African history showed very simplified though: if a country is poor, or the less the country owned and physically possessed, then it is not so interesting for warlords or such African terrorists, but if the country is rich there is always something to fight for. Despite the fact that the conflict in the DRC has reduced the production of minerals substantially since its economic peaks in 1970s, that yield and slag recovery operations alone are sufficient enough to motivate previously mentioned countries to fight for control of mineral producing regions of the country.[47] The UN mission in the area – MONUC, had and still has the main task to stabilise the region and restore security conditions. Troops have to also supervise the upcoming elections and assist in distribution of humanitarian aid. Another huge problem which is the DRC and all the Sub-Saharan region facing are diseases. HIV/AIDS and malaria are devastating the population, and the World Health Organisation (WHO) *inter alia* would be most probably extremely busy in its effort to reduce mortality caused by those fatal killers. Religions did not bring any major difficulties to the country. Both Islam and Christianity are present and peacefully coexisting. The country was ignored by media, economy, news and trade for such a long time. It should be changed, hopefully. But what is the state without the people. And people in the DRC held their breath for so long, which resulted in that the society almost cracking. Nevertheless, despite the brutality, slavery and huge life losses ordinary people stayed nice, friendly and hopeful. What else do they have? Common people believe in values like justice and that education gives freedom, but nothing is free. Infrastructure progress is visible, railways and roads have already been reopened - thus reconnecting people. Hydroelectric capacity of the country has increased by opening new hydro power station blocks on the Congo River in Matadi. The future of the country does not look as depressively as it did in the past.

---

46 Butts & Bradshaw, *Op. Cit.*, p. 37.
47 *Ibid.*, p. 5.

What could be done by the international community? The UN presence (MONUC) in the area remains crucial. Regardless of the huge mission cost, MONUC operation has had a very positive effect. Further international mediation of the situation in the DRC could also contribute to restore stability in the region and involve the West. Finally, there is a necessary to establish multifaceted, possibly power sharing governments, at least at local levels. This would probably be the most difficult task, as war and genocide memories are still in minds of not only Congolese, but Hutu and Tutsi in particular.

Evaluating mentioned international projects and given an example of one Sub-Saharan country – the DRC, it is time to look forward. It is highly important to find and introduce tasks for the future. Despite the fact, projects like the NEPAD or the UN MDGs initiative would naturally have their ideological opponents, the West should carry on. From the economical point of view, it is clear that Africa's macro economy is far more different than the western one or at least how it is understood by the West. Command economies in Africa would not work, as previously seen in Angola, Ethiopia, Mozambique and Tanzania. On the other hand, liberalisation would necessarily need some governance reforms but it could generate the capital required. Re-structuralisation of the aid which flows to Africa is another condition that should be considered by the West, as well as trade policy towards Africa. Black Africa's stability and prosperity depends on how the situation would evolve in Kenya or Zimbabwe. This should particularly be the focus of the West. South Africa has successfully crossed the border when evolved to multiracial governance and democracy. Nevertheless, other Black African governments should secure conditions for access to the contributions of the white capital, foreign investment and western know-how.

In terms of security challenges for the future, this part of research will examine what could be done by African countries themselves, as well as what is possible for the future shape of the state and leadership, especially in the Sub-Saharan region. The effective way to address Africa's security challenges also lies with regional and international partnership at all levels. In the modern world, where security has become universal, even superpowers need minor, weak partners, to effectively tackle security problems in order to prevent an escalation of those.

When examining the aid which goes to Africa, it would be useful to mention the theories and statements released by the World Bank. According to them, progress has been already achieved in lifting people above the absolute poverty line of US $1 per day. Success rate of the World Bank projects reportedly increased from 60 per cent in the late 1980s to 80 per cent in 2002. However, giving any figures of success rate would not present a real picture and fail to reflect the situation correctly. Exact figures were talking about hundreds of thousands people in years of 1997 and 1998, but there are millions starving in Africa. As expressed by Ross Herbert: "*...would it not be more efficient and effective just to fly planes over Africa and push money out of the doors*?"

Conclusion

According to the World Bank, aid has helped in Africa when the policy environment has been 'good' or receptive. The quantity of aid that countries received has no effect on the quality of their macro-economic policies.[48] It clearly means that successful use of aid is directly influenced by cooperating and reasonably successful governance. But the question remains what should come first, aid or 'good' policy? This in reality shows that first step for many African nations is to work out how to use aid better, especially given high levels of dependence on this source of national income. Instead of simply taking aid, it would be much more constructive to establish what projects could at least add value to the GDP.[49] It is also necessary to realise what was done wrong in the past, by both donors and recipient states, to avoid previous failures in terms of political will and conditionality. Finally, it has to be recognised what is required to attract international investment, again in terms of political environment but also in terms of what private local and foreign sectors need. Despite the fact that a lot was already spent on African regional integration, a great effort should be focused on understanding and accessing the global market by Africa in the future.

The aid and its volume is not a problem in African development. Nevertheless, Africa itself should realise that future political stability could

48 www.worldbank.org/research/aid/africa/release/aid.html
49 Herbst & Mills, *Op. Cit.*, p. 67.

be only achieved through economic prosperity. The best way to deliver this effect is by improving trade access.

According to the World Bank, rich countries maintain protections in the areas of agriculture and labour-intensive manufactures. These are exactly the areas where developing countries have comparative advantage and there would be large gains to poor countries if these are reduced.[50] For example, the cost to developing nations is more than US $100 billion per year, almost twice the total aid from the North to the South. But while poor countries are asked to remove subsidies from agriculture, subsidies for farmers in rich countries – approximately US $1 billion a day - representing six times more than their total foreign and aid budget.[51] All the facts show that discrepancies are common. Nevertheless, signals which could meet African demands are on the table. Omar Kabby, the President of the AfDB has been very forthcoming: ...*"if all the rich countries could raise their Overseas Development Assistance to 0.7% of GDP, if they can open up their markets and also cancel the debts, these measures alone could release enough resources for revitalisation of Africa's development"*.[52] International community should open up its markets, re-structuralise its policy of subsidies and encourage market reforms. It was already estimated that such new approach could lift 320 million people out of poverty; such process would be five times more effective than simply providing aid.[53]

Another factor for African development and further economic integration of Africa, as well as a security condition, is the sovereignty of states. African states mainly exist within boundaries as they remain since the colonial era. The example from the DRC and the Great Lakes Region shows that boundaries themselves are part of the problem, while describing causes of that particular conflict. Tutsi majority in the east DRC and the Great Lakes Region attacked by Hutu elements of the Rwandan Army resulted in huge genocide. This tribal-ethnic unbalanced situation could cause an escalation in the future, if it would not be put into a deep consideration by international community. It is also necessary to say that if Kinshasa, as well

50 Collier & Dollar, *Op. Cit.*, p. 19.
51 *Ibid.*, pp. 8-9.
52 Awvonda, *Op. Cit.*, pp. 32-33.
53 Herbst & Mills, *Op. Cit.*, p. 69.

as Rwanda's and Uganda's leaderships were not able to control their territories and protect their population, these countries could not be called sovereign. Having said all of that, one of the big questions for the AU and the NEPAD remains whether any progress in terms of security and integration can be achieved without changing contemporary frontiers.[54] Nevertheless, Africa also needs to have a partnership for peace at the level of various sub-regions and at the continental level. Instability in one country tends to have broader consequences for security and prosperity across its borders. So, it should be a mutual interest of neighbouring countries to create and consolidate partnership for peace and stability, regardless of how well they manage their domestic affairs or how much cooperation they receive from international partners.[55]

Future problems in such establishment of regional partnership could possibly lie on personal qualities of African leaders. They are often better off personally remaining as head of a sovereign state, even if their country is at war, than entering into what will inevitably be an uncertain power-sharing arrangement during peacetime.[56] Africans have demanded African solution to African problems for a very long time. The NEPAD now offers a great opportunity for them in terms of how development and security should be promoted. The process is clearly in their hands now. They could prove why they have been so disappointed by the Western activities. However, the leaders have to be realistic and have to recognise what the NEPAD could bring to the African countries. Future leaders should have a vision, but with practical impact on their countries and not avoid reality. They have to be willing to launch fundamental domestic reforms and face difficult decisions in reorganising ineffective domestic structures. However, an idea that the stereotype of colonial authority should be replaced by African "big man", like Nelson Mandela in South Africa, does not seem to be absolutely necessary. History shows that success of the country is not orchestrated by a single person. It is usually, if ever, reached only by enormous collective effort with remarkable external contribution.

---

54 *Ibid.*, pp. 72-73.
55 Cobbold & Mills, *Op. Cit.*, p. 172.
56 Herbst & Mills, *Op. Cit.*, p. 75.

When summarising such terrorist background or support in Africa, one has to agree that it was and still is possible. Osama Bin Laden and other terrorists were successful in the past also on the African soil. The essay has tried to show the reasons for that. Several factors of instability and insecurity projected into weak or failing states did allow such activities. Starvation and hopelessness of Africans were misused by local warlords/leaders to gain the power. Corruption on all the governmental levels has created a room for survival of various dangerous suspects, as well as for incredible misusing of international humanitarian aid.

Nevertheless, the future perspective should not be so bright for terrorism. If the world concentrates its effort to stabilise Africa in all aspects, terrorists would not succeed. And this will be a huge step forward in the term of war against terrorism. Future stabilisation and prosperity of Africa are the key words which should be discussed across international, as well as regional forums.

Chapter IX
African Governance Initiatives

Introduction

The world is beginning to acknowledge the growing international importance of the African continent and that global security hinges on the developed world's actions in this region. By 2010, Africa will be a major provider of oil, natural gas and other natural resources to the US, China, India, Europe, and other nations competing for access to these resources. The world is also beginning to recognise the investment potential in Africa, as they seek out opportunities and build political support on the continent. The Global War on Terror has also been played out on African soil. Osama Bin Laden has previously based his operations in Sudan and terrorists struck U.S. embassies in Africa years in advance of the '9/11' attacks. Africans have also been actively recruited for terrorist operations in South Asia and the Middle East, including Iraq. Domestically, mass killings in the Darfur region of Sudan and the persistence of conflict on the African continent challenge the world's will to deal with such events. Africa is also at the centre of the greatest health pandemic facing the world: HIV/AIDS. With these thoughts in mind, the developed world must do more to establish lasting stability in Africa. To facilitate such an initiative, the policies of the countries of the North must change to reflect Africa's growing importance, and properly integrate the continent into the globalized world economy.

The concept and importance of good governance in Africa are well understood, but there is growing concern – particularly among aid agencies - that existing African governance initiatives are not realizing the anticipated economic growth and societal development. These noble initiatives are doomed to failure, because the basic determinants of successful statehood still evade many of the poorest states on the African Continent. At present, Africa is trying to 'run before it can walk', as leaders pursue an aspirational model of governance, while many states struggle to establish stable conditions for security, growth and sustainability. Many of the governance issues discussed in this research merely distract African leaders from the root causes of Africa's problems: AIDS and famine, crippling debt, conflict and state failure, and corruption. Until Africa can resolve these basic issues, much of the literature published under the banners of initiatives such as the African Union (AU) and the New Partnership for African Development (NEPAD) will remain wishful rhetoric.

This research will review the recent history of Africa and explore the influence of colonialism on the continent, before considering the concept of governance in detail. Following a brief review of the most recent reports on African governance, the research will seek to contradict the optimistic views of the United Nations (UN) and AU, by focussing on the core problems facing Africa, which 'Governance' improvements alone cannot resolve. The research will address each issue in turn, by providing a brief background to the problem, followed by a current assessment and possible solutions.

The research will show that the African continent has been greatly influenced by the western liberal democratic model of governance imposed during the colonial period, and subsequently by western financial institutions during the post-colonial era. African society has evolved over the last 40 years under the aegis of the west and its institutions, and the research will show how the resulting governance structures sit uneasily within societies that do not conform to western liberal ideals.

In defining governance, the research will show how two of the main arbiters of good governance: the World Bank and the UN, measure this function by gauging issues such as participation, accountability, effectiveness and responsiveness, rule of law, control of corruption and vision. While current governance initiatives address these issues, the research will argue that they fail to deliver the development necessary, despite progress reports to the contrary. By citing aid agency reports and other commentators, the research will show that existing governance initiatives do not address the core problems undermining African development discussed below.

HIV/AIDS threatens to overwhelm Africa, by altering the African Demographic and eradicating the most productive element of society. Consequently, economic growth has suffered and the continent can no longer cope with external shocks such as famine and drought. Debt is stifling African development, as many states spend more on debt maintenance than on health and education. While African states focus on debt, they are unable to trade themselves out of aid dependency. Conflict, sparked by ethnic tensions and competition for natural resources, has crippled vast regions of Africa, resulting in widespread human rights abuse, while weak government has perpetuated the 'failed state' phenomenon. African citizens have also been deprived of the basic right to protection by the State and have been repeatedly exposed to poverty, dislocation and in the worst cases, genocide. Corruption is also endemic in African society, and is seen as the 'African way' by many who seek to exploit positions of power at the expense of the majority.

These basic ills account for Africa's underlying problems, and only by solving these issues can Africa bring its existing governance initiatives to fruition. By tackling HIV/AIDS, relieving debt, resolving conflict, fostering legitimate and effective government, and eradicating corruption, the African authorities can resolve the current malaise and promote the stable conditions necessary to sustain good governance in the 21st Century.

The research will conclude with a summary of possible corrective actions, which could provide a 'route map' to recovery for the African continent and a stepping stone to more effective governance under the auspices of the AU and NEPAD.

Africa and the Impact of Colonialism

Any study of Africa must first consider the history of the Continent, to establish why it has evolved as it has. Pre-colonial African society developed to support the different cultures and traditions that prevailed. Low population densities and lack of economic development on the Continent limited the emergence of structured societies, but there was still clear evidence of order in African society. Whilst permanent trappings of civil society did not emerge, African peoples developed effective forms of representation and justice, with the formation of 'tribal confederations' in many regions to provide security and a sense of community.[1] The concept

1 Thomson, *Op. Cit.*, p. 8.

of 'kinship' also emerged in early African culture and the power of lineage, which tied ethnic groups into tightly-knit communities based on ancestral links and kin.[2]

As African economies developed, communities began to generate economic surpluses, allowing them to fund political structures and governments. Communities built up around religious groups, monarchies or military prowess (e.g. the Zulu Nation). In many African states 'non-hegemonic' power systems emerged, which were tailored to - and reflected - the loose boundaries in place. Typically, power emanated from the village centre and dissipated quickly as one moved further away. In the absence of firm boundaries, and given the abundance of relatively uncontested territory, disputes could easily be settled by simply moving away.[3] This lack of hegemonic heritage may partly explain the difficulties that African states have experienced when making the transition to modern statehood, as defined by western liberal democratic society.

By the late 19th Century, competition among European nations for land and resources in Africa brought pressure for agreement on ownership of territory. Deals struck at the 1884 Conference of Berlin demarcated Africa into colonial states along boundaries that have remained in place ever since.[4] The following eighty years of colonial rule changed the complexion of Africa permanently. The colonial period can be divided into 3 overlapping phases: the period from 1884 to World War One; the inter-war period; and the period from World War Two to independence. This chronology applies to most colonial powers, with the exception of Portugal, which allowed its territorial control to lapse at various periods throughout the European colonial era.[5]

Following the 'scramble for Africa', formalised by the 1884 agreement, the colonial powers lost interest in their territory, often appointing small teams of administrators to rule these nations. Ronald Robinson refers to British colonial administration at the time as a 'gimcrack effort run by 2 men and

---

2 *Ibid.*, p. 10.
3 *Ibid.*, p. 9.
4 *Ibid.*, p. 11.
5 Tordoff, *Op. Cit.*, p. 33.

a dog'.[6] These teams overcame local resistance to establish administrative structures and to enforce the rule of law. Taxes were imposed to fund investment in infrastructure and cash crops were introduced. African land was commandeered for commercial purposes and as plantations were established, natives were employed as labour to work the plantations.[7]

The inter-war period began with the sharing of war spoils, as Belgium, France, Britain and South Africa claimed territory formerly held by Germany under a League of Nations mandate.[8] Colonial administration expanded to include provision of medical, educational, agricultural and veterinary services. However, these services remained largely inadequate for the needs of the African population. Colonial powers began to construct key infrastructure such as roads and harbours, but this work was curtailed by the depression of the 1920s and 1930s.

During World War Two, Africa became a net provider to the European war effort. Countries such as Rhodesia, the Belgian Congo and Tanganyika generated significant trade surpluses with mainland Europe, which gave them a significant 'head start' in the post-war period.[9] The first signs of independence came in 1946 when the Gold Coast and Nigeria were granted the right to representative government. An ideology that led the Allies to fight the Hitler Regime now sat at odds with the principles of colonialism, and rising African nationalism encouraged the colonial powers to review their position. However, they opted for different exit strategies. While the British, French and Belgians ceded control of their territory relatively peacefully during the 1950s and 1960s, the Portuguese resisted independence claims, resulting in a protracted struggle before independence was finally granted.

As the Europeans withdrew, they handed over countries reliant on former colonial masters, due to legacy trading arrangements, and economic stability was underpinned by multinational companies (MNCs) wielding disproportionate influence over local governments. Colonialism also left

---

6 Kirk-Greene, 'The Thin White Line', 'African Affairs' (January 1980), cited in Tordoff, p.33

7 *Ibid.*, p. 34.

8 *Ibid.*, p. 35.

9 *Ibid.*, p. 36.

behind a clear imbalance between the 'haves' and 'have nots' in African society and post-independence politics often sustained this nepotism. Following independence, a brand of African nationalism emerged that differed from European nationalism, as it evolved primarily from anti-colonial sentiment and lacked ideological substance. This ideology was reactionary and stressed the need for self-determination, human rights and equal distribution of wealth, but to date, the majority of African states have failed to deliver these espoused goals, which are considered pre-requisites to civilised existence. In many states, political function declined following independence, as the State and incoming military leaders (as was often the case following military coups) gained greater control. Many states opted for central control in preference to popular participation, as the latter required meaningful political interchange, which was difficult to achieve in early post-colonial Africa.

In the 1980s liberalization took hold, as pro-democracy movements began to gain ground on existing single-party governments and this tide of democratization gathered pace in the 1990s. Western banks and governments also began to impose western liberal democratic doctrine and policy on Africa, as a condition of investment.[10] The 1989 World Bank Report 'Africa: From Crisis to Sustainable Growth' criticised the quality of governance and argued that, in future, aid would not be forthcoming without significant improvement – code for insistence upon a shift towards 'Breton Woods'[11] ideals.[12]

By the 1990s, post-colonial boundaries were weakening, and war was being waged in the Democratic Republic of Congo (DRC), supported by Rwandan and Ugandan troops. Ethiopia and Eritrea also began to clash. During this decade, genocide went unchecked in Rwanda, when elements of the Hutu majority – the so-called 'Interahamwe' - slaughtered 800 000 Tutsis and moderate Hutus, spurred on by government-sponsored rampant ethnic hatred.[13] Africa's response to globalization during the 1990s was also poor

10 *Ibid.*, p. 114.

11 Institute credited with formulation of globalized economic policy

12 Sub-Saharan Africa. From Crisis to Sustainable Growth. A Long-Term Perspective Study (Washington, DC: The World Bank, 1989), p.192, cited in Tordoff, p.115

13 'Rwanda: how the genocide happened', (1 Apr 2004), http://news.bbc.co.uk, (accessed 22 February 2013)

and there was a lack of enterprise-level training to exploit the opportunities that it brought. Those states with functioning democracies were able to agree quickly on a response to globalization, but the typical African response to the pressures of a 'shrinking world', and an increasingly globalized marketplace seeking to exploit Africa's valuable resources, has been poor.

Defining Governance

The World Bank broadly defines governance as 'the traditions and institutions by which authority in a country is exercised'.[14] More specifically, it is 'the process by which governments are selected, monitored and replaced; the capacity of the government in question to effectively formulate and implement sound policies; and the respect of the citizens and the state for the institutions that govern economic and social interactions among them'.[15] The World Bank articulates these principles further, into 6 clusters of 'governance indicators', which it uses to measure state performance.[16] These are:

a. Voice and accountability.
b. Political stability and absence of violence.
c. Government effectiveness.
d. Regulatory effectiveness.
e. Rule of law.
f. Control of corruption.

The UN defines governance as 'the exercise of economic, political and administrative authority to manage a country's affairs at all levels'.[17] It comprises the mechanisms, processes and institutions, through which citizens and groups articulate their interests, exercise their legal rights, meet their obligations and mediate their differences. The UN identifies the following characteristics of good governance:

---

14 Kaufmann, *Op. Cit.*, p. 2.
15 *Ibid.*
16 *Ibid.*, p. 3.
17 'Governance for Sustainable Development', http://magnet.undp.org/policy/default.htm, accessed 22nd Feb 06

a. Participation.
b. Rule of Law.
c. Transparency.
d. Responsiveness.
e. Consensus orientation.
f. Equity.
g. Effectiveness and Efficiency.
h. Accountability.
i. Strategic vision.

The UN has further classified these characteristics into three strands of governance: Economic, Political and Administrative. Economic governance addresses a country's economic activities and trading relations with other economies and considers equity, poverty and quality of life. Political governance deals with policy formulation and administrative governance focuses on policy implementation.

Review of Current Governance Initiatives – Are They Working?

Studies undertaken by the UN Economic Commission for Africa and the World Bank suggest that African governance – whilst not perfect - is working. This research will look at two current initiatives and assess their impact on the governance of the Continent.

The AU

The AU was formed in July 2002, when it superseded the Organisation of African Unity (OAU). With a membership of 53 states, it has pan-African participation. The AU is a significant step forward from the OAU, which was viewed as a 'Dictators Club' and was often criticized for failing to protect African citizens from their own leaders. Col Qaddafi of Libya pioneered the reformation of the OAU, following his vision of a 'United States of Africa', and the organization was launched with a Constitutive Act and aspiration to engage the African Diaspora, to build an effective unified African continent.[18]

18 AU Constitutive Act', http://www.africa-union.org/root/au/AboutAu/Constitutive_Act_en.htm, (accessed 2 February 2013).

The AU has established a number of official bodies to provide the governance functions required. These include: the African Court of Justice, to rule on human rights issues; the Executive Council, to rule on trade, industry, social security and communications issues; the Peace and Security Council (yet to be ratified), which aims to monitor and intervene in African conflicts; and the Economic, Social and Cultural Council, comprised of professional and civic bodies. The AU has also affiliated 3 financial institutions: the African Central Bank; the African Monetary Fund; and the African Investment Bank. These institutions hope to provide fiscal advice to underpin AU development initiatives.[19] As a force for good, the AU has deployed troops to the Darfur region of Sudan to suppress conflict (supported by the European Union), and its influence is reported to have forced elections in Togo. Furthermore, the AU's opposition to the coup in Mauritania in August 2005 may have forced the ruling Mauritanian Military Council to commit to elections.[20]

Economic collaboration between AU states continues to be hampered by civil war and conflict; however, the AU is forging ahead with its goals of free trade regions, customs agreements, single market policies and economic and monetary union, which it hopes to achieve through the African Economic Community (AEC). The questions remain as to whether – given this backdrop of continued conflict – widespread economic development can be expected to materialise within a reasonable timeframe.

NEPAD

Reportedly the brainchild of Thabo Mbeki, the President of South Africa, and Abdoulaye Wade, the President of Senegal, NEPAD aims to improve the capacity of African states to govern and implement a collective strategy for development. The goal of NEPAD is to equip Africa for sustained growth and development and to strengthen its position in an increasingly globalized world. It outlines a course of action that includes the following priorities:

The creation of peace, security and stability.

Investment in people, through a comprehensive human resource strategy.

---

19 Melber, *Op. Cit.*, p. 4.

20 *Ibid.*, p. 5.

The harnessing of competitive advantages, as part of a revised industrial strategy.
Diversification of African production and exports.
Investment in Information Technology to bridge the 'Digital Divides' (individual to business / business to business / State to society / Africa to Rest of World).
Development of infrastructure – primarily energy and transport.
The creation of effective financial mechanisms.

As an economic development programme of the AU, NEPAD concentrates on education, health, regional infrastructure, agriculture, and preservation of the environment and market access.[21] Many observers recognize the value of this initiative, which is underpinned by the work of the AU, and subordinate initiatives - such as the African Peer Review Mechanism (APRM) - also provide useful governance tools, which aim to standardize best practice within participating states and in this respect it has been effective. The APRM also aims to ensure that the standards of governance published in NEPAD's Declaration on Democracy, Political, Economic and Corporate Governance are maintained throughout the Continent.[22] The 5 key principles of NEPAD – reinforced through the APRM – are: good governance; peace, stability and security; sound economic policymaking and management; effective partnerships; and domestic ownership and leadership.[23]

Assessment of Existing African Governance Initiatives – Optimism vs. Reality

African governance initiatives appear to be high on rhetoric and aspiration, but deliver little to the poorest African states. The World Bank and the UN judge African progress towards good governance favourably, as their annual reports show, but their assessments are optimistic.,[24] The metrics identified by both organizations reflect the predominant 'western liberal democratic' paradigm that developed nations have imposed on Africa and these are not necessarily reliable indicators. The Colonial governance model enforced

21 'History of NEPAD', http://www.nepad.org/2005/files/inbrief.php

22 Deegan, *Op. Cit.*, p. 364.

23 UNECA report 'Strategies for promoting Effective Stakeholder Participation in the African Peer review Mechanism (APRM)' (14 April 2005)

24 UN document 'Striving for Good Governance in Africa' (2005)

prior to Independence still permeates Africa, and the Western perception of Africa remains largely unchanged after 40 years, despite evidence of significant 'ideological drift' between Africa and the West. Western misconceptions about African progress will persist until the UN, the World Bank and the governments of the Developed World recognize this 'drift' and diagnose the real problems afflicting Africa. This research will now look at these 'real problems' and identify possible solutions to them, to create a better platform upon which African governance initiatives can build in the longer term.

African Governance – An Alternative View

Many commentators perceive governance initiatives such as the NEPAD as a sop to the nations of the North, as they seek to exploit African resources and industry, in a new form of economic imperialism.[25] One of the basic tenets of NEPAD is that external investment form 'the North' is needed to 'kick start' Africa, but this is contested by those who merely see this as a second opportunity for the developed world to exploit Africa.[26] The initiative has had a mixed reception among many African leaders and political commentators, who believe that Mbeki and Wade did not consult widely enough within the Continent, before developing the structure and content of the Partnership. As a result, it lacks credibility in certain quarters.[27] Furthermore, some of the more valuable initiatives have lacked uptake among African nations. At present, only 24 states have signed up to the APRM, due mainly to poor 'marketing'. For NEPAD, the APRM and governance best practice to be effective in Africa, the private sector and civil society needs to be engaged more effectively in the process.

OXFAM supports the work of the AU and NEPAD, but has expressed concern about Africa's poor progress towards good governance. The agency is alarmed by the situation emerging, where over 300 million people subsist on less than US$1 per day, life expectancy is 48 years and falling and 28 million people are infected with HIV / AIDS. OXFAM representatives

25 Nabudere, *Op. Cit.*, p. 4.
26 *Ibid.*, p. 25.
27 *Ibid.*, p. 6.

conducted a series of workshops in the 'Horn', Central and West African regions, and concluded that many serious internal issues persist, which must be addressed.[28] Its analysis has highlighted the following trends:

a. The growth of 'war economies' based on competition for Africa's most valuable natural resources (minerals, oil, gold, lumber etc). In many cases, multinational companies are complicit in the systematic exploitation of these precious natural resources.
b. A growing culture of impunity and lack of respect for human rights and the rule of law.
c. Widespread corruption.
d. Evidence of an unchecked HIV/AIDS pandemic.
e. A decline in international support offered to Africa, and the skewing of international trade relations to exploit the Continent.

These findings reinforce the theme of this research, which argues that, whilst the governance initiatives underway in Africa are inherently positive, they will not succeed until the basic issues bedevilling the continent are addressed (AIDS and Famine, crippling debt, conflict and state failure, corruption, and the negative effects of globalisation).

Dealing with Famine and HIV/AIDS

HIV / AIDS threatens to overwhelm Africa's development programme completely. OXFAM assesses the pandemic to be the biggest threat facing Africa today. Over 16 million people have died from the disease since the epidemic began and over 28 million children and adults live with the disease.[29] In 2005 alone, 2.4 million Africans died from AIDS.[30] It has slashed African economic growth by as much as 4 % per annum and its impact across society is immense.[31] Such is its impact that it has rendered much of the Continent incapable of responding to the 'normal' challenges of African life. In particular, it has drastically altered the African demographic, by effectively

28 OXFAM Briefing Paper No 19, p. 7.
29 OXFAM Briefing Paper No 19, p. 16.
30 'The Impact of HIV and AIDS on Africa', www.avert.org/aidsimpact.htm, accessed 8th March 2006
31 *Ibid.*

ripping the economically productive 'heart' out of many communities. Young professionals in the military, the police, education and the health sector have been particularly hard hit.[32] The longer-term effects are as yet unknown, but the more obvious consequences are discussed below.

Africa is no stranger to famine, brought about by drought and crop-failure-induced food shortages. Many states in the region have suffered in the past 40 years, perhaps most notably Ethiopia and Darfur in recent years. Sadly, this situation is compounded by the effects of HIV/AIDS. In particular, the disease is adversely affecting Africa's ability to survive such crises and break the cycle of drought and famine. Writers such as De Waal and Whiteside have coined this phenomenon 'New Variant Famine', which is brought about by 4 key factors: changes in dependency patterns within African family units brought about by AIDS induced morbidity and mortality; loss of assets and skills associated with high adult mortality rates; the increased burden of care associated with treating sick adults and orphaned children, and the combined effects of malnutrition and HIV infection.[33]

HIV/AIDS makes it extremely difficult for communities in Africa to cope, and morbidity and mortality have greatly reduced the productivity of the adult sector. This sector is, traditionally, most capable of coping with water and food shortage, by adapting and diversifying livelihoods and income; however, these coping skills are being lost, as adults die prematurely from AIDS. Webb and Mutangadura estimate that African households with a critically ill family member suffer reductions in annual income of up to 35%, as they are forced to adopt less labour-intensive activities which generate less income.[34] This leaves the family unit less resilient to external shocks such as drought and famine. Studies of farming communities in Zimbabwe in particular have shown that maize production by households which lose an adult to AIDS can drop by as much as 61%.[35] 'New variant famine' therefore threatens the very poorest of African society and crises can occur within states even when they are not suffering widespread food shortages, as AIDS-stricken family units often cannot acquire food, due to

---

32 *Ibid.*

33 De Waal & Whiteside, *Op. Cit.*, p. 4.

34 Webb and Mutangadura, *Op. Cit.*

35 Kwaramba, *Op. Cit.*

loss of labour and income potential. The situation is often compounded by a lack of state support for affected families.[36] This situation is reflected in Kenya today, where Kenyan citizens are dying from starvation, within easy reach of the tourist hotspots on the Kenyan coast. Furthermore, with such a bleak outlook for AIDS-infected countries, many victims lack the motivation to resist famine, given their long-term prognosis of inevitable demise. The care profile and burden of care in Africa has also shifted, with women in rural areas bearing the brunt of caring for sick relatives, as employers shirk their responsibilities for their workers and society forces the problem onto family members.[37] HIV sufferers are also more susceptible to malnutrition and the infection is more likely to develop into AIDS where malnutrition is present. Increased health spending has denied other areas such as education, infrastructure and security. This has slowed skills accumulation on the continent and altered 'productive' (i.e. educated and trained) labour force growth rates. The young adult population has been hit hardest and OXFAM quotes Zambia as an example, which is losing more teachers to AIDS than it can train.[38]

Whilst there are positive signs that a continent-wide education programme is beginning to reduce infection rates in the 15-19 year old sector, governing bodies need to do more to curb the disease and counter its impact. Action needs to be taken immediately, supported by the developed world, to provide primary care for HIV/AIDS sufferers. Africa must also bolster its education programme, to highlight the dangers of the disease to the extremely vulnerable African youth. Governments also need to address the problems caused by changes to the African demographic profile.[39]

Despite funding increases over recent years, the financial aid available to fight AIDS globally is still 50% short of the required target. In addition, shortfalls have been identified by African national agencies and NGOs, which need to be addressed. Work is in hand to provide antiretroviral drugs to Africa at affordable prices, but the developed nations of the North should provide the funding necessary to support an Africa-wide HIV prevention

---

36 De Waal & Whiteside, *Op. Cit.*, p. 4.
37 *Ibid.*, p. 6.
38 OXFAM Briefing Paper No 19, p.17
39 *Ibid.*, p.19

and treatment programme. Local governments, supported by developed nations, need to provide sufficient numbers of healthcare professionals to fight the disease, thus reversing the 'brain drain' of healthcare professionals from Africa to the more affluent countries. Kenyan authorities reported in 2003 that over 7000 health professionals were available to fight HIV, but were unemployed due to a lack of government funds.[40] Local governments need to implement a social development strategy to recruit, educate and support these professionals for the foreseeable future.

Swaziland is a case in point and an example of what can be achieved. In April 2004, the Nation reported the highest HIV infection rates in Africa. Since then, the country has launched an ambitious antiretroviral administration campaign, supported by a nationwide 'fostering campaign', for its orphaned children, and an education and feeding programme supported by UNICEF, to encourage young children back to school. The programme appears to be working, as school attendance figures are increasing. It is too early to say whether these programmes will have an enduring effect in reducing infection rates, but the Swaziland authorities are hopeful and the evidence is encouraging.[41]

Resolving the Crippling Debt Problem

Africa is aid dependent, with some states wholly dependent on cash inflows from aid organizations; however, this aid is not working. It is estimated that 34 of the world's heavily indebted poor countries (HIPCs) are from sub-Saharan Africa, so the problem of debt is a serious one. Within these states, the median debt to export ratio is 340%.[42] Many commentators view African debt as a 'charade', as outflows to service debt are matched by inflows of aid. The debt is – in effect – not being repaid, as donors are simply injecting funds to cover loan repayments. This culture and tradition of indebtedness is damaging for three reasons. Firstly, the debt deters private investment and limits political and economic reform. Secondly, debt management wastes political and economic capacity and detracts form the core business

40 'Africa: AIDS Resource Gaps' (April 2005)
41 'Swaziland: AIDS in Context' (April 2004)
42 *Ibid.*

of politicians and policymakers. Thirdly, these huge inflows of aid and related debt payment focus the eyes of the public on aid and debt, rather than macroeconomic development and growth.[43]

This cycle of African indebtedness must be broken. Developed economies have tethered African economic development, by micromanaging debt and by forcing inappropriate structural reforms on African states, based on western liberal models. A three-strand approach is required to address the problem of African debt and to enable development. Firstly, aid must be increased. OXFAM estimates that, in the last decade of the 20th Century, the developed nations reduced African aid by up to 40%, and sub-Saharan Africa saw per capita aid drop from US$34 to US$20, despite rising GDPs in most developed nations.[44] To compound the problem, much aid has been squandered to prop up corrupt governments and invest in ill-fated projects. Recent reports of alleged misuse of aid in Kenya are testament to this.[45] Secondly, whilst Africa could potentially trade its way to a better existence, unfair trade practices by developed nations hamper local economic development. Many western governments subsidise their industries to retain market dominance in sectors where African industry might otherwise be competitive. Furthermore, World Bank and International Monetary Fund (IMF) imposed structural reforms, and loosening of market controls in Africa makes the African economy more vulnerable to competition from established multinational companies (MNCs). Direct foreign investment in Africa favours the lucrative 'extractives' industries, and these relationships can sustain and prolong resource wars and conflict in the region. Africa must better regulate its trade with the rest of the developed world and 'reign in' the activities of western companies on the Continent. Thirdly, the HIPC initiative has identified those states unable to shrug off their massive debt burdens without external intervention. Despite considerable debt relief, at least 15 of the 34 countries involved are spending more than 10% of GDP servicing debt, while two thirds spend more on debt repayment than health care. Action is in hand to write off much of this debt and at their 2005 Summit, the leaders of the G8 nations – spurred on by a vocal 'drop the debt' campaign, resolved to tackle the issue.

---

43 *Ibid.*, p. 8.

44 OXFAM Briefing paper No 19, p. 19.

45 'Kenyan Vice-President Interviewed Over Fraud', Daily Telegraph, 23rd February 2006

Unfortunately, despite reassuring sounds at the 2005 G8 Summit, promises of debt relief to Africa have yet to materialize and the Paris Club of creditors[46] has recently angered the aid community, by striking a debt relief deal with Nigeria, which will remove some two thirds of the debt outstanding, but leave the country with debt of over $12 Bn; money that Nigeria can ill-afford to repay. Many aid agencies argue that debt cancellation is now more important than further aid and their logic is irrefutable, when countries like Nigeria – even after partial debt relief – will still be facing interest charges of over $1 Bn per year. Debt cancellation, coupled with increased opportunities for free and fair trade would allow Africa to 'trade itself' out of debt permanently. Furthermore, African nations need to develop employment opportunities to help generate economic growth and 'Keynesian' style economic development.[47] If states can develop labour-intensive industries, they can provide access to the labour market for their poorest people. In concert with such initiatives, local governments must remove the barriers to market entry facing private enterprise and encourage ethical local and foreign direct investment. The development of an effective social development programme will also help to educate and train people and support economic development.

Countering Inter-State / Ethnic Conflict and State Failure

Over the last 40 years, nearly 20 African countries (some 40% of sub-Saharan Africa) have experienced at least one period of civil war.[48] In 2001, it was estimated that 20% of the population of sub-Saharan Africa resided in states at war, and low intensity conflict has become a way of life in many others. Whilst tribalism and ethnic conflict have contributed to these conflicts, failures in economic development are equally to blame. In their work on the prevalence of war in Africa, Elbadawi and Sambanis argue that the high incidence of civil war is due not only to extreme ethnic friction, but also to high levels of poverty, heavy dependence on resource-based primary exports and, more frequently than not, failed political institutions. Many

---

46 Group of 19 largest aid donors to Africa

47 'Demand-driven economic theory named after John Maynard Keynes'. Assumes that employment generates demand and corresponding economic growth

48 Elbadawi & Sambanis, *Op. Cit.*, p. 1.

commentators postulate that the most effective way to reduce conflict is to initiate political reform and effectively manage the socio-cultural diversity of African societies, enabling them to harness this diversity, rather than allowing it to generate friction.[49]

Africa is highly dependent on natural resource exports and many states are completely dependent on them for survival.[50] Poverty levels in Africa are also greater than most other developing regions (GDP per capita is 50% of the Asian figure and 12.5% of the European figure).[51] Many warlords see access to valuable natural resources as the key to escaping poverty and securing power in the Region, and many war economies have developed from competition to secure these resources. Victorious warlords inevitably monopolise these resources and collude with MNCs to secure export avenues for their 'booty', which are beyond the control of local or regional government. These 'resource wars' are fought without regard for the civilian populace and frequently generate dislocation and genocide.[52] Furthermore, war economies often exist in the absence of effective government. Where administrations survive, they are often guilty of misusing foreign aid on patronage and corrupt activity and this can heighten the probability of internal conflict. Mismanagement and corruption often favours one side of the community and exacerbates ethnic tensions; these issues must be addressed if such conflict is to become a thing of the past.

In other cases, corrupt governments may be exploiting a region's natural resources for its own benefit, at the expense of the local community. Many Nigerians in the Delta region believe that the Nigerian government – in collusion with the oil industry – is exploiting national oil reserves for its own gains, without regard for biodiversity or local economic prosperity in the regions where production is – and arguably the socio-economic benefits should be - greatest. Oil 'bunkering' in the region is also widespread and armed gangs – often in collusion with government officials – are operating without sanction.[53] Militants in the Delta region have taken action into their

49 *Ibid.*, p. 9.

50 *Ibid.*, p. 10.

51 *Ibid.*

52 OXFAM Briefing Paper No 19, p. 7.

53 Illegally siphoning off oil from wellheads, for onward sale on the black market.

own hands and have begun to kidnap western oil workers in the region, in the hope of securing better terms for local inhabitants or more favourable terms for their illegal activities. The responsibility for ending the cycle of resource wars lies with both the governing bodies in Africa and those states sponsoring the MNCs that collude with the warlords. The Organization for Economic Cooperation and Development (OECD) has already made headway in this area, with its 'guidelines for MNCs' and the UN human rights initiatives are ongoing. However, they need political support if they are to have an impact.

Many authors view Africa's ethnic diversity as a possible cause of conflict, but the opposite may also be true, as such diversity prevents the emergence of regional ethnic superpowers. Societies which become polarized into ethnic factions are often more likely to suffer conflict, and experience in East Timor and Sri Lanka, and closer to home in Northern Ireland, substantiates this.[54] Another case in point is Nigeria, where long-standing frictions between Muslims and Christians have been reignited, following 'anti-cartoon' protests and violence against Christians in Nigeria's northern cities. Christians have retaliated by destroying numerous mosques, and the Christian Igbo group in the South East and the Muslim Hausas from the North of the country have clashed. This crisis has prompted further calls for the fragmentation and ethnic cleansing of Nigeria into 3 regions.[55] For ethnically diverse states to be effective, they need strong democratic government. Collier has also shown that, ethnically diverse societies have a much greater need for a functioning democracy than more ethnically homogeneous ones. Elbadawi and Sambanis endorse this view and add that the influence of strong political institutions can mitigate the effects of ethnic diversity.[56]

Throughout much of Africa, aid agencies observe that the rule of law has lapsed. Serious crimes go unpunished and individuals' rights are violated daily. Very often, the International Community has turned a blind eye to these injustices. Legislation exists to counter human rights abuses, but this is not enforced in many parts of Africa.

---

54 Elbadawi & Sambanis, *Op. Cit.*, p. 11.

55 'Sectarian Killings Strain the fragile Unity of Nigeria', the Daily Telegraph, Saturday 25th February 2006.

56 Elbadawi & Sambanis, *Op. Cit.*, p. 15.

International law, the Universal Declaration on Human Rights and the UN Charter are not enforced for the protection of those who need it most. Lack of justice leads to more conflict, as individuals and groups take the law into their own hands, thus fuelling the cycle of violence. The African Commission on Human and Peoples' Rights (ACHPR) has been in existence since 1987, but it lacks effectiveness and is not taken seriously by those states it is intended to monitor. More recently, the AU Constitutive Act has proposed the African Court of Human Rights, but this has yet to materialize.[57]

Kaplan argues that many African governments have ceased to govern effectively, as they have succumbed to poverty, disease, crime and anarchic violence.[58] Miskel and Norton introduce the analogy of 'ailing and fallen trees' to characterize the decline of states towards ultimate failure. They have devised a series of characteristics to indicate state failure, based on an assessment of poverty, literacy, mortality, social mobility, inflation, emigration and infrastructure (economic conditions and private sector health), and government strength (i.e. border control, law and order, government action). These factors can be used to predict state failure and many African states score poorly against each of these categories.[59]

Kaplan uses Miskel & Norton's analogy to argue that the 'soil' – the social fabric of African society – is poor in failing states. By contrast, Helman and Ratner argue that the 'roots' of African society are too shallow, as states created following independence are not equipped to deal with 21st Century challenges.[60] Kennedy contends that the vicious cycle of state decline is often brought about by trans-national problems such as environmental degradation and AIDS. More advanced states can adjust to such external threats, as they have the wherewithal to evolve, but the weaker states often suffer and decline as a result.[61]

On balance, the predominant cause of conflict appears to be competition for valuable natural resources, whilst weak government, the presence of

57 OXFAM Briefing Paper No 19, p. 11.
58 Norton & Miskel, *Op. Cit.*, p. 2.
59 *Ibid.*, p. 5.
60 Norton & Miskel, *Op. Cit.*, p. 3.
61 *Ibid.*

powerful MNCs and the greed and desire of local warlords conspire to perpetuate such conflict. The solution rests not only with local governments and warlords, but with the leadership of those nations whose MNCs provide a market for these valuable resources. Oversight and regulation is required to prevent exploitation or misappropriation of these resources. Efforts to limit exploitation of African natural resources need to be accompanied by a conflict resolution programme in hotspots such as the Sudan, the Democratic Republic of Congo and the Mano River Basin. The arms industry also serves to fuel the conflict in these regions, so steps must be taken to limit the production and trafficking of weapons to these regions, to coincide with other demilitarization initiatives. Local government cooperation will be essential to this process, given the obvious financial benefits that arms trading can bring to those in public office.

Africa – through the work of the AU and the NEPAD – also needs to do more to assist failing states. The APRM provides a vehicle for the migration of best practice and improvement in state governance in 4 key areas: democracy and political governance; socio-economic development; economic governance and corporate governance. In concert with other improvement initiatives, the APRM will provide a mechanism for governments, NGOs, external stakeholders and civil society to build consensus on effective governance at national and continental level.[62] By tackling each of the features of failed states in turn (poverty, literacy, mortality and morbidity, inflation, emigration, infrastructure, border control, law and order, and government effectiveness), the APRM could enable poorer nations to quickly close the gap on more prosperous African states. However, for the APRM to be effective, many more African states need to sign up to the process.

For peace to prevail in Africa, the African people must learn to manage conflict without resort to violence. Furthermore, external aggravating factors, such as the willingness of foreign MNCs to exploit African natural resources, by negotiating directly with warlords under corrupt trade arrangements needs to be eradicated. Four steps could be taken to alleviate the risk of conflict in Africa. Firstly, fighting must cease and disarmament, demobilisation and social integration must occur immediately, to defuse the

62 African Union Progress Report and Initial Action Plan (2002), p.11.

situation. Secondly, public bodies and institutions such as the military, the police and Judiciary need to be reinstated and rehabilitated in failed states as soon as possible. Thirdly, inclusive political reform must occur, to aid the establishment of a meaningful constitution in troubled states and instil truly accountable behaviour. Finally, to break the cycle of conflict, economic and social welfare reforms are essential, to remove the spectre of recurring conflict permanently.

Tackling African Corruption

Corruption in Africa is often thought to stem from a clash between traditional values and imported norms that accompany modernisation and societal development, and as such it is viewed as an unavoidable outcome of development.[63] Bayley defines corruption as 'the misuse of authority as a result of considerations of personal gain, which need not be monetary.'[64] Harsch sees African corruption as 'outright theft, embezzlement of funds or other appropriation of state property, nepotism and the granting of favours to personal acquaintances and the abuse of public authority and position to exact payments and privileges'.[65] However one defines it, corruption is endemic in African society and threatens to derail current governance initiatives completely. Bureaucrats exploit their positions to benefit themselves, their families and ethnic groupings, while political groups and national elites capture the instruments of power and exploit them for their own gain, erecting barriers to potential competitors through legislation and restricted access to resources. Gould and Mukendi blame the acceptance of this on the 'soft state' characterized by weak national interest, and lack of commitment to serve the public good, a trait common to developing countries.[66]

Poverty, deprivation and inequality also encourage corruption in Africa, where loyalty to family and ethnic groups is often more important than individual rights or personal accountability. Interestingly, 'public choice

63 Alam. *Op. Cit.*, pp. 441-456.
64 Bayley, *Op. Cit.*, pp. 719-732.
65 Harch, *Op. Cit.*, pp. 31-48.
66 Gould and Mukendi, *Op. Cit.*, pp. 427-457.

theorists' argue that this behaviour is perfectly natural, as they believe that corruption is a function of government control and regulation of economic activities, and that politicians govern inherently for their own gains.[67] OXFAM believes that widespread corruption in Africa results in lost investment, unacceptable human suffering and severe impoverishment.[68] Within Africa, Nigeria, Uganda, Kenya and Tanzania are ranked among the most corrupt. Independence and globalisation brought a 'Gold Rush' mentality to Africa, which encouraged the more powerful interest groups to exploit their position and broaden the wealth gap between the corrupt minority and the impoverished majority. Whilst more prevalent in post-colonial Africa, this behaviour is not new and much of the nepotism and corruption emerged under colonial administration. Bureaucratic corruption in Africa stems from widespread opportunism by bureaucrats and civil servants, keen to influence and exploit the socio-political environment for personal gain.

Gillespie and Okruhlik have identified 4 approaches to removing corruption from society and these apply particularly well to the situation in Africa today.[69] These strategies comprise societal, legal, market and political initiatives. The societal strategy introduces a moral 'yardstick', against which corrupt activity can be easily identified and measured. Legal action may involve the introduction of special legislation and investigators to weed out malpractice and penalize the perpetrators, as a deterrent to others. Those engaged in corrupt activity often seek to exploit regulations to gain unfair advantage in the marketplace (preferential treatment, grants, subsidies etc). By removing unnecessary legislation, governments can free up markets and thereby reduce the scope for such corruption. A 'small government' approach such as this would allow the laws of supply and demand and competition to properly shape the market economy. Corruption also arises from political sources, where too much power is vested in too few people. This can be countered by distributing power as widely as possible within the political system and encouraging public representation in the political decision-making process at all levels.

---

67 Mbaku, *Op. Cit.*, p .5.
68 OXFAM Briefing Paper No 19, p. 1.
69 Gillespie and Okruhlik, *Op. Cit.*, p. 80.

Looking again at the societal approach to combating corruption, Brennan and Buchanan argue that effective rules are essential.[70] Individuals must have rules that enable them to co-exist and prosper with fairness and equality alongside their fellow citizens. Many rules in force in Africa have a colonial legacy and do not reflect the true values and norms of African society. This divergence promotes and sustains corruption. Moreover, where constitutions were reformed after independence, this process was traditionally conducted by the - often western-educated - ruling elite, and the resulting constitutions often do not reflect the majority view. Development of a universally agreed and recognized constitution would therefore be the starting point for the elimination of corruption in Africa.

Perhaps most importantly, to counter corruption, political leaders must serve notice to society that it is no longer acceptable and the leaders themselves must be prepared to embrace participative political reform. African leaders must demonstrate the political nerve to reform, and the political process itself must be seen to be beyond corruption. Isaac Umunna reinforces this point and highlights another problem afflicting African politics, where incumbent leaders appear increasingly reluctant to cede power. He cites evidence that a number of leaders, such as Bongo of Gabon, Museveni of Uganda, Mugabe of Zimbabwe and Conte of Guinea may have skewed elections to remain in office.[71] Finally, African society must shrug off its acceptance of corruption as 'the African way'. A 'bottom up' campaign will be required to inculcate these standards and values in African society.[72]

Other Reasons Why Current Governance Initiatives Fail to Deliver

Adejumobi's 'culture theory' of conflict posits that the African culture is predisposed to violence and conflict and that pre-colonial African society was characterized by inter-tribal and intra-communal warfare, where cattle

70 Brennan and Buchanan, *Op. Cit.*

71 Umunna, *Op. Cit.*, pp. 22-25.

72 OXFAM Briefing Paper No. 19, p. 14.

raiding, inter-town rivalry and factional struggles were commonplace.[73] This theory implies conflict and warfare of this nature is the price a developing society has to pay, as it evolves into a modern civilised state. On a similar theme, Bobbit argues that western liberal democratic society emerged, painfully, from several centuries of conflict and perhaps the conflict observed today in Africa merely reflects the growing pains that the continent is experiencing.[74]

Several commentators argue that existing political systems in Africa are flawed and cannot deliver the economic conditions for sustained growth.[75] Many, like Chabal, believe that any effort to sustain the existing system will merely prolong the current inequity and widespread corruption. However, whilst the end of the Cold War may have signalled the 'Triumph of Liberal Democracy' heralded by Fukuyama,[76] prompting a widespread adoption of western liberal multi-party politics in Africa, there is no evidence to suggest that Africa is best suited to a western political model. Adoption of western liberal democratic ideals has also become a condition of aid to Africa, but in many states effective political structures do not exist to utilize this aid effectively.[77] Chabal stresses that – rather than democracy – African states are looking for political accountability. This involves more than merely presenting the illusion of democracy through elections and multi-party politics, which provide no guarantee of accountability, particularly when the election process is 'fixed' to preserve the interests of the ruling party. Effective and legitimate forms of accountability - where African people know their rulers are accountable to them for their actions - are required, rather than the mere ritual of the election process and the trappings of multi-party democracy. African states need to take the initiative to create an accountable political system that meets their needs and protects their values and traditions. Should the emergent political system no longer resemble the

---

73 S. Adejumobi, "Conflict and Peace Building in West Africa: the Role of Civil Society and the African Union, Conflict, Security & Development," *Car fax Publishing*, Vol. 4, No. 1, April 2004, p. 64.

74 P. Bobbitt, *The Shield of Achilles: War, Peace and the Course of History*, (St. Ives: Clays Ltd., 2002), pp. 69-242.

75 P. Chabal, "A Few Considerations on Democracy in Africa," International Affairs, Vol. 74, No. 2, 1998, p. 294.

76 Cited in Williams, *Op. Cit.*, pp. 83-122.

77 P. Chabal, *Op. Cit.*, p. 294.

western liberal ideal, then the developed world must adapt to accommodate this model, rather than continue to force western liberal ideals on Africa.

Engel and Mehler argue that the crisis of state failure facing many African states is due mainly to the transfer of the 'monopoly of violence' from government to other parties such as warlords or other social identity groups.[78] As stated above, many commentators view Africa through a 'Westphalian liberal democratic lens', which considers statehood to be underpinned by this monopoly on tax raising and violence. However, it is unreasonable to assume that – without colonial influence - African society would have evolved to fit such a model. Indeed, pre-colonial governance models in Africa varied widely from 'acepholy' to 'polykepholy',[79] to 'empirical statehood'. Over the last 15 years, many African states have disintegrated through violent conflict and states have declined as a result of deliberate or unintentional transfer of power to warlords and other such sub-state actors.[80] In parts of Nigeria, the monopoly of violence has been transformed into 'functional oligopoly', where different actors provide security against different kinds of threats from different kinds of aggressors, from political social identity groups (e.g. youth and ethnic militias, such as the 'Bakassi Boys' of Onitsha, Nigeria, or the 'West Side Boys' of Sierra Leone).[81] Any effort to restore stability in Africa must seek to return the 'monopoly of violence' to the state, by force if necessary, and put measures in place to retain this power. Such initiatives will again depend on the African authorities implementing the four steps discussed under the heading of 'Conflict Prevention' (reconciliation of fighting elements, institutional reform, political reform and socio-economic reform).

Conclusion

The role of Africa in the world is changing. By the end of the decade, the world's nations will be competing fiercely for her scarce energy resources,

---

78 U. Engel and R. Olsen, *The African Exception: Contemporary Perspectives on Developing Societies*, (Aldershot: Asgate Publishing, 2005), p. 91.

79 Bierschenk & de Sardan, cited in Engel & Olsen – meaning multiple figureheads

80 *Ibid.*, p. 94.

81 *Ibid.*, p. 96.

while the major powers jostle for opportunities to invest in the region and garner political support on the continent. The spectre of terrorism hangs over the continent and it continues to suffer bitter internal conflict, left unchecked by the developed world. Africa is also the epicentre of a global HIV/AIDS pandemic which threatens the sustainability of the continent. The developed world must act now to stabilise the region and do what it can to acknowledge Africa's growing importance, deal with her problems, and properly integrate her into a globalized world economy.[82]

Effective governance is key to the successful development and growth of Africa, but existing initiatives fail to deliver, as the basic conditions for successful societal development do not exist. Unless African leaders address the core problems of AIDS and famine, crippling debt, conflict and state failure and corruption, the continent will not realize its full potential. Eighty years of colonial rule have moulded Africa into a quasi-western liberal democratic society, where western ideals sit at odds with underlying pre-colonial culture and traditions. Consequently, the governance structures in place merely espouse the principles of governance, while behind the scenes traditional African power politics, conflict and corruption prevail. The World Bank and the UN have broadly defined governance – according to western liberal ideals – as a process of governing that embodies participation, accountability, effectiveness and responsiveness, rule of law, control of corruption and vision. Indicators based on these ideals are used to measure performance and thus provide assurance to aid donors that investment – through aid and other forms of direct investment – in Africa is working. World Bank and UN reports focus heavily on subjective assessment against these 'governance indicators' to present a positive image of African development. However, these reports do not tell the full story.

The AU recognizes the need for governance and - through its numerous bodies - it hopes to create the conditions for successful development. Its military activities have also drawn praise as it attempts to resolve disputes in the Sudan, Togo and Mauritania. Whilst the AU is making some progress, civil war and corruption still hamper the work of the Union and it fails to address the key issues of HIV/AIDS, debt, conflict and state failure and

82 Haass, cited in Lake, *Op. Cit.*, pp. 13-14.

corruption effectively. NEPAD is a promising development that aims to concentrate on education, health, regional infrastructure, agriculture, the environment and market access. Most notably, the APRM aims to spread governance best practice throughout Africa, but this can only succeed if states sign up to it. At present, only 24 of the 53 African states have joined, as many leaders are sceptical of NEPAD and see it as a strategy that will lead to thinly-veiled neo-colonialism.

HIV/AIDS threatens to stall African development completely, as it strikes at those in African society traditionally most able to cope with the challenges facing the continent, such as drought and famine. In many parts of Africa, AIDS is killing 'productive' workers faster than social development programmes can generate these workers. The continent is also locked in a cycle of debt management that stifles internal investment in health, education and welfare and stunts economic development. Aid donors perpetuate the status quo, by providing a stream of funding to meet debt repayments. Conflict - be it ethnic or based on competition for scarce natural resources – is endemic in Africa and the problem is compounded by weak government and state failure in conflict hotspots.

Whether state failure contributes to, or is a consequence of, conflict is a moot point, but the devastation from such conflict is preventing development and the ultimate victims are the African citizens who suffer poverty, human rights abuse and – at worst – genocide. Corruption is also widespread throughout Africa and its existence is often attributed to the clash between the imported 'colonial norms' and African traditions. Poverty, deprivation and inequality, coupled with prevailing opportunism also promote corruption in Africa. Such corruption became embedded in modern African society during the 'gold rush' era following independence, where interest groups sought to secure political and financial gains at the expense of the majority.

If Africa is serious about promoting good governance, it must tackle the HIV /AIDS crisis by increasing access to primary medical care and medication, and implement a continent-wide education programme. African debt must be eradicated and social and market conditions must be established to enable the continent to trade its way out of debt. Only when the debt is lifted will Africa be able to focus investment on the education, welfare and governance initiatives necessary to break free from the current stalemate of crippling debt payments offset by external aid. Africans must also learn to manage conflict without resort to violence. Where resource wars prevail the developed nations must do more to curb 'demand side' activity by MNCs, and collusion with warlords and corrupt governments. For conflict to be resolved permanently, disarmament, demobilisation and social integration must be encouraged, and public bodies and institutions in conflict hotspots will need to be reinstated as a matter of priority. These measures, coupled with democratic, economic and social reforms may resolve conflict in Africa permanently. Finally, to eradicate corruption, African political leaders will need to embrace a more transparent and accountable political framework, ideally based on democratic process.

Notwithstanding the proposed solutions discussed above, it is important to remember that, in terms of socio-economic evolution, Africa lags behind the developed nations of the North, whose own political systems have taken centuries to evolve. The world must be careful not to expect Africa to run before it can walk. However, the developed nations and the more advanced African states, have a duty to help the continent move forward quickly, to close the gap on the rest of the developed - and rapidly 'globalizing' - world. It is no longer acceptable to sit back and lament the failure of the western liberal democratic model in Africa. Once the basic conditions for sustainable development have been established, the developed nations of the world must strive for a system of governance that matches the traditions and culture of the continent. A uniquely African solution will be needed.

General Conclusion

The origins of African instability cannot be attributable to one single cause. However that the European colonial powers dissected the continent irrespective of cultural, ethnic and tribal considerations remains a historical fact and any speculation as to quite what an Africa devoid of these colonial influences would look like, would be so speculative as to be deemed utterly irrelevant. That this research led to an interstate patchwork of ethnic and tribal minorities that created 'tension' and conflict is also a recent historical fact. However although these 'borders' were a factor that might have contributed to broad instability, it was never the initiating cause of African conflict. That trigger clearly lies with the post colonial cultural dynamic of African 'patrimony' and 'corruption' combined with the low hanging fruit afforded by an abundance of 'resource rent' temptations offered to inexperienced and untested political elites.

With the all too sudden removal of colonial control and its associated checks and balances, African states found themselves vulnerable to the post WW2 dynamic of Cold War competition for influence through 'proxy states'. This entrenched the perception of the 'acceptability' of patrimonial corruption that in some areas lasts, undiluted, to this day. It was this combination or 'resource rent' disenfranchisement, corrupt 'patrimony', the Cold War entrenchment of political elites and to a lesser extent the influence of colonial borders that has led to 'Africa's Bloody Twentieth Century'.

If the colonial era offered the world its first' Scramble for Africa', the Cold War its second then the twenty-first century re-engagement of China, Russia and the West is offering Africa its third' Scramble for Africa'.

Ironic though the statement may seem, Africa's abundance of natural resources is not going away. Indeed on current projections it is likely to increase as rising commodity prices, 'Peak Oil' and increasing demand from both industrialized and industrializing nations encourage greater exploration and technological innovation aimed at bringing these commodities to market. These increasing demands on ever scarcer resources, will inevitably see the world's great economic powers once again in a state of competition on the African continent in the aforementioned third 'epoch' of the 'Scramble'. However unlike the Cold War era none of those involved in this third epoch, have any vested ideological interest in conflict. Indeed conflict adversely affects not just the subjected country but also the associated global power. China, whilst committed to supporting the Government of Sudan, would be significantly better off operating in a Sudan at peace with itself.

Against this resource driven competition, the West's preoccupation with its Global War on terror will be of comparatively less relevance. The formation of AFRICOM and the associated stabilizing benefits, will have a notable effect for the better on the continent however the primary focus and indeed driver for change will remain Africa's resource phenomenon. Whereas the modern version of this competition is likely to actively promote peace and stability, it will also remain vulnerable to the effects of unrestrained corruption and the reaction to this of 'disenfranchised' minorities or electorates. Active engagement, anti corruption policies, the promotion or good governance and responsible Security Sector Reform remain Africa's best hope for a peaceful twenty-first century.

Whereas the AU is unlikely to develop into the sort of effective and genuinely capable 'force for good' that both Africa and the International community might wish for, it will remain a useful tool of the United Nations. For the same reasons of competing resource interests that will mitigate the full development of the AU, it is likely that the UNs 2005 'Responsibility to Protect' mandate will remain largely un-deployable.

However, in the face of all these 'epochs' and 'pulses' there will remain an enduring patience of a continent that continues to retain a certain magic all of its own.

Overall, this research has explored challenges faced by most African countries; though looking stable Africa can again be seen as destined to conflict due to the presence of conflict trigger issues in most parts which may throw it into chaos. This research has again enlightened areas where the world can help Africa. The world should take a leading role in efforts towards democratising the political system in African countries with all her partner organisations being supportive to the initiative.

This research also has demonstrated that despite the fact that the African Union has been widely condemned as a failure in this conflict, the international community and the UN have contributed to some of those perceived failures. The structures of the African Union have been analysed as being in their infancy stage and that certain third party intervention measures were taken hasty without proper planning. However, it has been demonstrated that some of such decisions were taken due to external pressures from powerful countries who wished not to support the activities through the UN but preferred this done by the African Union.

African governments should also embrace democratic ideals which should guarantee good governance, transparency, rule of law and accountability. It is high time African people realised and appreciated the different ethnic communities, religious affiliations and their historical backgrounds. Africa should appreciate its development, the national, religious, cultural and economic diversities existing amongst them.

Regional bodies such as ECOWAS should be strengthened on regional basis and then strengthen the African Union as a mother body. All the structures in the African Union should be empowered to function as they were designed to work. Meanwhile, the African Union and all the regional organisations should revisit their definition and understanding of the concepts of territorial integrity, sovereignty and their self determination.

Conflict prevention should be realised in the African military forces at national level and regional integration as seen with the example from SADC Brigade. While appreciating that conflict cannot be totally eliminated in the world, the challenge for Africa which is prone to intra-state conflicts should be to manage it in constructive ways so as to prevent recourse to violence. African leaders, Governments and the people should realise that the primary responsibility for conflict prevention in Africa remains within Africans themselves. While International mediators only help to achieve this desire and objective. Democratically elected African governments should therefore accommodate legitimate opposition while all parties should avoid creating instability in countries.

Africa faces a lot of challenges from poverty, hunger, ethnic wars, diseases, religious issues, drugs and organised crimes, illiteracy, resources, immature democracies, world politics and globalisation. The world can assist African countries in many ways as discussed but could also use influence through UN and other International and regional organisations to come forth into African course in various ways as training the African conflict prevention.

Africa still needs a lot of things but the hope for the future will be the only lasting and helpful for today's Africa. And through Africa's future, the world will enjoy prosperity in more advanced ways and all these initiatives are only for African people, but to all the people of the world.

Index